Meeting
Freud's Family

ALSO BY PAUL ROAZEN

Freud: Political and Social Thought

Brother Animal: The Story of Freud and Tausk

Sigmund Freud (editor)

Freud and His Followers

Erik H. Erikson: The Power and Limits of a Vision

Helene Deutsch: A Psychoanalyst's Life

Walter Lippmann, *The Public Philosophy* (editor)

Encountering Freud: The Politics and Histories of Psychoanalysis

Louis Hartz, *The Necessity of Choice: Nineteenth Century Political Thought* (editor)

Helene Deutsch, *Psychoanalysis of the Sexual Functions of Women* (editor)

Victor Tausk, *Sexuality, War and Schizophrenia* (editor)

Helene Deutsch, *The Therapeutic Process, The Self, and Female Psychology* (editor)

Meeting Freud's Family

PAUL ROAZEN

University of Massachusetts Press

AMHERST

Library of Congress Cataloging-in-Publication Data
Roazen, Paul, 1936–
Meeting Freud's family / Paul Roazen.
p. cm.
Includes bibliographical references and index.
ISBN 0–87023–873–6 (hard : alk. paper)
1. Freud, Sigmund, 1856–1939—Family.
2. Psychoanalysts—Austria—Biography.
I. Title.
BF109.F74R64   1993
150.19′52′0922—dc20   93–22734
[B]   CIP

British Library Cataloguing in Publication data are available.

For Bernard and Sheila

Contents

Meeting
Freud's Family

Looking Back on How I Began

In the fall of 1964 I had completed writing my Ph.D. thesis on "Freud and Political Theory," and was waiting for Harvard formally to award my degree. With a background in social philosophy, I approached Freud's work with the same care I would have brought to bear on the writings of such giants in the history of ideas as Jean-Jacques Rousseau or Edmund Burke. It would have raised fewer eyebrows in my profession had I been working on the thoughts of St. Augustine or St. Thomas Aquinas, for example, but Freud's theories seemed sufficiently commanding to deserve my full-scale attention.

Political science continues to treat psychoanalytic thinking as an annoying stepchild. This is particularly striking since as early as 1930, a pioneering political scientist wrote *Psychopathology and Politics*,[1] a book that relied on clinical evidence in developing its argument. As an undergraduate I had been intrigued by the ideas of Walter Lippmann, for he had been absorbed by the implications of psychoanalytic theory for viable democratic convictions. He asked, for example, to what extent are voters able to fulfill all the ideals of the eighteenth- and nineteenth-century proponents of participatory democracy? And on what grounds can one expect leaders to respond to the needs and demands of the public? Notions of self-interest and calculating advantage turn out to be trickier than they might seem; otherwise, much of human history would simply be reducible to a sequence of mistakes and errors. All of Freud's ideas had laid down a challenge to assumptions about the power of rationality and the extent to which people act realistically.

Having finished my Ph.D. dissertation, I was about to be promoted from graduate teaching assistant to full-time faculty member. My formal education had been grounded in political science, and since as an undergraduate I had been interested in psychology and politics, it was a short step to becoming committed to the interdisciplinary nature of all the social sciences, and to the specific relevance of psychology for social thought.

During that same fall of 1964, I started to attend a year's worth of clinical psychiatric conferences at one of the best training centers in the city, the Massachusetts Mental Health Center. That forbidding-sounding place had an honorable heritage as the direct successor to the Boston Psychopathic Hospital, which was venerable as part of the history of modern psychiatry. The Massachusetts Mental Health Center was then, and will probably always remain, affectionately known within psychiatric circles by its nickname "Psycho."

In 1964 the Center's teaching staff boasted a considerable roster of senior psychoanalysts. As is the practice elsewhere, newly admitted psychiatric patients were automatically assigned to inexperienced residents. Psychiatry was taught in large part by means of staff conferences. Therefore, small meetings were convened, during which a patient's condition was discussed with the staff connected to the various psychiatric wards. Each resident's job was to present his or her case to an experienced senior psychiatrist, who was usually also a leading psychoanalyst. The patient was then interviewed in public by the consulting psychiatrist. The clinical material would be used not only to recommend a specific treatment, but also to offer generalizations about the significance of the case itself. That patients willingly cooperate in such appearances, which inevitably compromise their privacy, is a sign of the immensity of the distress they are laboring under.

The time I spent at clinical psychiatric conferences before earning my degree in the late spring of 1965 was crucial to my understanding of the strengths and limitations of psychoanalytic psychology. My interest in psychoanalysis, indeed in any form of psychology, was, as

I have indicated, viewed as an aberration in my field of political science. Political scientists like to think of themselves as tough-mindedly concerned with the successful pursuit of power. The history department at Harvard, or the people who then made up the interdisciplinary Department of Social Relations, would have been more sympathetic to my preoccupations. Conceptions of plausible psychological behavior are often unspoken and implied, and a special sensitivity is needed to perceive the ways in which new perspectives can shed light on old ways of thinking. I had always assumed that the social sciences formed a basic unity, and that academic distinctions as they existed among departments were the result of accidental university forces. I was proceeding on the premise that a theory of human nature was essential, and that Freud's concept of the power of unconscious forces was a memorable step in intellectual history. In the course of my training in social philosophy, it was widely agreed that all past political thinkers, beginning with Plato and Aristotle in ancient Greece, had had distinct conceptions about the nature of psychology and what accounts for motivation.

Yet when I told one senior member of my own department about what I proposed to do at "Psycho," sit in on case conferences, the reaction to my novel enterprise was so grimly unfavorable that there was no reason for me to repeat the unwelcome news to anyone else. I was sternly warned that I was jeopardizing my career and that no one in my department would support my work. In spite of such disapproval, I was determined to continue what I regarded as a significant part of my education. I knew enough to realize how ignorant I was of practical clinical issues. Although I had a fairly heavy teaching schedule, I did have some extra time on my hands since my dissertation was completed, and I was passionately curious about what I might be able to learn.

In October 1964 I saw a posted announcement that a public meeting of psychoanalysts would be held at a large lecture hall at the Massachusetts Institute of Technology in Cambridge, Massachusetts. Today's reader needs to be reminded that in those days, psychoanalysts were at the head of the American academic psychiatric profession. Over the past quarter of a century, biological psychiatry has made some remarkable advances, so that efficient drugs are now available that at the time were not even dreamt of. And since those earlier days, we have benefited from the so-called antipsychiatric movement, which alerted us to how medical metaphors could disguise the ways in which social norms might be imposed on patients in behalf of combatting what were misnamed as illnesses. The dominant world view on all issues connected to mental health has changed since 1964, even if it is not easy to remember what were once taken to be commonplaces.

Biological psychiatry has been resolutely in favor of what medical science can teach, while antipsychiatry has reflected a deep suspicion that medicine is merely window-dressing for reinforcing conformist social values. Although diametrically opposed, each movement has something important to teach. This is all the more reason to recall that back in 1964, full-time psychoanalytic treatment was a prominent therapy, conducted almost entirely by doctors, and is still a common procedure for those who consider themselves in the vanguard of progress. Psychoanalysis involves patients lying on an analyst's couch, free-associating, for four or five sessions a week—each lasting about fifty minutes—over a period of some years. The analyst is supposed to remain relatively distant and neutral. In 1964 psychoanalysis was avidly used for the relief of emotional problems, as well as for the purpose of training future practitioners in the healing professions.

Today there is still a large gulf between those clinicians who rely on purely psychological treatment, which means words and the power of rational insight, and those practitioners who are committed exclusively to organic cures, which usually involve the use of various drugs. A remarkable degree of sectarian conflict, or philosophic disagreement, has persisted throughout the fields of psychotherapy and psychology. Different schools of thought have too little to do with one another; often they do not even read each others' writings. It is frequently the case that because of the role of competing ideological convictions, the significance of the communication between patient and therapist gets lost in the shuffle. Entirely aside from Freud's stature in the history of ideas, I think that clinically he will continue to matter because the therapeutic relationship is what psychoanalysis characteristically focuses on. In spite of the many controversies that have raged, it is important to recognize Freud's genuine accomplishments, even as it is also necessary to acknowledge the defects in his own special approach.

Back in 1964, even short-term psychotherapy, with more limited goals than full-scale psychoanalysis, was heavily influenced by psychoanalytically based reasoning. That has remained true even now. Therapists can understand and beneficially use psychoanalytic principles without actually conducting analyses themselves. So in 1964, whether one ambitiously sought to reconstruct one's childhood in an analysis in the hope of overcoming adult difficulties, or instead went for brief counseling assistance, the teachings of Freud were paramount in the climate of opinion then prevalent.

Freud actually anticipated that future pharmacological innovations might render his own preferred form of psychological treatment redundant. In the 1920s he warned his followers in Vienna that they had to hurry in their pursuit of knowledge, for Freud feared that new methods of helping people would bypass the study of psychology.[2] He repeatedly worried that the investigation of human conflicts would be undermined by the need to offer quick therapeutic assistance. He saw the pursuit of scientific knowledge as at odds with the quest for devising successful means of therapy.

Until his death in 1939, Freud remained committed to the fundamental importance of his own fascination with purely psychological dilemmas. Yet, throughout his career he had been convinced that emotional stress could ultimately be traced to underlying physical processes. He had started out in the 1880s and 1890s convinced of the significance of what were then known as "constitutional" factors in personality development. Despite his creation of psychoanalysis, I think he never budged from his earlier conviction about the fundamental power of purely physical processes.

In 1964, however, the main hopes for enlightenment and therapeutic cure seemed to rest—at least among the people I knew—on what the psychoanalysts themselves were up to. Analysts were still relative newcomers to the field of mental healing, trained at their own separate institutes apart from psychiatric centers of learning, and often determined to displace old-line psychiatry from its traditional position of authority. The old-fashioned psychiatrists had been associated mainly with custodial care and therapeutic pessimism; in 1964 not much time had passed since electric shock-treatment, and even more drastic surgical remedies, had been fashionable.[3] Within what were then considered, among those I associated with, as the most progressive circles, any use of electrical, surgical, or biochemical forms of treatment was regarded as inhumane and retrogressive. Despite all we have learned about biochemistry since then, the warnings of the traditional analysts are still valid concerning the dangers of overmedication. Accordingly, in 1964 psychoanalysis and humanitarianism appeared to be closely allied.

Although announcements for the public meeting to be held in 1964 at MIT made no reference to the specific reason for its taking place, I soon learned that the occasion was intended to honor the retirement of Dr. Grete Bibring. Dr. Bibring was the founding head of the Department of Psychiatry at one of Boston's finest hospitals, Beth Israel, and had held that position for almost twenty years. When she, as a psychoanalyst, had begun her career there, Freud was medically in the forefront of the concerns of leading progressive psychiatric practitioners.

Today Freud's stature seems more purely humanistic. On the one hand, his standing in the history of ideas is securer than ever, for he succeeded in transforming our conception of human nature, and he has therefore influenced how we think about a wide variety of problems. Everything from child-rearing to marriage-counseling has been affected by his ideas; literary critics and historians are especially indebted to his insights. Yet at the same time that the literature about Freud has mushroomed internationally over the last generation, psychoanalysis as a method of treatment has lost much of its glow within American psychiatry. Because Freud himself had been more interested in creating a secure body of knowledge than a therapeutic procedure, he was wary about the predominant interest in America of using his work in a practical, healing context. Thus, he might not be displeased that today's medicine displays a relative lack of interest in his contributions.

In 1964 there were fewer doubts about the feasibility of psychoanalysis as a preferred treatment. Paradoxically, its heavy expense added to its stature, since it would not appear surprising if the best form of therapy turned out to be the most costly and time-consuming. Grete Bibring as a person symbolized what was then the psychiatric establishment.

The general public naturally finds it difficult to keep up with the changes in this important area of knowledge. It was confusing to me in 1964, and it remains so even now, that Freud himself was never qualified to be a practicing psychiatrist. In old Vienna there was a contrast between the kinds of office cases that a trained neurologist like Freud was apt to work with, and the far more troubled patients, now called psychotics, who wound up in the hospital facilities staffed by psychiatrists. In his training to become a physician, Freud had had only the briefest acquaintance with psychiatric problems. He evolved his new technique of psychoanalysis out of his experiences as a neurologist, and invented the category "neurosis" to cover the problems of the patients he chose to see. Although Freud sometimes came across psychiatric cases, he was not always able to diagnose them. Occasionally he persisted in seeing them, despite his own warnings against trying to treat them psychoanalytically. Even if his patients did not get better and wound up in institutions, he could relate to them better than many psychiatrists of that era.

In America there has never been any such clear-cut professional distinction between neurology and psychiatry. The healing professions were so open to new ideas that psychoanalysis, which in Europe remained on the fringes of medical respectability, was welcomed in America as a fresh way to assist patients. At the end of World War II, when Grete Bibring started off as chair of psychiatry at Beth Israel, it would have been unheard of abroad to have psychoanalysts heading up a major psychiatric facility. And yet in 1964, it was still the case that, in Boston at any rate, all the major hospital departments of psychiatry were once headed by psychoanalysts. This fact had to have added significance since Boston was an established model for medical education elsewhere.

Grete Bibring successfully transplanted the latest Freudian thinking to the setting of a general hospital. Creating a training program for medical residents, she applied psychoanalytic principles in order to address the broad spectrum of needs that she encountered at Beth Israel. Although the hospital's in-patient facilities were small, even the problems brought by out-patients were more varied than those encountered in private psychoanalytic practice. Although Bibring was thoroughly attached to orthodox psychoanalytic theories, she could never have accomplished her goals had she been clinically rigid. So, that 1964 meeting at MIT meant much more to me than the end of the academic career of one professor of psychiatry, even though I later found out that she had been the first woman to hold that title at Harvard Medical School.

Grete Bibring's accomplishments at Beth Israel, one of Harvard's teaching hospitals, were only part of her story. In 1925 she had joined the Vienna Psychoanalytic Society as an associate member, and was therefore a member of the circle around Freud in his final years. She had been prominent enough in Vienna to have been appointed as a training analyst, one who was trusted to oversee the analyses of candidates who hoped to become analysts themselves. She left Vienna in 1938 when the Nazi occupation of Austria finally drove Freud and his entourage into exile in London.

After a brief period in England, Bibring left for Boston after Freud's death; the British realistically feared a Nazi invasion, and she had two children to worry about. Her husband, Edward, who died in 1959, was also prominent within Viennese psychoanalysis, although originally from Romania. He was not a physician, but then Freud had not wanted to confine psychoanalysis within medicine, and Edward Bibring became one of the major psychoanalytic theoreticians of his generation. Grete and he had entered Freud's circle at the time when Freud was already old and stricken with cancer of the jaw. He was therefore distant toward new pupils, and they had little direct contact with him. Because of her career and her marriage, Grete Bibring retained the aura of psychoanalysis's central-European past.

No matter how famous Freud ultimately became, when Grete Bibring started out as an analyst in the 1920s he was still an outsider to Viennese medicine. He had been trying not only to revolutionize the clinical approach to mental suffering, but also to challenge traditional Western ethics. Before the First World War, Freud had been much taken with Carl G. Jung, and for a time made Jung his "Crown Prince" within psychoanalysis. His choice of Jung as a successor had many determinants beyond their personalities, and their friendship as well as their falling-out influenced the future course of Freud's work.

Jung had come from the ranks of Swiss hospital psychiatry, and Freud sought to add that school to his own growing movement. Freud had hoped that Jung as a Gentile could ensure Freud's standing outside the narrow confines of Freud's own status in Vienna, for he was afraid that his movement would be too closely identified with Jews like himself. Consequently his eventual disappointment with Jung was proportionate to the great hopes Freud had had for him. Even though the quarrel between the two men took place during 1912–14, to the end of his life Freud remained intransigent about what he considered the "loss" of Jung from his following. Because Jung became one of Freud's most perceptive critics, the confrontation between Freud and Jung remains an enduring debate in the history of ideas.

Throughout most of Europe, neurology and psychiatry have retained their separate identities. Freud's creation of the entirely new professional discipline of psychoanalysis left the local Viennese highly dubious, even at a time when he was attracting numerous patients and disciples from abroad. The general influence of his teachings in America was a tribute to the power of his writings. The devoted work of his disciples who, like the Bibrings, emigrated to America, helped ensure the eventual success of his ideas on this continent.

In addition to supervising the residents at Beth Israel Hospital, Grete Bibring was also a leading training analyst in Boston. Unlike in Vienna, candidates here who were ambitious academically also sought professional instruction in psychoanalysis and often followed her advice about their own treatment. Ever since 1925 the rule had been formalized within Freud's school that all prospective analysts be themselves analyzed. This procedure was first proposed by Jung before World War I, at a time when it seemed innovative. Freud was, I think, less than enthusiastic about the idea, but eventually agreed to the necessity of training-analyses as part of the education of future analysts.

Psychoanalysis also attracted those who were interested in learning about the subject without themselves wanting ever to practice. It was widely known, for instance, that Professor Talcott Parsons, a famous Harvard sociological theorist, had been one of Grete Bibring's most prominent analytic patients. In the early 1950s he became a special member of the Boston Psychoanalytic Society, and his occasional participation in meetings symbolized the Cambridge intelligentsia's involvement in the analytic movement. Parsons had tried to integrate psychoanalytic ideas into his own special system of thought, and he was in the forefront of those social scientists who were fascinated by the implications for their work of Freud's ideas about human nature.

The period immediately after World War II marked one of the high points of Freud's influence in America. Just as the First World War had stimulated special interest in the work of psychoanalysis because of problems of so-called shell shock, so too did World War II highlight the field of military psychiatry and promote governmental involvement in psychoanalysis. One analyst even became a general. Thus, a widespread demand for psychoanalytic training existed after World War II; and the postwar benefits for veterans meant that indirectly the federal government was helping to subsidize psychoanalysis. Private foundation money was also available for psychoanalytic training.

In 1956 the 100th anniversary of Freud's birth coincided with the publication of an official three-volume biography by Freud's British follower Ernest Jones. (Jung's own centenary in 1975 was allowed to pass without an authorized biography. His family still refuses to allow a full-scale study, using all the private documents that are said to exist, to be undertaken. Even the editing of Jung's texts, compared to what has been done for Freud, has remained decidedly perfunctory.) All the literature about Freud that came out during the mid-1950s did much to stimulate interest in the history of Freud's struggles and the movement he had led. Although Grete Bibring herself never published enough to explain fully rationally the kind of local reputation she had acquired, in 1964 her name evoked the respect and awe which were then associated with Freud's immediate disciples.

Thus, it had not taken any special purposefulness on my part to decide that I would most likely learn something new by attending that MIT meeting. Many analysts from Boston were scheduled to speak on a variety of topics. I took no notes, but I remember that the most unusual aspect of the occasion was that at the time Boston analysts, although the acknowledged leaders of the psychiatric powers-that-be, rarely appeared outside a strictly professional context. I had never heard of them presenting themselves before an open, general audience. The people at the MIT meeting were drawn from a wide variety of backgrounds, and the discussion was not intended to engage only those who planned to go on in psychoanalytic training.

Unlike psychoanalysis practiced in most other cities in America, Boston psychoanalysis was then, despite existing tensions among its members, exceptional in being united in one organization for teaching purposes. Most places had two or more such centers, and New York City surpassed everywhere else in the country with its multiple training facilities. When a breakaway group from the Boston Psychoanalytic Society was formed in 1974, Grete Bibring—continuing to practice as an analyst after her retirement from Beth Israel—was one of the few leaders who decided to join it.

At one point during the crowded MIT proceedings, in a question-and-answer period after some papers had been presented, an energetic old woman volunteered from the floor to say a few words; she was instantly invited to the podium on the stage. Although her name had not been listed on the program, she turned out to be Dr. Helene Deutsch, then eighty years old, who was famous for her clinical papers as well as her two-volume *The Psychology of Women*. However elderly she might have seemed, she survived Grete Bibring and lived to be ninety-seven. Helene Deutsch had tried to disarm the enthusiasm of her reception by saying that she was not a good speaker, but the warmth of the audience's spontaneous response was a sign of her legendary stature. Later on, when I got to know her, she modestly proposed that people received her with such approval because they were personally relieved that someone could be so old and still retain her faculties.

Helene Deutsch came from a generation of Freud's followers that

was distinctly older than Grete Bibring's. During World War I
Deutsch was an assistant at the University of Vienna to Professor
Julius Wagner von Jauregg, the only psychiatrist ever to win a Nobel
Prize. (He developed a fever therapy for curing general paresis [neu-
rosyphilis], once thought to have had psychological origins.) Not
only had Deutsch, then on Wagner-Jauregg's staff, been accepted for
analysis by Freud himself, but in 1924 she had become the founding
director of the Training Institute of the Vienna Psychoanalytic Society. A certificate co-signed by Freud and Deutsch had given Grete
Bibring the formal credentials to graduate as a psychoanalyst. In
1935, Deutsch immigrated to Boston to help start up its own Institute. An eminent neurologist, Dr. Stanley Cobb, was opening the
first full-time psychiatric unit at a general hospital, the famous
Massachusetts General; Cobb wanted Deutsch on his staff. By the
time I first saw Deutsch in 1964, her prolific clinical writings,
combined with the teaching of generations of analysts and other
professionals, had earned her a secure place in the history of what
Freud had dubbed the psychoanalytic "movement."

That day at MIT, Helene Deutsch confined her remarks to some
surprisingly personal reminiscences about old Vienna. Her English
was not easy for me to understand. It was some time before I realized
that she had originally come from Poland. With the name Deutsch,
and being a follower of Freud's in Vienna, I did not at first realize her
true national identity. Yet it was so important a part of her that
Edward Bibring once remarked that Helene Deutsch spoke five
languages, all in Polish.

At the MIT meeting she recalled how, at a Viennese medical
gathering, she overheard some colleagues scoff at her late husband
Felix because of his special interest in psychoanalysis. Felix had been
an internist, for a time served as Freud's personal physician, and
afterwards in Boston he had helped advance the fields of psycho-
somatic medicine and interviewing technique. Much later I found
out that Felix, who had tried unsuccessfully to establish himself at
Beth Israel before Grete Bibring got there, felt he had been outdone
by her. It also turned out that the Deutsches and the Bibrings led rival
psychoanalytic factions in Boston. Like other fields, psychoanalysis
has its political struggles, and the two couples had their own separate

circles with favorites they tried to advance. Although it is not always acknowledged, senior analysts have their protégés, usually people they have analyzed, much as thesis supervisors try to promote the academic careers of their students. Despite the veiled animosities among Freud's followers, the importance of the 1964 meeting was itself a sign of how successful the "cause" of psychoanalysis had become.

My curiosity was aroused by Helene Deutsch's willingness to make some unguarded references to the early days of analysis; and I knew that she lived, as I did then, in Cambridge. I had been aware for some time that the few surviving people who had known Freud well, his pupils and patients, must have an untold story to tell. An outsider like myself was bound to perceive as enlightening those features of their stories that they probably considered unexceptional.

In that fall of 1964, I had just interviewed another elderly analyst, Dr. Abram Kardiner, at his Park Avenue apartment in New York City. When I started studying Freud in the early 1960s, I read everything about him that I could lay my hands on. But the whole purpose of conducting my own interviews with those who had known Freud was to have a look for myself. Kardiner had written some important books on social thought, and he, like Helene Deutsch, had been personally analyzed by Freud. The question of who had analyzed whom was more than a matter of any social pecking order; the fact that Grete Bibring had only been analyzed by a contemporary of Helene's, instead of by Freud himself, said something about Grete's relative standing in Vienna; it meant that she was accorded less importance as a source of information about the early days of psychoanalysis.

Kardiner had encountered some serious difficulties with the New York Psychoanalytic Society, as had others who could lay claim to have had a special "in" with Freud, but he went on to help found the Psychoanalytic Institute at Columbia University's medical school. Boston analysts may have played a special role in American medicine, but their colleagues in New York had a unique cultural power if only because they lived in the center of the publishing industry; an editor who chose a particular analyst for his or her personal treatment could lend a special weight to the clinical proceedings. Despite

Kardiner's lofty reputation, I found him direct and down-to-earth, every bit as impressive as his many books on a variety of serious issues might have led one to expect. I was then trying to get some human feel for what the circle around Freud had been like, in order to understand what his ideas amounted to. So the possibility of my speaking with Helene Deutsch presented me with another special opportunity. I wrote her a short letter after the MIT meeting, explaining my interest in seeing her. She quickly sent back a note accepting my request.

I could never imagine that I would be lucky enough to interview some of the key members of Freud's immediate family. As I will explain, Helene Deutsch was integral to my success. This book is an attempt to re-create—based on my understanding of the place of psychoanalysis in intellectual history—the world of Freud's family life. I relied specifically on my contact with the people I met. Someday there will be far more written evidence made available to the public; for example, there are over a thousand letters from Freud to his future wife that are still embargoed to scholars.

In the following meditations, I have tried to invoke the special immediacy of my association with the individuals I interviewed. Being aware of my own limitations, both cultural and personal, I have tried to give a balanced account of what Freud's family members seemed to me to be like.

What I want to report now is not so much a sentence about something, or even a phrase, but rather the whole ambience surrounding these people, and how their lives said something special about Freud. As one scholar has recently observed about Freud, "virtually his entire lifetime was spent within large families."[4] What were these people like? I decided to find a different sort of evidence than can be gained from the written record, which itself may raise contradictory or unfathomable points.

These interviews taught me something important about the human origins of ideas—so important that I found it impossible to return unchanged to the traditional field of intellectual history in which I had been trained. For I came to understand that even the most elaborate doctrines do not exist in some idealized abstract space, apart from the human actors who conceived them. The creative acts of individuals take place in a special social and cultural setting, which can require considerable effort to recapture. After conducting these interviews, I became far less inclined to take at face value written words, either in books, articles, or even in personal letters. It is, I believe, critically important to attend to the human dimension underlying all formal communications.

Although my interviewing style unfolded only gradually, enough time and distance have now passed for me to present in an organized way some selections from this experience. Before I began this work, I had spent all my adult life with books, never having conducted any sort of interviews. I was therefore a novice at what I had undertaken to accomplish; despite the passage of over twenty years since I started meeting people who had known Freud, the whole enterprise I undertook remains my formative intellectual adventure.

1

Helene Deutsch Gets My Foot in the Door

I will be recounting how I met three of Freud's children, each of whom came to play a unique part in the psychoanalytic movement as a whole. After I went to see, on Helene Deutsch's recommendation, Anna Freud, I arranged on my own initiative to interview her older sister Mathilda, and then their brother Oliver. I also met Freud's sister-in-law—his younger brother's widow. One of Freud's two daughters-in-law whom I came to know was exceptionally informative. To round out my contact with the Freud family, I was able to meet one of his grandchildren, some nieces, a nephew, and a grandniece. Helene Deutsch remained a key figure in my work, since I regularly brought her interview material to talk over.

As I headed off to meet Helene Deutsch in the fall of 1964, I had no idea that I was beginning a process that would bring me into contact with many members of Freud's family. But for me and for others at that MIT conference, Helene Deutsch represented a direct link to Freud. It was not so much that she, like so many other analysts, had a photo of Freud on her consulting room wall, although it was an unusual and striking one. We knew how intimately involved she had been in the development of psychoanalytic theory. She knew, for example, exactly how often and in which precise contexts Freud had cited her own writings. Her work formed an integral part of the history of psychoanalytic doctrine as it had evolved in Freud's lifetime.

Helene had made another distinctive contribution, for she was especially interested in those psychological phenomena that did not neatly fit the preexisting categories of either neurosis or psychosis. Throughout her long career she insisted that the most important clinical issues could not conform to cut-and-dried conceptual distinctions. Probably her most famous clinical paper was concerned with what she, over Freud's objections, had called the "as if" personality.[1] Her interpretation of "as if," or imitative, behavior was part of her interest in how the self develops. The years since then have witnessed a flowering of concern with the more general problems of authenticity and identity.

In the years following our first meeting, Helene Deutsch's reputation would suffer the slings of feminist criticism. Detractors of Freud used her, often unfairly, as a special point of reference. As a loyal disciple of Freud's, Deutsch was often viewed as a traitor to her sex. If Freud was, as some have thought, an enemy of female emancipation, then Deutsch—a psychoanalytic pioneer—could be considered one of his collaborators in this reactionary endeavor. The special niche she had achieved in Freud's world served for a time to detract from the progressive nature of her accomplishments.

In 1964, however, these debates lay largely in the future. Then she was a towering figure in the history of psychoanalysis whose theories of femininity were to me, as a relatively young man, complicated and abstruse. She was singularly lacking in the ability to simplify her ideas. A contemporary of Helene's, Karen Horney, was journalistically if not psychoanalytically the more talented of the two. Although by 1940, *Time* magazine had singled out both Deutsch and Horney as "the outstanding women psychiatrists in the U.S.,"[2] Horney has turned out to be far more popular.

Horney had criticized Deutsch in print; Helene chose not to fight back, except for a response buried in a footnote at the bottom of a page. In 1964 it was not yet clear that Horney would pull so far ahead of Helene. For in contrast to Deutsch, who had such a special relationship with Freud, Horney practiced in Germany before moving to the States and had had no personal contact with Freud. Helene felt secure about her position, partly due to the confidence that she knew Freud had placed in her. I am not sure she ever fully realized the extent to which, because of the feminist criticism directed at her, she had slipped behind an old rival like Horney. In her own time Helene had been in the vanguard of feminist thinking, so it was not easy for her to understand how some later feminists could be so short-sighted as to ignore her pioneering achievements.

Horney had founded an independent school of psychoanalysts in New York City, whereas Deutsch remained organizationally a loyal-ist. My knowledge of past controversies in the history of psychoanaly-sis only heightened my admiration for Helene. After all, Horney had died in 1952 at the age of sixty-seven, and here was Helene Deutsch, still vital and able to answer my questions. And I found that Helene's ideas did not fit the stereotypes often attributed to her; they were genuine expressions of her own life and experiences. Whatever the differences between her and Horney, the field of psychoanalysis had allowed both women to become prominent. To me Helene Deutsch's entire career illustrated how far ahead of its time Freud's psychoanalysis had been in enabling women to play prominent professional roles.

I was to spend hundreds of hours interviewing Helene Deutsch about Freud and the history of psychoanalysis. In the process we also became friends. She came to my wedding in 1967, and later (1978)—long after my writing had caused professional contro-versy—she agreed that I should write her biography. At the begin-ning of our relationship, I was so cautious and tentative that it took a good while for it to sink in that she was eager to have me come back. I now think that from the outset she must have sensed that for me, every interview was dazzling.

In those days, there was not much literature about the story of the development of Freud's school. Among Helene Deutsch's earlier stu-dents was a young man named Wilhelm Reich. Since Reich became wayward and finally died in a U.S. federal prison in 1956, Deutsch wryly commented how he had been a protégé of hers. Helene was exceptionally good at making fun of herself, and excelled at pithy sayings. Like all intelligent people of advanced years, she was wor-ried about losing her mental capacities. There were, she joked, three stages to senility: first, you feel that something is different, then oth-ers observe that things have changed, and finally only others do so.

Her former students never forgot the liveliness of her presentations. When at a coffee shop I ran into noted analyst Erik H. Erikson, who was then still teaching at Harvard, I told him whom I had been interviewing. Erikson said Deutsch had been his first teacher at a seminar on psychoanalysis in Vienna. As an insider himself, he cautioned me to be careful about how I used what I would learn from her, implying that since she had been one of the founders of the movement, I bore a special responsibility toward its future.

Erikson's own reputation was by then already immense. He was so influential that in 1970, *Newsweek* ran a cover story about him. No matter how successful an analyst may become professionally, few ever attain the prominence of an Erik Erikson. Bruno Bettleheim would later eclipse Erikson's standing, although Bettleheim's death in 1990 started a controversy of its own.[3] (In 1964 Bettelheim was already famous; I remember Helene laughing about the confusion she had inadvertently caused when she had invited Stjepan Betlheim, an analyst from Zagreb, to a gathering.)

I think Helene must have appreciated how important I felt it was to understand her technical works within the context of the history of ideas. More than once I had to struggle to unravel the categories of thought that were bound up in the past. I had immense respect for the calling that she stood for; when Helene became an analyst, it was not a job but a spiritual mission. Perhaps it was snobbish on my part, but it struck me as more significant that a great intellectual like Simone de Beauvoir in *The Second Sex* had relied on Helene's work than that Betty Friedan later on in *The Feminine Mystique* could not appreciate Helene's subtleties.

As sophisticated and skeptical a European psychiatrist as Helene was, she and some of her friends had sought individual salvation through the practice of analysis. Many of the most famous controversies surrounding psychoanalysis were fueled by the "religious" convictions that these innovators entertained. In spite of the many criticisms leveled at Freud's recommended treatment procedure, Helene upheld his belief that the couch was a sound vehicle for enabling patients to relax and open up. And she agreed that the analyst should seek out a patient's apparently random thoughts in the course of their free associating. She also felt that the analyst had a unique vantage point from which to perceive the hidden connections between apparently disparate thoughts. And she was firmly convinced that the insights gained from achieving distance toward one's feelings, made possible through psychoanalysis, brought the patient a measure of freedom and control over unruly emotions. The analyst's interpretations, once tactfully communicated, enhanced a patient's ability to make personal choices.

The more I got to know Helene, the more I learned how deeply disillusioned she was about some key aspects of psychoanalysis as a form of therapy. She thought, for example, that analyses tended to last much too long; analyses that go on for years and years, she held, undermine the very autonomy that they are intended to promote. People who need such extended support are entitled to a different form of treatment.

Along similar revisionist lines, Helene also proposed that it was only out of insecurity that analysts were apt to rely on hocus-pocus to achieve Freud's stated ideal of the analyst's "neutrality" toward patients. Neurotics, she thought, can bring their own emotional distortions to the therapist without the therapist having to construct an artificial treatment setting. Helene's reservations about "orthodox" analytic technique were either privately held or expressed only obliquely in her writings. She was far less reserved in expressing her acute distress at both the increasingly bureaucratic nature of psychoanalytic training, and at the course that theory-making had taken. She repeatedly cited Freud's own regret—especially after getting cancer in 1923—that he had moved in an abstract direction. She had hoped to rely on the evidence supplied by case histories, but felt that such material was rarely offered in the literature. Instead, complex speculations, detached from clinical cases, had become the unsettling fashion.

Despite her reputation as an orthodox psychoanalyst, I found Helene to be thoroughly independent-minded. She thought she knew Freud so well that she had scarcely looked at Jones's authorized biography. In fact, she viewed Jones as an opinionated, tight-lipped outsider to events in Vienna, and she did not contribute to his endeavors. Jones was so difficult that he rarely made close friends;

others later told me that Jones had communicated neither the spirit of the Freud they had known nor the social environment in which he lived. While as a beginner I had found Jones's books invaluable, increasingly I came to see how his own distinct prejudices shaped the way he framed the course of Freud's life. Still, there is no single source about Freud, apart from his own writings, that I have gone back to more often than Jones's texts.

I was surprised to learn that Helene did not even own the celebrated *Standard Edition* of Freud's works in English, which began publication in 1953. I felt I should tactfully conceal this fact from its translator and general editor, James Strachey, when he directly asked me whether she had ever acquired it. Strachey was justifiably proud of what he had accomplished with his edition of Freud, but he was uncertain if someone of Helene's stature would rely on his interpretation of Freud. It turned out that Helene had actually memorized some of Freud's more obscure papers. It was striking to me, then, that when I examined her early German editions of Freud's works, she had never felt the need to underline anything in them; this may have been a reflection of her central-European respect for the printed page, but I suspect it was also due to her almost religious reverence for Freud's writings.

At our first meeting, Helene had immediately picked up on my own immense respect for Freud as a pivotal figure in the history of ideas. During our subsequent talks, I tried to master all the available literature, but I also was especially attentive to her spontaneous reactions to my questions. She was wonderfully lively and unusually expressive, with remarkably communicative eyes, and she grew relaxed and uninhibited during our talks. As I look back on it now, each meeting left me exhilarated, and I looked forward to every subsequent session with special anticipation. I later learned that she had joked to a close friend of hers that each evening before our meetings, she had to put her mind to thinking about the "assignment" of providing me with some fresh historical material.

Although I did not really understand it then, in the fall of 1964 Helene was in the process of remaking her life after the death of her husband earlier that January. Both had been the same age and had been married for fifty-two years; toward the end of his life, his ill

health had taken up a lot of her energy. At the time of our first
meeting, the period of mourning had largely passed and the atmosphere was right for the two of us to get together. As eager as I was to
enlarge upon my research, I was also a college teacher, and as it
happened, she had been fascinated for years with the problems of
youth. She was now deeply concerned about the reaction to her
husband's death of one of her grandsons, a student at the University
of California at Berkeley. Because of these family worries, as well as
what she thought would be her own short life expectancy, she was
undertaking a special study of adolescent emotional conflicts. She
found that with such youngsters, even the briefest therapeutic intervention on her part could produce manifestly good results, and she
appreciated their gratitude.

Although I could not then realize how much longer she would
live, I knew enough about psychoanalytic tradition to present Helene, as a matter of courtesy, with a copy of my dissertation, which, it
so happened, cited many of her more obscure articles. In such a way
had Otto Rank introduced himself to Freud in 1906, with a manuscript of his own. Rank became a special favorite of Freud's and a
close personal friend of the Deutsches; Rank's first wife, Beata,
known by her Polish diminutive "Tola," turned out to be Helene's
best friend in Cambridge.[4]

My punctuality, and my precision in calling her only at specified
times to set up our appointments, was an unspoken agreement
between us—although to anybody but a Freudian of that era, such
exactness might have seemed obsessive. Freud's own sense of time
had been as precise as that of other middle-class gentlemen of his
culture; doubtless he had to be that way to accomplish so much.
Since Freud's customary pattern was so settled, a student like Theodor Reik could always plan to meet Freud on his walks. Helene's life
was also orderly, and she still had a good-sized clinical practice.

At first I saw her monthly. She was alert and lively, full of interesting anecdotes, every bit as "zingy" as people remembered her as having been many years earlier, when she arrived in the United States. It
is not necessary to dwell on the obvious unfortunate aspects of
growing old—the losses of friends and loved ones, as well as the de-
clining capacities associated with aging. But fortunately for Helene,

as with many extraordinary people, her creativity extended to this phase of her life. For example, she was then transforming the office of her late husband, who also had practiced at home, into a separate apartment for company. At one point, a woman and her small child occupied the apartment, providing Helene with the kind of companionship she could not get from a housekeeper. Although she lived to be nearly 100, Helene never had to enter a nursing home.

In my second interview with Helene, I was surprised when she offered to recommend me to Freud's daughter Anna in London, England; more than once, Helene was to repeat this inviting proposal. Anna, the only one of Freud's children to become a psychoanalyst, was not only the author of numerous well-known texts but also the acknowledged leader of the Freudian movement. For Helene to introduce me to Anna Freud, who was then living in the same house Freud had died in, was an attractive inducement for continuing to see Helene. But even though Anna was the symbolic head of psychoanalysis, the fact is that my working relationship with Helene was rewarding enough for its own sake. Just getting to know her personally brought me in touch with early psychoanalysis and Freud himself; that human contact gave me an invaluable context in which to reconsider the written evidence I found in books and articles.

Although it was only one facet of my interest in Helene, I took it for granted that she had abundant personal knowledge of Freud's family. Not only did she know some of Freud's other children, as well as his wife, but Freud had referred one of his own nieces to Helene for analytic treatment. Although Helene tried to deny that there was any special significance to her having named her only son after Freud's eldest son, it is hard to ignore this parallel. Many of Freud's other disciples acknowledged naming their daughters for Anna Freud.

It did not even cross my mind to press Helene about her son's name, since she was so cooperative about everything that mattered most. At one point she casually asked me to attend a meeting at the Boston Psychoanalytic Society, where a younger friend of hers was coming from out of town to present a technical paper. I was reluctant to attend, a reaction consistent with my unhappiness with the general direction of American analysis. One basis for my special interest in the MIT meeting was my eagerness to meet and interview people like Abram Kardiner, and Helene herself—an older, idealistic generation more interested in ideas than in professional advancement. I appreciated how culturally sophisticated and well-educated the Europeans had been, and I later discovered how discontented Helene too had become with the narrow interests of her American students.

In a spirit similar to my own dissatisfaction, I heard that the Viennese analyst Ernst Kris, an analysand of Helene's and also a personal favorite of Freud's in his last years, was reported to have been unhappy with how analysts had turned into what Kris had disdainfully called dentists—clinical practitioners capable of earning substantial sums of money but with little knowledge of theory or history, common on this side of the Atlantic.

As an outsider, I faced bureaucratic obstacles in attending the Boston meeting, and anyway, I was dragging my heels about it. To accomplish her objective, Helene went ahead and formally submitted my name to an appropriate committee; without any further effort on my part, I was given the privileges of a guest at the society. Not only could I attend future formal meetings, but my new status also made it easier for me to use the society's library.

As time went on, I felt strengthened by the knowledge that came from my interviews with Helene, and I began to seek out others who had known Freud. Helene made no effort to encourage me in this direction, but in time I found her fascinated by what I had been able to find out. I was determined to make my own way, despite hearing some discouraging predictions that either analysts—out of loyalty to Freud—would be unwilling to talk about him, or that there was nothing new to be learned.

In the spring of 1965 I traveled to Chicago, where I met five more pioneering analysts. Even though they were old and experienced I found they still seemed to appreciate the recognition; and despite their well-known names and established reputations, they found the time to see me. They had dealt with each other for years, and were often interested in what I had already been told. I had the advantage of being a newcomer, in that all sorts of unspoken assumptions had to be spelled out for my benefit. Gradually I got used to their accents and the peculiarities of their sentence structures, as well as some of their characteristic attitudes about Freud. A few key details that I could supply proved to be immensely helpful in jarring their memories. Thus, my book-knowledge of the circumstances surrounding the publication of certain of Freud's papers, my familiarity with the names of pre-World War I neurologists and psychiatrists, and my knowing in which cities early analytic meetings had been held, proved surprisingly effective in providing the context for these people to talk freely.

I found the interviewing immensely rewarding, although each new meeting demanded that I use all my capacities to allay any doubts they might have about an intrusive outsider. These challenging encounters were complicated by the fact that none of them could anticipate what I was apt to consider important. Sometimes they would regard certain areas as off limits and would label them "personal." I was not trying to pry into their private lives or uncover the emotional problems that might have sparked their initial interest in psychoanalysis. But the lines between their personal and psychoanalytic identities were always hazy, which had to be the case for the pioneers who had adopted Freud's approach to understanding and alleviating human dilemmas.

They were often surprised at my fascination with their casual comments and asides which seemed to me, as an inquirer, to express far larger themes. How exceptionally good the water tasted in old Vienna might seem an insignificant and unusual detail, but by absorbing this kind of trivia, I established my credibility as a researcher who knew something of the world I was inquiring about. A discussion about the expense of analysis raised the matter of what Freud had charged, and then how this compared to what other items at the time might have cost. That Freud shook hands before and after every analytic session was just a central European custom, one which was never established in America, even though in Vienna hand-shaking provided a significant element of supportive reality to Freud's own therapeutic practice.

The idiosyncracies of Freud's approach, including his constant cigar-smoking, his antique-filled office, or the presence of his chow dog while he saw patients, took awhile to sink in, and I am not sure I ever adequately appreciated how special a therapeutic environment Freud offered. Depending on how a patient adjusted his pillows, it was possible to almost sit up on Freud's analytic couch. If those I interviewed were apt to be unsure about what I was after, so was I; it always seemed that the people I was working with were sharing in my research which was really a quest for knowledge. I never knew exactly what I was going to do with the material I was collecting, although one of my unspoken concerns was always the issue of what makes for good therapy.

These early analysts were more devoted to Freud's framework of ideas than were succeeding generations, and it would not be an overstatement to say that they had staked their lives on Freud's school. As much as Freud might have liked to think that he had created a neutral scientific technique, the commitment to his work was almost religious in nature; he aroused the kind of loyalty among some of his followers that can only be compared to the fanaticism found within certain cults. Thus, if Freud severed relations with someone, or if a former student chose to go off in an independent direction, it was tantamount to betrayal and heresy or to breaking a family bond. Carl Jung, Alfred Adler, and Otto Rank, for example— at least at the time when I was actively pursuing my interviewing— were all regarded as beyond the pale; the writings of these former Freud allies are still not assigned to analysts in training today. The situation among analysts remains embattled; to say that someone's work in the field is reminiscent of any of these early heretics is like singling out a Trotskyite in pre-Gorbachev Soviet politics.

While those I interviewed shared in the same mythology about the struggles Freud encountered while creating his discipline, they were all remarkably flexible in how they chose to manipulate psycho-analytic concepts. I have never satisfactorily resolved the fact that whereas they could acknowledge that Freud, at his best, treated every patient as an exception, ignoring his own written recommendations about proper therapeutic technique, they themselves would not publicize his individualistic practices.

Psychoanalytic doctrine can be considered an elaborate and com-plicated form of theology. Not only are nuances involved in using

Freud's system properly, but even arguing about its merits and limitations makes demands on one's ability to reason within the terms he devised for us. The profession that Freud's disciples advanced after his death did become enormously successful. But whatever their material motivations were for becoming psychoanalysts, and some of them did become wealthy, I always felt that their original interest was based on their concern for the fate of the human soul—that of their patients as well as their own.

Despite the obstacles I encountered, I kept on interviewing because the people I met were so interesting. Entirely aside from the process of trying to reconstruct Freud as a man and a thinker, each of his followers had something special to tell me. I found in the end that many of the ideas of early psychoanalysis were outdated, and that materialistic considerations, including pressures to conform as the profession became more of a trade union, played a larger role than I had anticipated.

In the course of my work I arranged to see a number of Freud's "heretics" as well as his apostles. Although Jungians and Adlerians, for example, could not be expected to give me any first-hand accounts of Freud, since they had been reared at a distance from him, they could all give me critical insight into the kinds of questions I might like to keep in the back of my mind. There is an old German proverb which says that hatred can lead to intelligence, and as I proceeded in my work I assumed that even Freud's enemies might have something important to teach. Their reservations were sometimes sound and respectful, legitimate objections that were not recognized in the available literature.

I wanted to put aside the old partisan wrangling; just as Freud had behaved differently than his public pronouncements might have led one to expect, the contrast between what his disciples did as opposed to what they said was itself instructive. However dogmatic their stated principles, they often proved flexible in their actual behavior; this was true in the practices of both Grete Bibring and Helene Deutsch. As individuals, Freud's pupils were a remarkable band of people, and I admired their dedication to the idea that how we think affects the way we live.

In the years since I conducted my interviews, the literature about early psychoanalysis has proliferated. If in America today psycho-analysis is subject to skepticism, its significance as a cultural influ-ence throughout this century remains unchallengeable. Today's Pa-risian intellectuals are more fascinated than ever with all things psychoanalytic; there are some sixteen Freudian organizations func-tioning in France. Based on personal experience with the pioneers in this field, they are genuinely worthy of the attention they have been given. Their cultural background stands in broad contrast to that of their bread-and-butter American successors, both within psycho-analysis and the most traditional forms of psychiatry itself.

I also was deeply touched by the emotional involvement of Freud's disciples. Their religiosity bespeaks their concern with essentially spiritual issues, ones I could easily relate to. Although this religious devotion also led to the bothersome sectarianism that has marred the field, it is impossible to have one's cake and eat it too. So if they held their beliefs with a conviction that could border on fanaticism, this intolerance also led to an especially deep introspection. These twentieth-century puritans tried to live by ideals that were almost by definition impossible to implement. I found this devotion to be unusually touching.

In the end I got to know more than seventy people who were personally familiar with Freud. Because they were all quite elderly, many of them living in Europe, I felt I had to work fast. Unfortu-nately, virtually everyone who had known Freud has now passed away. It is sad when I look over the list to realize that only a handful are alive today. In addition to meeting those who had personally known Freud, I also arranged to see many others who were either especially interested in the history of analysis or had themselves taken part in the early analytic movement. I was able to talk to twenty-five of Freud's analytic patients, about whom I plan to write in the near future.

If I am to put first things first, it is important to report next about my contact with Freud's immediate family; all the other interviews I did prepared me for meeting them. Freud actually made the whole psychoanalytic movement a kind of extended second family. From among his students he chose surrogate children, celebrating their birthdays, helping to finance their educations, and offering them both patient referrals and direct advice. His disciples, in turn, would transfer to him the feelings one would naturally have for a biological parent. Because of this closeness, it was not unusual for them to name their children after Freud's own sons and daughters. And it was not surprising that their familial dependencies could foster deep resentments and interfere with their relationships to Freud.

2

The Family Freud in Perspective

Whether Freud was conscious of it or not, the bulk of his theorizing was to become a challenge to traditional family life. From today's perspective, it may appear that Freud, as the founding psycho-analyst, was a patriarch writing in behalf of traditional family values. The passage of time does give us an added perspective from which to appreciate the special sort of moral convictions Freud was endorsing. Genuine historical understanding allows us to get beyond the preju-dices of our own era and to learn something about ourselves which only the past can offer.

Freud was born in 1856. Looking back over so much time is bound to create special hazards, yet we have no choice but to view his-tory through today's preconceptions. Accordingly, I respected Helene Deutsch for the prominent role she had played historically. And the fact that Freud was such a significant influence on twentieth-century thinking helped me justify the kind of interviews I conducted with some of the key members of his immediate family.

The approach I took did not necessarily imply any universal moral progress since Freud's time. Medical science has made advances, and technological improvements have taken place, but such changes do not mean that our own beliefs are better than those of our predecessors, who often had unique strengths of their own. So it would never have occurred to me, for example, to expect Freud to behave toward his children as one would expect a good parent to do

32

nowadays. The time he spent with his wife must also be understood with an almost anthropological tolerance for what would have been customary in his day.

How Freud behaved has to be put in the context of a middle-class physician counting on his wife to manage a household with an abundance of servants. It would be unfair to chastise Freud for not being more like ourselves, and anachronistic to expect him to fulfill our own standards of conduct. The value of studying history involves going beyond congratulating ourselves for our own supposed superiorities. After all, the fact that a century earlier someone like Thomas Jefferson personally owned slaves does not mean that in the context of his own times he did not promote human liberty. The real point of examining the past is that it can give us some perspective on the inevitable blind-spots of our own convictions.

Within the terms of Freud's own culture he was, I think, rejecting the fundamental principles that defined normal family life. He was trying to understand how people can suffer from the effects of parenting which has gone wrong. One of the sources of Freud's enduring appeal, I believe, is that he so often took the side of the suffering child. Although Freud could be manipulative and identify with parental authority, he also underscored that the kind of neurotic suffering he labored against was a direct consequence of family life.

One of the most influential features of Freud's new psychology was that it criticized accepted patterns of raising children. Psychoanalysis held out the noble ideal that human anguish could be lessened through psychological knowledge. It is tempting to believe that there are experts in the human soul, people who can tell us how we ought to live. Psychoanalysis has flourished partly on the hope that we can improve on past concepts of child-rearing. Freud did succeed in pointing out problems which had too often been swept under the rug; he showed how a child's perceptions could be at odds with what adults were apt to anticipate. Even if his specific examples no longer have much relevance, he deserves credit for trying to identify with those who are the natural underdogs in life.

No matter how hard it might be to overcome our own preconceptions of what is "natural" in families, Freud's personal life has to be a matter of key significance. In truth, it was he who first acknowledged the importance of his own familial relationships. For example, at a number of strategic points in his writings, he referred to the influence of his father, Jacob. While Freud never credited his father with having directly contributed to the creation of psychoanalysis, Freud did propose that his most enduring theorizing—about the meaning of dreams—could be directly related to his reaction to his father's death in 1896.

No one has ever satisfactorily explained why Freud took dreams so seriously in the first place. One suspects that Freud's use of cocaine, both before and after its addictive qualities were known, might have played some part in heightening the vividness of his own dream experiences. Freud had started experimenting with cocaine as part of his medical research, and was bitter that he missed out on discovering its genuinely useful properties, which earned a Viennese acquaintance of his a Nobel Prize. Freud never discussed cocaine's relation to his dreaming, but instead related the composition of his *The Interpretation of Dreams* (1900) to Jacob Freud's dying.

Freud sometimes complained that he wished his father could have behaved differently toward him, for Freud had dallied for some eight years when studying medicine at the University of Vienna, having toyed with the idea of also pursuing a degree in philosophy. Another kind of father might have helped Freud be more decisive during that youthful phase of life. As we shall see, Freud behaved differently at a corresponding point in the life of his middle son Oliver. From the earliest years we can track, Freud was full of ambition, so it should not be surprising that he supposed that had his father been better educated or more socially prominent, then perhaps Freud's own career might have followed a smoother path.

We still do not know how Jacob Freud supported his family in Vienna. The family had moved there when Freud was a boy of four, after his father had been financially ruined as a businessman in Moravia—later a part of Czechoslovakia. It is likely that various relatives on both sides of the family helped out; at one point Freud's parents took in a lodger. A niece reported that as an old man Jacob spent a considerable amount of his time studying the Talmud, and a literature has arisen over how much Freud knew about Jewish customs and Hebrew in particular.[1] According to one of Freud's sisters, Jacob was "a self-taught scholar" who was "really brilliant."[2]

Freud wrote much less about his mother, Amalia, than his father, and despite Freud's having published in 1925 a formal autobiography, he told us relatively little about either of his parents. His special reticence about his mother may have been in keeping with what was culturally acceptable in the society in which Freud was reared. But Freud's reluctance to describe his mother is striking if only because she lived until 1930, when she finally died at the age of ninety-five. At that time Freud was already suffering from cancer of the jaw, and outlived his mother only by some nine years. At her death he reflected in letters to friends that now he too might feel free to die, since she was no longer alive to suffer from his loss.

It is a sign of his immense power that Freud's disciples expressed little interest in the character of Freud's mother. Apparently, since Freud chose to highlight other aspects of his childhood, excluding his mother's role, his disciples showed no special curiosity about the nature of her personality. This is a valid generalization even if Sandor Ferenczi, an important Hungarian student of Freud's, chose to dare to think about the effect Amalia might have had on her eldest son during a period when Ferenczi was himself troubled about his relation with the man he considered his master. As Ferenczi wrote in his diary in 1932, close to the end of his own life:

> The ease with which Freud sacrifices the interests of women in favor of male patients is striking. This is consistent with the unilaterally androphile orientation of his theory of sexuality. . . . The author may have a personal aversion to the spontaneous female-oriented sexuality of women: idealization of the mother. He recoils from the task of having a sexually demanding mother, and having to satisfy her. At some point his mother's passionate nature may have presented him with such a task.[3]

Ferenczi was writing during a period of disillusionment with Freud, and it probably took such a mood to allow him to dare link some of Freud's characteristic biases to Freud's special tie to his mother. Ferenczi was one of the first to raise the issue of the masculine tilt in Freud's psychological system; that is what he meant by the "unilaterally androphile orientation" of Freud's theory of sexuality. Others have, especially over the last generation, commented on the sexism built into traditional psychoanalysis. But Ferenczi was unique in being so early to trace Freud's "idealization of the mother"—as a defense against specific feelings toward the opposite sex, which might now be labeled as "chauvinistic"—to Freud's particular involvement with Amalia. It sounds as if Freud had so strong a need to be the paternal head of his own family, perhaps in contrast to his father, that it was especially difficult for him to tolerate the presence of maternal trends within himself.

Ferenczi, like others in Freud's intimate circle, would have had some personal contact with Amalia. She not only came to the official celebration in honor of Freud's seventieth birthday in 1926, but it was not unusual for Freud's special favorites to pay courtesy calls on the old woman. As bold as Ferenczi was in using some of Freud's own concepts to untangle the master's character and theoretical shortcomings, Ferenczi did not raise the one perplexing issue: why did Freud choose not to attend his mother's funeral in Vienna, instead sending his daughter Anna as his "representative?" Presumably the rest of the family understood why Freud preferred to stay home working instead of being at the service.

The founder of psychoanalysis has, even now, escaped thorough psychoanalytic inspection. Most analysts have followed Freud's example by concentrating on his relationship to his father and ignoring Freud's mother. If there is one lesson that psychoanalysis should have taught us, it is that everyone necessarily suffers from self-deception. Therefore, Freud's own account of his life ought in principle to be only a surface treatment, and one that should be subjected to close scrutiny. Like Jung before him, Ferenczi did object that Freud felt "he is the only one who does not have to be analyzed."[4] But even Ferenczi was hampered by how far he felt he could comfortably go in probing the nature of Freud's own hidden psyche.

More recent psychoanalysts, and historians who have taken their cues from official literature about Freud, have been even less inquisitive than Ferenczi, who was exceptional in his intuitive gifts. Nearly everything we know about Freud's childhood comes from comments he made in his own writings. These autobiographical disclosures have been largely accepted at face value, as if they were concrete, verified facts. Even Freud's reports of his dreams, and the associations he gave to them, have attracted an immense but largely uncritical degree of attention.

Otto Rank, another pupil of Freud's and a contemporary of Ferenczi's, also made some insightful remarks about Freud's selectively defensive use of his recollections. Like Ferenczi, Rank was inspired to interpret Freud psychoanalytically because of Rank's difficulties in dealing with Freud. Rank suggested, for example, that when Freud wrote about the immense impact his father's death had had on him, Freud was actually using this bit of family history to evade and disguise a falling out he was having with a father substitute—his mentor, Josef Breuer. Rank's point that Freud could use his past to avoid facing up to a crisis in his life has not been taken seriously by most of those who have studied Freud's life and career. (One consequence of Freud's influential teaching is that we now tend to overrate the claims of infantile conflicts instead of seeing them as excuses for adult misconduct.)

The little objective information we have about Freud's family tells us that Amalia was only nineteen when she married Freud's father, who was a mature man of forty. Jacob's first wife, whom he had married when he was seventeen years old, had died three years earlier; he briefly had a second wife, although there is some mystery here. In any event, when he married Amalia, they were still living in Moravia. Jacob Freud had two grown sons by his first wife, one of whom had a son older than Sigmund. According to what a nephew of Freud's told me, Jacob's first family had been the source of his financial distress; Freud's two older half-brothers had invested in South African ostrich-feathers, and when the market for them collapsed with a change in women's fashion, Jacob wrecked himself bailing them out. The half-brothers later settled in England; presumably they helped Jacob by sending money back from England.

The great psychologist came into the world as part of a complicated family setting; his nephew was his elder. For the rest of his life Freud was enmeshed in a large family constellation. He appears to have had little difficulty in standing out amidst all his family members. He was his parents' first child, and they went on to have five

daughters and then another son. Still Freud retained a special significance within the family circle. And as I have already mentioned, in
championing psychoanalysis Freud created an extended family, one
that fostered new allegiances and responsibilities and that in the end
created most of the famous controversies now connected with his
name.

In his own time Freud was a notable rebel, so it is plausible that he
would attract others of a similar persuasion. Wilhelm Reich was
among those analysts who took Freud's child-oriented line of reasoning to an extreme. The implications Reich drew account in part for
Freud's decision to wade in and specifically counteract the influence
Reich threatened to exert over psychoanalysis as a whole. In the
1920s Reich was a well-trained psychiatrist and a brilliant Marxist
theoretician. Freud was taken aback when this follower of his chose
to indict the whole middle-class family as the source of neurosis.
Instead of attempting to cure isolated symptoms like Freud was trying
to do, Reich proposed to abolish traditional, middle-class families
and substitute collective forms of child-rearing. Whatever implications Reich drew from Freud's theories, Freud's own world was one
in which numerous relatives were taken for granted. Reich heralded
the future in that he was concerned about the quality of life under
changed social circumstances.

These innovations were troubling to Freud, partly because he
feared that the public would accept Reich as a representative of
Freud's psychology. Also, Reich had couched his ideas precisely in
Freud's own biologistic-sounding language, which was why Freud
found Reich so threatening and irritating. Freud had indicted late-
nineteenth-century sexual mores as a source of neurotic conflicts,
and Reich went even further in behalf of sexual emancipation.
Freud's *Civilization and Its Discontents* (1930) provided a retort to
Reich's work. In that book Freud explained that he thought the
nature of human problems could not be traced to social institutions,
whether the structure of the family or the nature of capitalism.
Instead, Freud found troubling how fundamentally discordant human passions were.

Freud's psychology was one of drives inherently at odds with one
another. He saw aggression, or what he called the death instinct,

pitted against sexuality. Further, Freud proposed that aggressive impulses turned against themselves, and that inner self-division could explain not only the existence of guilt feelings but also the phenomenon of conscience itself. Perhaps most disturbingly, Freud proposed that even the sex instinct was necessarily self-divided, and that therefore sex could never be wholly satisfactory. Freud's vision, unlike Reich's utopianism, was a tragic one.

Reich, like Ferenczi, thought that Freud suffered from certain sexual inhibitions which helped account for the nature of some of his central ideas. (Later we will examine what is known about Freud's relationship with his wife's sister Minna, who lived with them for many years.) And like Ferenczi, Reich was inclined to think in terms of Freud's being "relatively impotent."[5] Both Ferenczi and Reich might have been in error about Freud's sex life, although as we shall see, it may be better to accept the idea that they were on the right track rather than propose that Freud actually engaged in an illicit sexual liaison.

Freud's own teachings entitle us to inquire into the nature of his upbringing and what his parents and siblings might have meant to him. By examining the nature of his family—he married in 1886 and fathered six children in the next eight years—I believe that it should prove possible to conjecture about his background and the personalities of the people who helped shape his early life. Freud taught that in each of us the child becomes father to the man; and therefore Freud's earliest years, and the family from which he came, had to play a decisive role in accounting for the person he was, as well as the theories he developed.

As a figure in history, Freud now assumes an almost mythic stature. One cannot overestimate either the significance of his impact or how he looms over the modern consciousness. It has even been suggested by a famous literary critic that Freud is the single greatest modern writer: "No 20th century writer—not even Proust or Joyce or Kafka—rivals Freud's position as the central imagination of our age."

> Freud was one of the greatest Western speculators, and was certainly the most suggestive myth maker of the last century. Asserting that his new science was firmly founded on evidence, on practice and observation, Freud nevertheless imagined a new map of the mind, or else he

discovered remarkable ways of mythologizing a Western map of the mind that had been developing for some centuries. Seeing himself as making a third with Copernicus and Darwin, Freud actually may have made a fourth in the sequence of Plato, Montaigne, and Shakespeare. The neurologist who sought a dynamic psychology seems today to have been a speculative moralist and a mythologizing dramatist of the inner life.[6]

Freud's standing is assured; his life and struggles seem emblematic for many. For instance, D. M. Thomas's best-selling novel, *The White Hotel*, begins with letters that read as if they were written by Freud, Jung, and Ferenczi themselves, and not the imaginative creation of a talented novelist. Readers had no trouble getting into Thomas's novel, which began with the occasion of Freud's brief but memorable trip to America in 1909, accompanied by Jung and Ferenczi. The success of *The White Hotel* is but one indicator of just how well-known Freud's career, and his capacities as a letter-writer, have become.

Yet the problem is that too many people regard Freud as either a demon or a saint, extremes that make it very difficult to approach his life with anything like dispassionate curiosity. Those with a specifically biological orientation in the field accuse Freud of holding back scientific progress; they regard his emphasis on the role of early childhood as a fairy tale at best, or as a narrative reconstruction of the past that provided patients with only a fictive sense of coherence and continuity. In an era when both therapists and suffering patients were both at sea, it was no small achievement that Freud had offered them some way to bring order to a seemingly incoherent set of problems. Unfortunately, however, there are still those true believers who take deep offense at any criticism of Freud's accomplishments; they regard any attempt to treat Freud as a legitimate object of historical inquiry as a sign of disrespect, if not debunking.

The general literature about Freud is largely composed of books about books. The professional psychoanalytic journals are even more disappointing, in that they customarily extract those quotations from Freud's works that serve to support the most current clinical practices. It is difficult for today's practitioners to acknowledge just how different Freud actually was from their idealized version. It is tempting to smooth out discontinuities between the present and the past and to rely on Freud's words as a classic authority for recent innovations. The result is bound to be a form of mythologizing. For in reality Freud was wholly unlike the character fostered by organizational propaganda. His originality and daring, which one might think of as an obvious quality, has been downplayed for the sake of using his memory to support those conventions that are currently acceptable.

Without ever verbalizing it, in retrospect I had had enough of the myths surrounding Freud, and I sought to meet the people who could tell me something directly. I will now describe a few of his family members—those who were still alive in the mid-1960s and who agreed to see me—and I will try to pass on some of the knowledge about Freud that I acquired.

I feel a special responsibility to record the interviewing material, for not only are these people no longer alive, but when they agreed to be interviewed on behalf of the Freud Archives in New York City, those transcripts were locked up in the Library of Congress in Washington, D.C. All of the dates restricting access extend throughout the next century and are arbitrary, since imposed at the whim of the Freud Archives itself.

In the case of Anna Freud, she not only never wrote an autobiography but also refused to allow herself to be tape-recorded about her father. I did not fully appreciate how fortunate I was to have been granted an audience with Anna based on Helene Deutsch's letter of introduction. Anna's brother Oliver, who did agree to be interviewed by the Freud Archives, has had his material locked up until the year 2057. Such a date may sound awesome, but based on my own interviews with Oliver, which will be recounted in Chapters 11 and 12, there is no reason to believe that there is anything other than the eccentricity of the Freud Archives behind the 2057 date. There is no reasonable relationship between the date and the sensitivity of the material he was willing to discuss. Even Freud's final will is sealed at the Library of Congress until 2007, although it has been a public document since it was probated in London in 1939; I even published it in a journal in 1990.[7] Thus, the need to protect Freud, stemming from unrealistic idealizations of him, is a whole story in itself.

Anna Freud was cautious even in her dealings with Ernest Jones.

Only after he completed a draft of the first volume of his Freud biography did Anna give him copies of the precious love letters between her parents. But some members of the family, like Anna's sister Mathilda, were opposed to exposing Freud's private life. I think that the reserve on the part of the Freud family has partly stemmed from a conviction that Freud's own wishes were unlikely to have been in favor of such disclosures; he had not even wanted an authorized biography of himself. The family only agreed to that proposal when they were unhappy about the growing body of literature which they regarded as unduly unsympathetic.

It is my hope that this account will be helpful not only to general readers interested in learning more, but also that in the future, specialists may use this account to better understand all the documentation that will finally be released from the Library of Congress.

I have of course relied on my detailed interview notes, as well as my knowledge of Freud's writings and the plethora of published material about him. Vignettes from the life of someone like Anna Freud, who was dedicated to her calling as a psychoanalyst, can be as interesting as any of her explicit teachings. I have intended here to be immediate and personal, concerned with my reactions to the people I actually met. In my earlier publications it seemed only appropriate to allude to this interview material, as I extrapolated from it—along with other historical evidence—in order to explore those issues I could understand only indirectly. This time I have written mainly about the people I saw and heard, using this evidence to understand more about the general area of Freud's family life.

When those who were personally involved with Freud, his pupils as well as his family, read his works or thought about his ideas, they automatically sifted out what seemed to them subjective or distorted. Many of the concepts that have occupied some of Freud's disciples, like his theory of a primitive death instinct, were dismissed out of hand by the people who knew him best. I came to conclude that the essence of what Freud had accomplished through his written works constituted a memorable autobiography, a great self-confession. The fact that those who used his techniques often came to different conclusions does not diminish his stature. In fact, I believe that he succeeded in contributing to the advancement of science; for to utilize his approach to achieve different results, and to puncture new myths, means that he created something sufficiently beyond himself to be independently useful to others. This characteristic of Freud's work helps account for the fact that his stature has continued to grow over the last few decades.

In the long run I think Freud will be regarded as a striking genius, even if not all of his particular recommendations remain viable. The German Marxist thinker Theodor Adorno once said of psychoanalysis that "only the exaggerations are true," and I wish early on I had appreciated his insight. For as an artist, Freud created a whole world; the distortions he engaged in and the extravagances he promoted were necessary to establish his particular vision. In the end, the man Freud, with all his inevitable frailties, is more worthy of emulation than the petrified god that some appear to need in order to support their idealizations of the creator of psychoanalysis.

Even if in the end I cannot accept many of Freud's theories, Freud the man can be much more interesting than many of his concepts. For example, his energy level was so high as to be in itself special. I am reminded of one pupil who was amazed to walk alongside Freud in the mid-1920s; he had to struggle to keep up with Freud, who was then almost seventy years old and had already undergone several operations for cancer of the jaw. If Freud is this strong now, thought the student, what might he have been like much earlier?

A former patient of Freud's thought it remarkable not just how hard Freud worked, but how effortlessly he did so. Freud's vigor not only lay behind the quality of people he was to attract, but also helps explain the continued vitality of his ideas throughout the twentieth century. The French are only the latest group to respond with whole-hearted enthusiasm to the force of Freud's innovations; he is now required reading for high school students in France who intend to go on to college. It is a tribute to the intensity of the French response to Freud that some of the most original psychoanalytic thinking is now going on in Paris.

But we must always remember that Freud was a person with fallibilities and, therefore, we have to accept the fact that he sometimes behaved disappointingly. While some of his accounts of human troubles are difficult to defend, his life is still a monument of fascinating contradictions and anomalies. In keeping with the complexities of the whole story, we will find that within his family circle, Freud behaved differently than one might expect of the first psychoanalyst. With any great figure in intellectual history one wants to be able to move from the work to the life, and then back again. So it is essential to remember that his world of old Vienna is long gone. The Hapsburg Empire that flourished for some 700 years until the end of World War I completely collapsed in 1938, with the annexation of Austria by the Nazis. Thus, to try to comprehend Freud without considering how radically things have changed, would be a historical fantasy.

As I indicated at the outset of this chapter, Freud cannot ever be our contemporary, and it would be ahistorical to flatten out or to ignore the central contrasts between the genuine Freud and ourselves. Yet seeing how different Freud and his immediate circle were from ourselves makes the subject particularly valuable. History teaches the most when it offers us alternatives to life as we already have known it. Freud, to the extent to which we can begin to understand him in the context of a vanished world so different from our own, becomes both more important and useful in emancipating us from preconceived notions of how life might possibly be experienced.

3

Maresfield Gardens

The Freuds stayed in Vienna until after Hitler invaded Austria in March 1938. Many of Freud's followers had tried to persuade him to leave much sooner, and it has often been thought that Freud's political naivete about the dangers he and his family would face explained his delay in getting out. Ever since the Nazis had come to power in 1933, German psychoanalysts had been in trouble, and Freud knew that Hitler's regime took a dim view of his work. Yet he was irritated when any of his followers chose to leave, as the Deutsches did in 1935, and he was determined to keep the center of psychoanalysis in Vienna.

Freud was almost eighty-two when Hitler annexed Austria, and a man of his years cannot have looked happily on the prospect of being uprooted from the city that had been his home for so long. I think that he remained there so resolutely largely on medical grounds; he knew that his Viennese doctors understood the complexities of his cancer case. In fact, his health rapidly declined once he got to London.

Freud had waited so long to leave that when the political crisis finally broke, he had to count on the assistance of powerful allies abroad to get safely out of Vienna. One of his former patients was William C. Bullitt, then America's ambassador to France, and the U.S. Department of State was actively concerned with the problem of protecting Freud's safety. The Princess Marie Bonaparte came from Paris to help, as did Ernest Jones from London. The issue was not merely rescuing Freud, but how to obtain exit permits for some eighteen more adults and six children. Freud himself was only allowed to leave in June, the central figure in the exodus that took place immediately around him. But his health was such that others like Anna were essentially in charge of the migration.

Holland may not have seemed far enough from the Nazi menace, and Switzerland would have been considered too closely associated with Jung. Jones took care of the necessary British papers, and the Freuds were deeply indebted to him for his help at this critical juncture. In London, the Freuds first stayed at a house rented by Freud's youngest son Ernst on Elsworthy Road. In July the new house on Maresfield Gardens was purchased for some £6,500. Freud, however, was unable to see the house until mid-August and moved there in late September, by which time many of his books and all his antiquities had been shipped from Vienna.

Maresfield Gardens is a street located in a suburban neighborhood. Technically, the Freud house was in Hampstead, which was supposed to be an exceptionally fashionable place. But when I first saw Maresfield Gardens, I could not understand why anyone could think Hampstead at all interesting. Although I had once been a student at Magdalen College in Oxford, the isolation of that academic experience had left me unfamiliar with London as a city. Some years later, after I had been actively conducting my field research on Freud and early psychoanalysis, I finally got around to touring the fascinating area around Hampstead Heath. All the shops and restaurants there made me realize that the Hampstead of the Freuds was only a minor aspect of that part of the city.

Freud lived at #20 Maresfield Gardens during the last year of his life, in 1939. It was an impressively large, ivy-covered house built around 1920. No wonder, I thought to myself at the time I first saw the house, that Freud, having been driven out of Vienna by the Nazis, had joked "Heil Hitler!" when he saw the accommodations that were finally found for him in London. In Vienna he had lived for decades in a spacious but dark rented apartment in a modest part of town, and over summer holidays the Freuds regularly stayed in comfortable but rural settings. Now in London he had an immense free-standing home. Freud's sense of irony could be mordant; according to one account he actually had raised his palm in the infamous "Heil Hitler!" salute, which would be shocking to even his most sophisticated admirers. After Freud first got cancer it hurt him to talk; some even still write as if he had had cancer of the tongue rather than the jaw. Each of his sayings was to become legendary among his followers. *

Helene Deutsch had told me in 1965 that after Anna Freud's death, the house was to be transformed into a public museum. It may seem hard to believe, but when I first went to see Freud's old apartment on the Berggasse, which was on the same floor as his consulting rooms, both sides of it were being occupied then by a private family and a seamstress's shop. In this a typically small Viennese residential building, Freud had for years taken the whole second floor for his work and his family; the Berggasse itself was, as an observer later accurately described it, "a dull and undistinguished street in a nondescript part of the ninth district of Vienna."[1] The same words could essentially be used to describe the nature of Maresfield Gardens within greater London.

The Berggasse building was notable also for the fact that Dorothy Burlingham, an intimate friend of Anna Freud's and in analysis with Freud for over a dozen years, lived in an upper story. Dorothy was an American, from the immensely rich Tiffany family, and had established a private telephone line to Anna in the Freud family apartment.

I had heard from an academic colleague of mine that an old

---

*At least one expression of Freud's sardonic sense of humor, which became famous later, turns out to be a myth. Before Freud was given final permission to leave Vienna, the authorities had requested he sign a document testifying that he and his family had been well treated. According to Jones, "Freud had of course no compunction in signing it, but he asked if he might be allowed to add a sentence, which was: 'I can heartily recommend the Gestapo to anyone'" (Ernest Jones, *The Life and Work of Sigmund Freud*, vol. 3, *The Last Phase, 1919–1939* [New York: Basic Books, 1957], p. 226). The actual document signed by Freud has now been unearthed and no such postscript appears on it. (See the *Journal of the International Association for the History of Psychoanalysis*, English ed., no. 8 [1989]: 13–14.) Those words, which in the meantime became, thanks to Jones, a commonplace among Freud's disciples, may have been spoken by Freud, and perhaps can surface in one of his as yet unpublished letters. Such a comment would have been a subtle take-off on how one might have recommended a former servant in those days.

neighbor of the Freuds was still living upstairs at the Berggasse, and so I visited there a widow, Mrs. Oschner, whose husband had been a physician. The furniture and decor of her flat bore such a striking resemblance to the photographs taken of the Freud family's apartment that it made me think that she had been frozen in time. Mrs. Oschner recalled how some of the Freud women would on occasion, around Christmas time, bring children to her place since they did not have such holiday decorations at home. And she knew about Dorothy Burlingham, whom she had mistaken for an Englishwoman because of the starkly stylish way she dressed.

Mrs. Oschner clearly remembered when the Freuds suddenly left in the 1930s, taking "all their furniture with them." She repeated this point unlike any other. She obviously knew the Freuds were Jews, but seemed to have no recollection of the political events that precipitated their flight. Years earlier, when I was a youngster traveling in Europe, a Viennese had confided to me how in 1938 the citizens of Vienna had welcomed the invasion by the Nazis. Although a plaque on the exterior of the apartment building acknowledged Freud's having once lived there, my taxi-driver had no knowledge of the significance of the address he was taking me to. But when I knocked on the door, the inhabitants of Freud's apartment guessed right away that I must be a visiting American. Only subsequently was a museum founded there, partly with Anna Freud's help. In London itself, after Anna Freud's death in 1982, it took until July 1986 for the Freud Museum to be officially opened.

By the 1960s Freud's house at #20 Maresfield Gardens in London had become a mecca to all who sought to follow in his footsteps. Being invited to the house was, I soon found out, a sign of being accepted within the inner circle of the leaders of the psychoanalytic movement. Those who had written on the subject of psychoanalysis, but for some reason had not been received at the house in which Freud had spent the last months of his life, knew that they were stigmatized as unwelcome. I later encountered a Los Angeles analyst who had never been invited to the house, despite all he had written about Freud, and this slight obviously rankled him.

I had a small grant to continue my research in Europe during the summer of 1965, so Helene Deutsch kept to her initial promise and went ahead that spring to set up an appointment for me with Anna Freud. The reply seemed to come by return mail. Freud had been an avid and conscientious letter-writer, from at least as early as a youth of fifteen, and that trait endured until he died at the age of eighty-three. Though lacking Freud's stylistic genius, Anna Freud inherited his determination to communicate promptly through letters. As soon as Helene Deutsch heard from Anna, she excitedly telephoned me the news.

At my next interview with Helene, which she was more eager than ever to hold, she read aloud the letter recounting Anna's having put the June date and time on her calendar. According to the arrangements that Anna outlined in agreeing to see me, I was supposed to confirm in writing the suitability of the day and hour she had proposed. Helene was obviously delighted that she still retained her influence with Anna; they had known one another for approximately half a century, but had not seen each other for some years. (Helene had gone to England in 1956 on the occasion of the centenary of Freud's birth.) I also think that as one of the great teachers in the history of psychoanalysis, Helene was pleased at being able, even at her extremely advanced age, to sponsor with Anna a newcomer to analysis.

Helene Deutsch had been unhappy with the quality of her students since her 1935 arrival in America. Her most satisfying period as a teacher had been in Vienna when, as head of the Training Institute, she had been able to rear a whole generation of future leaders. Before joining Freud's circle in 1918, Helene was already well-established within Viennese psychiatry. She already held a secure niche within both psychiatry and psychoanalysis before Anna Freud started to emerge in the 1920s as a figure in Freud's school.

Helene explained to me that for an analyst, visiting Anna Freud was like a Catholic going to see the Pope. For example, American analysts who had long since completed their professional training, often went to Anna for brief but formal analyses, what Helene termed "polishing up." Once trained, it is difficult for analysts to get further help for themselves in their own cities. Freud had thought that a psychoanalysis involved a subordinate's submitting to a higher authority. While I have every reason to think that Anna was less formidable a presence than Freud himself, still her role as a therapist of last resort helped secure the power she was able to wield. Throughout her lifetime Anna Freud remained the most significant living symbol of Freud's heritage.

Inasmuch as Helene Deutsch had been responsible for getting me in to see Anna Freud, it was some time before I appreciated the scope and intensity of their old rivalry. At the outset I had detected no divided feelings in Helene toward Anna. Yet the more I pursued my research and the less blinkered my initial conception of Freud grew, the easier it was to understand how Helene rather relished, in the way my work was evolving, a kind of quiet, second-hand challenge to Anna's authority.

In time I came to understand that Helene saw Anna not just as Freud's daughter but as a former student of her own, and one about whom she had complicated feelings. Yet, when in the late 1970s I was working on my biography of Helene and had free access to all the papers in her study, I never came across any sign that she had saved any of Anna's letters to her. (I later learned that some letters are held under restrictions at the Library of Congress.) Since there would have been so few occasions for them to correspond, one might have thought that Helene would have at least kept Anna's letter about me; Anna, it turned out, had kept Helene's letter recommending me. Yet, not only toward Anna but even in relation to Freud himself, Helene had been determined to maintain her independence. While she lived in Vienna and like others, communicated with Freud by mail, she regularly threw out his replies. She did remember some of them about patients, and she still could appreciate Freud's wit. She never would have dreamt of calling him up, for in that era the telephone had different connotations than now; only on the rarest occasions was Freud known to have made use of it.

In the course of my general research during that summer of 1965 in London, I found out that Anna admitted in writing to being jealous of the various women who were important to her father. But I think that she had special reasons for being competitive with Helene. Once, after attending an evening clinical presentation of Helene's in

Vienna, Anna had spent a sleepless night, explaining to a close friend that she would never be "as good" as Helene. Helene had an abundance of natural fire and vivacity, whereas Anna seemed to go out of her way to show off her plainness—"backing into the lime-light," according to one London analyst critical of her.

Both Helene and Anna were the youngest daughters of beloved fathers, but Anna never underwent the medical education that Helene had. Anna possessed none of the psychiatric credentials Helene attained, and never even enrolled in the traditional gymnasium educational institution which in Vienna would prepare one for the university. Helene, on the other hand, had had private tutoring to make it possible to enter, some years before Anna would have been at the appropriate age, the University of Vienna. Some women successfully defied the conventional odds against them; Helene had to struggle against her mother's wishes that she marry early, and Helene's father only backed her reluctantly. No such split took place between Freud and his wife over Anna. (Although both Helene and Anna were to die in the same year, 1982, Helene was over ten years the elder; she was born in 1884, and Anna in 1895.)

Thus, there were grounds for Helene, despite Anna Freud's subsequent stature, to be patronizing about Anna. Helene somewhat ruefully recalled a faux pas she had made after Anna's first talk in 1922 before the Vienna Psychoanalytic Society. In those days, one became a member by making a successful presentation, and Freud had, in cooperation with Anna, decided that she was ready. Anna's first psychoanalytic presentation is now known to have been largely autobiographical.* Helene's remorse was that she had been tactless enough to compliment Freud on Anna's performance. From his reaction, Helene immediately realized her mistake. Freud was not seeking any form of approval from Helene, and he had been mildly offended at the liberty she had taken in expressing an opinion about Anna to him. Yet his defensiveness may also have reflected his

---

*At the meeting, one of Freud's students had "induced a momentary panic by suggesting that the girl she had written about was 'a totally abnormal person whose incompetence and inferiority would absolutely emerge in real life.'" Anna was so shocked that she remained silent, but Freud came to the rescue; as Anna wrote about the incident, "Fortunately Papa answered him and defended my little girl" (Elisabeth Young-Bruehl, *Anna Freud: A Biography* [New York: Summit Books, 1988], p. 108).

awareness of the doubtful quality of Anna's work. (Another prominent analyst once told me how embarrassingly inadequate Anna's
initial papers had been.)

Anna ultimately was to play a unique role in Freud's later years,
sharing in his work in ways which came to exclude early followers
like Helene. During her father's lifetime, Anna gained prominence
mainly as his personal gatekeeper after Freud first fell ill. As a relative
explained to me, the ladies in the family formed a bodyguard to keep
people away from him. Increasingly Anna performed the role of
Freud's private secretary. For years he had answered all his mail by
his own hand, and only little by little did he allow anyone else to take
dictation, or even to type some of his letters.

As time went on Anna became the decisive arbiter of Freud's time,
and he increasingly relied on her advice about whom he should see
and even whom he might decide to treat. And then there were the
medical problems connected with removing, cleaning, and replac-
ing the prosthesis he had to wear inside his mouth. Anna functioned
in part as Freud's nurse, and doubtless helped prolong his life.
Numerous operations had to be scheduled as the cancerous tissue
threatened to reappear. In these areas Freud's wife, Martha, as we
shall see, was not capable of helping him, and even Martha's sister
Minna, who had lived with the family since the mid-1890s, could
not satisfy all his needs either.

In the meantime, Freud was increasingly proud that Anna had
succeeded in carving out a separate sphere for herself in the area of
child analysis, a field from which he held himself back. He never
treated children directly, although he did write one of his most
famous case histories about "little Hans," a child who had been
treated by his own father, knowledgeable about analysis by virtue of
being a member of Freud's Viennese circle. It would not be long
before Anna's position as a child analyst was challenged by a rival in
the field, Melanie Klein. Freud vigorously took offense at Klein's
criticism of Anna, which he understood to be a thinly disguised
critique of himself. Once Jones took Mrs. Klein's side, Freud felt he
had even more of a battle on his hands. When Theodor Reik, one of
Freud's nonmedical disciples in Vienna, was sued under a statute
against quackery, Freud rose to the occasion by writing a pamphlet

designed to defend the practice of his profession by nonmedical analysts; his *The Question of Lay Analysis* (1926) was clearly designed also to defend Anna.

By chance, I was invited back to #20 Maresfield Gardens in 1984, before the museum was opened, to be interviewed by a Dutch television station for a program about Freud that they wanted to shoot in the house itself. They asked me to speak about Freud from his ground-floor study, even though the house was entirely empty because it was in the process of being renovated for the museum. The only piece of furniture in the room during my interview was an analytic couch.

It was a shock for me then to see the house's state of disrepair; all of the historically important pieces had been crated and temporarily moved out. In one corner, I recall being tantalized by the sight of a box filled with reproductions of Freud manuscripts. Anna Freud had always kept her father's original papers in the house with her; she had signed an agreement that after her death, they would go to the Freud Collection at the Library of Congress—originally set up, without any enthusiasm on her part, after World War II by Dr. Kurt R. Eissler in behalf of the Freud Archives, which he headed in New York City. (Oddly enough, Jungian money was originally a key financial resource of the Freud Archives.) There had once been a break-in at the house, during a period before copies of manuscripts had been made, but fortunately the burglars were not interested in the things that concern scholars.

I remember thinking in 1984 how strange it was that the place looked so shabby. I was eager to see the state of the kitchen, but a loyal family custodian refused to give me access, although otherwise I had the run of the empty house. I surmised that Anna Freud had spent little money on maintaining #20 Maresfield Gardens in all the years that she lived there. At the time I attributed the neglect to a characteristic European refugee attitude toward the upkeep of London property. Anna Freud also owned a countryhouse in Walberswick, where she and others in the family (including a Viennese analyst) owned property. And I knew she shared another house with Dorothy Burlingham in County Cork, Ireland, as in Vienna they had had a retreat for themselves outside the city itself. It never dawned on me at the time that Anna might have lacked the means to properly maintain #20 Maresfield Gardens.

I later found out that the expense of maintaining the house had grown too much for Anna during her last years of ill health, and that ownership had been prematurely transferred to the museum trust that was waiting to take it over. Money provided by her American friend Muriel Gardiner was a key to the whole arrangement. Gardiner may be best known as the supposed model for Lillian Hellman's "Julia," which ultimately became a Hollywood movie about a psychoanalyst in the anti-Fascist Viennese underground in the 1930s. Hellman denied she had relied on Gardiner's life-story, and although Hellman's capacity for telling tall tales was notorious there are independent grounds, from within knowledgeable Viennese left-wing sources, for doubting Gardiner's claims to have been the basis of "Julia."

Gardiner had her own ideological agenda which could cause her to tailor the truth. One of her avocations was keeping track of Freud's famous patient, "the Wolf-Man," who had subsequently been ana-lyzed by Ruth Mack Brunswick, also Muriel Gardiner's own analyst. Whatever the Wolf-Man himself may have said, Gardiner always did her best to put Freud's handling of the case in the best possible light. She was immensely rich and sent the Wolf-Man regular funds. (She also was for years the financial angel behind *Dissent* magazine.) Gardiner was so committed to Anna Freud's faction that she, or her foundation, could be called upon whenever Anna or the Freud Archives needed special grants of money.

Although, as we shall see, Anna Freud was able to raise extraordi-nary sums for her Hampstead Clinic, she did not die financially secure. Her father had left a net estate, after taxes, of some £16,000. In Vienna, the Nazis had looted Freud's safe of the equivalent of $840, and there was a ransom to pay that came to almost $5,000. In addition, before leaving Freud and his younger brother Alexander (who moved to Toronto) provided for their four sisters still living in Vienna the sum of over $22,000. Still, by the end of his life Freud was pretty well off. The bulk of his estate went into the trust he had set up for his wife Martha.

The future royalties on Freud's books went exclusively to his grandchildren; he wrote in a letter, perhaps with false modesty, that he hoped his publications would provide some "pocket money" for them. But Anna, who remained unmarried and childless, had to feel left out of an important source of future earnings. It is true that Freud helped make her into a leading analyst, and she had her own clinical practice. She had also received the specific bequest of Freud's analytic library and his collection of antiquities. I suspect that the ancient objects were greatly undervalued as part of Freud's final estate. But these were assets which under the circumstances she could not think of ever selling. Unlike Anna, her older sister Mathilda (also childless) could in 1973 sell a first edition of *The Interpretation of Dreams* for $1,300, which by today's standards seems a low figure.

According to a 1954 letter of Anna Freud's, "under pressure" from her two brothers in England, Martin and Ernst, their father left "a family estate from which my mother could draw at will but which did belong to the whole family." Anna's troubled relationship with her mother can be documented, but the testament itself meant that in later years there would be a conflict of interest between Anna and Freud's grandchildren. For example, when she sought to block the publication of the extensive Freud-Ferenczi correspondence, which her nephews wanted in print, she and they were at loggerheads. (The correspondence is only now starting to appear.) Anna thought of herself as preserving the dignity and integrity of psychoanalysis. As she wrote in 1979 about another of Freud's correspondences, that with his Romanian boyhood friend Silberstein: "I can never help feeling that my various nephews and niece who have nothing at all to do with psychoanalysis are really not the ones to be considered. Unfortunately, due to the testamentary dispositions of my father, this is the law." One of Anna's old friends confirmed for me that Anna, the last child of the Freuds, had been the result of an unwanted pregnancy, the effects of which may be hard to exaggerate. This friend thought that regardless of Anna's position in Freud's life, or in the world at large, at base she was left feeling unwanted.

It is not clear to me exactly how Anna Freud acquired ownership of the house on Maresfield Gardens in the first place, although in the end it had become a part of the power, real and symbolic, that she exercised within psychoanalysis. When Freud's final will was signed, the household was still temporarily established at Elsworthy Road nearby. Presumably the Maresfield Gardens property would have gone into the trust for Martha; after her death in 1951, one would have thought that her five surviving children would have shared in inheriting the house, or the asset it constituted. Yet, by some family decision, Anna had remained there, where she had already been joined by her old friend Dorothy Burlingham.

When I first visited the house in 1965, it was a well-furnished functioning home. While Freud memorabilia abounded, #20 Maresfield Gardens was still a place where people lived and conducted analytic business. Thus, when I saw it in its temporarily denuded state in 1984, I was dismayed by the dismantling of what once had been a living entity. By then, both Anna Freud and Dorothy Burlingham were dead, and hypotheses were openly exchanged about the alleged strangeness of their intimate relationship. Hints of their lesbianism became a common rumor.

I have myself always taken the view that the tie between Anna and Dorothy was a wholly sublimated one of the closest of friendships. Recently, some letters from Anna to an earlier intimate friend of hers, Eva Rosenfeld, have come to light, and they show both Anna's vulnerability and her capacity for tenderness and affection. No letters from Anna to Dorothy have been released. Anna succeeded in hiding from the outside world a side of her which was in stark contrast to her austere bearing.

The house was filled with historical ghosts, even in Anna's time. Her father had died there after years of heroically coping with his cancer. During her own last months, Anna sat in the same garden as her father had, even wrapped in one of his coats. And one of Dorothy Burlingham's daughters, who had been a patient of Anna's for years—along with her brothers and sister—both as a child in Vienna and as an adult in London, had committed suicide at #20 Maresfield Gardens.

It was in the spring of 1987 that I first saw the completed Freud Museum. The magic of the old atmosphere has been masterfully recaptured in the dual objective of restoring the house and displaying artifacts from the history of analysis. Culture clashes were, of course, inevitable. For example, I spotted a striking round table with a beautiful inlaid centerpiece. When I skeptically asked if that bit of furniture had really been in Vienna, a helpful museum official showed me a photograph from a book proving that it had been with the Freuds before they left in 1938. Yet in Vienna the table had been completely covered with a crocheted doily (which Freud's sister-in-law Minna specialized in), while the English had characteristically chosen to expose the attractive woodwork. It was equally Viennese to mask such a centerpiece.

The only real lapse in taste, as far as I am concerned, was the prominence in Freud's study of the death mask of the Wolf-Man, who finally died at a Viennese mental asylum in 1979. Plenty of controversy exists over Freud's treatment of the Wolf-Man, whose case history forms part of Freud's war with Carl G. Jung and Alfred Adler. Freud was determined to prove against his critics, by means of the clinical case of the Wolf-Man, that infantile sexuality existed as the source of pathology, and that childhood neurotic conflicts could be independent of the events in later years. Conversely, Jung had proposed that this so-called infantile historical material was merely part of a defensive maneuver by adult patients, eager to use the past to evade current life tasks. Jung—and many others since then—thought that analysts too would be glad to avoid discussing their realistic relationship with patients by attempting to reconstruct childhood.

Displaying the Wolf-Man's death mask so prominently in the Freud Museum, even though Muriel Gardiner had taken such a special interest in him, seemed to me anachronistic, since he had died so recently. It also begs the question of whether analysis had even been the right method of treatment for him. In his last years the Wolf-Man thought he should originally have been diagnosed as schizophrenic, which is not how Freud had initially seen the case. [2]

Aside from the fact that it had cost $1.5 million to set the Freud Museum up, some of the details of the restoration are arresting. It sounds to me almost unthinkable that £50,000 went into the house's initial rewiring so that each ceiling light would have its own transformer; the result was a series of spotlights hanging down, which was so unsuitable for re-creating the home's ambience that two weeks before the formal opening of the museum, the ceiling in Freud's old study had to be ripped out, and another £20,000 was spent to rectify the original architect's unsuitable lighting plans.

One reason it took so long for the museum to open was that the London Borough of Camden, with a left-wing commitment to public housing, moralistically insisted that a separate flat be carved out of the big house. As a result the whole third floor—which once housed Anna Freud's consulting room, a waiting room for patients, a room for a secretary, as well as a guest room and a bathroom (given people's nerves, a toilet is an essential constituent of an analyst's practice)—had to be separated from the museum. The elevator that was originally installed by Freud's architect-son Ernst to assist his enfeebled father, later took tenants to the third floor, which was rented out for the considerable sum of several hundred pounds per week to a vice president of a commercial banking firm. Freud was politically anti-utopian enough to have taken perhaps some wry pleasure in the curious upshot of the socialist idealism which delayed the opening of the museum.

By 1990 the museum's research activities had so expanded that the third floor was no longer rented out. I found it startling to find, during a terrible heat wave that summer, that a completely open-minded researcher, sitting with bare-feet at a computer, could be working in quarters once inhabited by Anna Freud. Such easygoing ways were in sharp contrast to the austere asceticism I still associate with #20 Maresfield Gardens.

Converting the homes of well-known figures into museums has often justifiably given rise to skepticism. In this instance, it meant that despite the fact that Anna Freud had actually inhabited the home for forty-four years, her own quarters were done away with historically, and the house where Freud had lived only so briefly was turned into a monument to him and his work. Yet I do not think that Anna would have minded, for her attachment to the house was immense. She used it as a reason for not traveling more, and it was a vital link to her father. I found it especially poignant that in thinking about one of her dreams, she once asked herself if she ever left the house for one her father did not know, how would he be able to find her in her dreams?[3]

The belief that houses have spiritual ghosts helps account for why people want to visit such museums. In the case of #20 Maresfield Gardens, the objectives of the museum have not been completely fulfilled. Originally the idea was to make it an open-ended center for psychoanalytic studies. Even after the brouhaha over Jeffrey Masson, whom Kurt Eissler in New York had selected as his successor to head the Freud Archives, the museum's future remains uncertain. Aside from Janet Malcolm's celebrated 1983 pieces in *The New Yorker*, asserting that Masson intended to establish at #20 Maresfield Gardens "a center of scholarship, but it would also have been a place of sex, women, fun,"[4] it was already clear even while Anna Freud was still alive that Masson was not the right person to live in her house.

Malcolm's attributing those exact words, within quotation marks, to Masson himself—"a place of sex, women, fun"—gave him the ammunition to file his libel lawsuit against her. When initially challenged, she declared that all her direct quotations were to be found on her tape-recorded interviews with Masson; but on legal discovery, a number of remarkable discrepancies turned up and she had to rely on the more general right of a journalist to recapture the spirit of someone's comments.

Masson first fell from power at the Freud Archives because of some 1981 interviews he gave to a *New York Times* reporter: it was his pet theory that the sexual seduction of children lies behind adult neurosis, and that Freud knew this was true in the 1890s but cowardly disguised his findings because of the hostile reaction he had received from the Viennese medical establishment. When Masson was fired by the Freud Archives, he sued them and won an out-of-court settlement paid for by Muriel Gardiner, whose money had helped hire him in the first place. Masson later sued not only Janet Malcolm for falsely quoting him, but also *The New Yorker* and Alfred Knopf, Inc., which had published Malcolm's articles in a book.

In 1991 the Supreme Court unanimously overturned the lower court decisions, and it reinstated Masson's lawsuit against Malcolm for having concocted libelous quotations and attributing them to him. According to the holding in *Masson v. New Yorker Magazine*, the Constitution does not guarantee free speech for fabricated quotations which materially change the meaning of what was actually

said. Now that Masson has been successful on the point of law, a jury
trial has been held, but ended unable to agree on damages.

The first director of the museum, once it was opened without
Masson, was determined to keep it free of sectarian squabbles. He
soon resigned to return to Canada, and his successor tried to maintain a policy of ideological tolerance. At least one party was held
there, for example, for an author of a book about Freud which
would, I feel sure, have outraged Anna Freud; the guest's lineage was
more Jungian than Freudian. The Freud Archives in New York,
although capable of exerting some informal financial control over
the Freud Museum, pursued a far more secretive course about Freud
manuscripts than the museum itself wanted to maintain. After Kurt
Eissler was removed as director of the Freud Archives because of his
poor choice of Masson, and Eissler's handling of the whole public
dispute connected with Masson, his successor decided to descend on
the Freud Museum to carry off precious documents to the Library of
Congress. Although the Freud Museum kept the copying machines
going virtually round-the-clock, it could not keep up with the hurried demands from the archives in New York. Material that was not
able to be copied was carried to the United States in American
Embassy diplomatic pouches.

In 1990, the second director of the Freud Museum was displaced.
The nature of the problems between him and the committee members officially running the museum, which led to his formal resigna-
tion, have not been revealed. But it is safe to speculate that central to
the allegations was that under his auspices, the museum had become
if not anti-Freudian, then certainly non-Freudian. Lectures presented by the museum were not orthodox enough to suit the powers-
that-be that control the ultimate purse strings. It remains to be seen
whether anybody respectable in the world of museum-directorship
can be found to suit the religious purposes of the aging authorities
who still strive to control what goes on at #20 Maresfield Gardens.

4

On First Encountering "Miss Freud"

Long-time family servant Paula Fichtl opened the front door for me when I arrived for my first interview with Anna Freud. Paula originally worked for Dorothy Burlingham and came to the Freuds in the 1920s. In Anna's old age Paula became difficult, but she was provided for in Anna's will. After Anna's death, Paula allowed herself to be extensively interviewed by a journalist about her fifty-five years with the Freuds. By then, Paula was living at a nursing home in Salzburg back on the continent; a volume of these conversations eventually came out.

In 1965 I was only beginning to become aware of Paula's "historical" standing. She took me upstairs by means of the elevator and we casually chatted. Of course, I was all geared-up for meeting Anna Freud. Outside there was a mildly miserable, typical London rain, and Paula asked me about the weather back home. For her, home still meant Austria, where she told me that the Danube had been flooding recently. A charwoman was washing the floor of the front entrance hall; by the time I returned to the home over twenty years later in 1987, when the museum was set up, that single vignette symbolized a commonplace of the old household establishment, now impossible in an era of public visitors.

To ensure being on time for the interview, I was about fifteen minutes early. As I sat down to wait (Paula went to notify Anna Freud of my arrival), I thought of trying to absorb the significance of the cases of books and antiquities that lined the waiting room, but Anna Freud graciously came out immediately to take me into her consulting quarters. She was almost seventy, and had the same slight stoop that I had been told her father had. I mainly concentrated on her deep-colored brown eyes, which I found hard to fathom.

Only later, when I saw her in public, did I notice how oddly old-fashioned were the immensely wide, ankle-length dresses she chose to wear. According to a niece of hers, she always sewed her own clothes by hand; apparently while conducting analyses she could either knit or work at a loom. The jumperlike dresses she wore were two sizes bigger than necessary, which lent her an unnatural but absolutely characteristic shape. Her close-cropped hair highlighted her facial features, which I focused on.

Despite her efforts to put me at ease, something in her bearing, or in the situation, had an intimidating effect. This was true, I soon found out, for others as well. In those days what one heard about her, especially in North America, was expressed in stereotyped phrases of idealization: she was, I was told by Helene Deutsch, "a wonderful peaceful" person who "hates fights." Although some still consider Anna Freud a kind of modern saint, beyond rational criticism, that summer I found out as I pursued my research that there were other sides to her personality. For example, in 1954 she had written about a BBC program on Freud: "I heard the talks in the 3rd Program last night only and was disgusted. Not only 'slimy,' but stupid, ambivalent, arrogant, contradictory, malicious, uninformed and unenlightened. The BBC should be ashamed of itself." In those days Anna Freud's correspondence was normally inaccessible, but this sort of protectiveness about her father did not ever encourage me to relax about her.

Anna Freud was the author of famous writings on child analysis, and how it had to differ from the treatment of adults. She and Melanie Klein took such different approaches that, although Klein was already dead, Anna would still not attend the presentation of a paper at the British Psychoanalytic Society by one of Klein's supporters. Neither woman, however, got rational criticism from within her own separate following, and if one re-reads Anna Freud's texts now, for example, what stands out is how remarkable it was that no one challenged her more while she was alive.[1]

Anna Freud's most outstanding book, *The Ego and the Mechanisms of Defense* (1936), was written while she was working most closely with her father. She was a pioneer in codifying the various defense mechanisms of the ego, leading a fresh approach to psychoanalytic thinking after Freud's death. Although she objected to many of the "compromises" with early psychoanalytic tenets proposed by others, I never noticed her repeat Freud's early contention that all neurotic symptomatology was an expression of repressed sexuality. To my knowledge, her own innovations were made without awareness that she was in any way departing from "the true faith." Her students were apt to complain that from their point of view she had been relatively reluctant to publish. When I first met her she had just published a book that distinguished between normality and pathology in children, yet she never acknowledged that Freud had once berated Adler as a renegade for being interested in normal phases.

I think it was partly the American tendency to romanticize childhood that helped ensure that each time she came to the States she could always count on everyone being at her feet. Despite the fact that she privately shared her father's well-known bitterness toward everything American, Anna was always able to come to the States to raise money for the children's clinic she and Dorothy Burlingham headed. The list of American foundations that at various times supported her work was an expression of her influence. She later received honorary degrees from Yale, the University of Chicago, the University of Vienna, Columbia University, and Harvard, and was offered other honors that she never cared to pick up.

In London Anna faced a different situation. The British knew her as a person and treated her accordingly, while the Americans never seemed to acknowledge how autocratic she could be. In France she provoked outright contempt. This was partly a consequence of her support for Freud's analysand Marie Bonaparte, the Princess George, during the French controversy over Jacques Lacan. For in the 1950s, Anna and her allies helped ensure Lacan's ouster from the International Psychoanalytic Association, founded by Freud in 1910. Lacan was such a charismatic leader that any bureaucratizing movement would have had trouble holding him; but he was also objectionable because his clinical practices were considered too "wild." He could dramatically cut the length of individual analytic sessions, and did not adhere to anything resembling the standard fifty-minute hour. Despite the unique training experiences that both Anna and Marie Bonaparte had had with Freud himself, they assumed that such privileged freedoms were only for the few, like themselves, and should not be recommended for others. Although it is unlikely that Lacan knew at that point how unorthodox were Freud's own clinical tactics, Lacan had absorbed the idea that to be creative a psychoanalyst had to break with all preexisting rules.

Despite Lacan's theorizing and complaints about conformism, especially by Americans, in practice he tried to win acceptance from the International Psychoanalytic Association, but Marie Bonaparte and Anna Freud stood firmly against him. I think it is a tribute to the characteristically French intransigence about ideas that they refused to share in the mythology about Anna, and actually tried to weigh and assess her writing on its merits. While Freud was alive, Anna had scarcely been considered a psychoanalytic thinker of the first rank, and when evaluated by the broadest kind of cultural standards the French found her work sadly lacking.

The analytic couch in Anna Freud's consulting room seemed to me extraordinarily prominent, not only unusually large but placed more or less in the middle of the available space. In America the position of the analyst's couch would almost certainly be next to the wall; sometimes it even seems so much a part of the ordinary furniture that it could be used for casual sitting. This physical layout in the States reflected the fact that American analysts did more psychotherapy, with patients in an upright position, than exclusive couch analysis. In London, psychoanalysis had then still retained its exceptional status, not yet having been incorporated into everyday psychotherapeutic life. For Anna analysis was a unique technique, not one among many, and it was obvious that she considered it to be a morally superior approach. Her placement of the couch implied that walls could not be used as a possible defense, and that patients need have no reliance on them; it also ensured that the patient was certain to appear to be the center of attention.

Sitting near her, we talked about questions I had about the history of her father's ideas and the movement as a whole. Anna had known most of the people I wanted to write about, and I was trying to pick up any leads she might offer. It was hard for me to press any subject too strongly, especially since Helene Deutsch had warned me specifically against raising certain themes—Freud's Jewishness and the place of Moses in his writings, for example—that I had freely discussed with Helene.

Freud as a Jew has always been a sensitive subject for psychoanalysts, if only because his Jewishness raises the spectre of possible cultural sources for some of his ideas. Orthodox psychoanalytic historiography has always preferred to regard the development of Freud's ideas as part of the forward march of a neutral science. To cite a recent example of such partisanship, one commentator has gone so far as to maintain about Freud: "the *origins* of psychoanalysis . . . are untouched by his historical situation."[2]

So my being unable to entertain with Anna Freud such an obvious subject as Freud's Jewishness had a general dampening effect on how free-ranging I felt able to be. Later I decided that Judaism meant altogether less for Anna than to her father, but I have been told that she did love *Fiddler on the Roof*. All his interests were broader than hers. When an international gathering of analysts met in Vienna in 1971, a city official got up to apologize for how Freud and his circle had been driven out in 1938. Instead of Anna's seeing the problem as involving much more, in fact all world Jewry, and after all she and the other analysts had been fortunate in having a profession which could be practiced elsewhere, she merely got up and accepted the apology in behalf of psychoanalysis. Although the fact of my own Jewishness may have been of little consequence to Anna Freud, I have the vague conviction that it played an important role in most of my other interviews. I do suspect that had I not been Jewish, it would have counted for something special with Anna, for like her father she sought to ensure that analysis would triumph within the Gentile world. (The Burlinghams were blond, blue-eyed aristocrats.) It is difficult to convey just how grandiose were the ambitions of all the early analysts.

Somehow the subject of the numerically large Japanese psychoanalytic group came up in my talks with Anna. She was a trifle defensive about what was going on in Japan in the name of her father's work, but indicated to me that when they came to visit her, she found they understood little of what was going on, and she also had difficulty following what they were up to. She presented this mutual lack of understanding as if it had successfully cancelled itself out. Since I knew how hard she had worked to expel Lacan, and I saw how cool she remained toward Klein, I thought that if the differences between her approach and that of the Japanese analysts were ever made clear they would have to be organizationally excommunicated. Yet the existence of a Japanese psychoanalytic group obviously helped support the claims that psychoanalysis was a doctrine that could be applied to all cultures, East as well as West. So, even if it meant some cost in terms of compromising the doctrinal integrity Anna Freud supposedly stood for, it was well worth it to keep the Japanese within the fold.

I was somewhat taken aback by her eagerness to gloss over the significance of what was happening in Japan in the name of psychoanalysis. Freud had himself enjoyed and welcomed early Japanese interest in his work; he did what he could to encourage it, just as he tried to promote a following that had got started in India as well. Oddly enough, although Freud took a particular interest in collecting ancient Chinese artifacts, China has to this day remained exceptional in the lack of interest it has shown in Freud's ideas. Anna Freud's attitude toward the Japanese, since she seemed to anticipate that I would know that what they were doing there was wholly unlike what was acceptable in London, struck me as opportunistic; it was a chance for analysts to claim that their findings had been verified cross-culturally.

As I took note of Anna's willingness to rationalize about the situation of psychoanalysis in Japan, at the same time I was surprised to find just how aloof she could be toward Helene Deutsch. Anna indicated to me that since Helene had written to her in my behalf, and I obviously had such a warm appreciation for Helene, she felt safe in assuming that I must have been analyzed by Helene. Having no special purpose in mind, aside from a general belief in truth-telling, I gently corrected Anna's misconception. I found that whatever the public pronouncements of analysts might be, they were well aware of the subjective components in their kind of work. So although they might like to think of psychoanalysis as a detached scientific endeavor, the first question they were apt to think of was who had analyzed whom. Instead of Anna recognizing the most obvious link between me and Helene, that Helene was pure gold for my historical inquiries, Anna was like others presuming that our friendship arose in a therapeutic context.

I thought that Anna could have tried harder to express an interest in Helene's well-being, if only for the sake of appearances, but like others, she found Helene to be a prima donna. Anna sounded noticeably much friendlier about Felix Deutsch, whom she said had once been her own doctor; she seemed especially pleased to reminisce about him. Helene too, in a different way, readily acknowledged that Felix had been in better human contact than herself, although I could never be sure that her judgment was not being clouded by the hindsight of her mourning.

Later that summer I found out about a 1956 article that Felix had written on Freud, but which he had suppressed in Anna's behalf. As Freud's physician when he first got cancer Felix was in a complicated bind, for Freud had chosen Felix as his doctor after Felix had requested Freud's advice about whom to pick as Felix's own analyst. It turned out that Freud was offended that Felix, in the course of being analyzed, had talked about Freud's serious medical condition. It is hard to know what else Freud could have expected. To further complicate matters, Felix had never leveled with Freud about the presence of a cancer. It is difficult to understand how Freud would not have known this, given his surgeries and radium treatments. Critics thought Felix had lost his objectivity toward Freud because of Felix's being in analysis, but that was one of the conditions for Freud having chosen Felix in the first place.

I was skating on the thinnest possible ice when, with Anna Freud, I alluded to Felix's fear that Freud would commit suicide, thereby justifying his being less than forthcoming about Freud's diagnosis. Felix and Helene had, as a couple, discussed how Freud's situation should be handled, and Felix consulted with the foremost leaders in the international psychoanalytic movement. When later Freud chastised Felix and complained to others about having been misled, Helene was offended by Freud's mistreatment of her husband. She was also irritated that Felix, as Freud's physician, threatened her own good relations with Freud. Freud later went out of his way to personally reconcile with Felix, but the incident proved a lasting trauma for Felix, from which he never completely recovered.

In 1956, Felix had wanted to publish his side of the story, but withdrew his article in deference to Anna Freud's objections. It may be hard for the reader today to appreciate just how touchy and possessive Anna could be about her father. She was so upset at the idea of John Huston's movie about Freud (the original screenplay was written by Jean-Paul Sartre) starring Montgomery Clift, that she spoke against it publicly at a meeting of British Psychoanalytic Society.

It should not be surprising, then, that people I later interviewed wondered if Anna would allow my own studies to proceed. Anna had a faithful circle around her in London, and her allies and former patients were also spread across America. One analyst in San Francisco could not imagine why I was continuing my interviews, since I had already seen Anna Freud herself; that one source, it was implied, should have been authoritative enough for me. Others wondered whether I would submit whatever I might write to Anna for her approval. Someone like Felix Deutsch, because of old loyalties, might have felt obliged to show his article to Anna Freud before publication, but as an outsider I was under no such constraints. As my knowledge increased, it became easier to mix me up with psychoanalysts who had to protect a clinical practice that required referrals. It is always a mistake to underestimate the power of intimidation, unconscious as well as conscious, on practicing clinicians.

Although with some interview subjects I could easily take notes in their presence, it would have been unthinkable for me to have done so in Anna Freud's case. In any event, I was concerned that an obvious attempt to record her remarks might introduce some bias into our exchanges. I already knew, for example, that Helene Deutsch was more candid and relaxed during our interviews than she sounded during taped conversations with others. The presence of a tape recorder has to distort any such encounter; thus, I sought responses that were as spontaneous and unguarded as possible; it was not so much my memory that I was willing to rely on as my ability to learn something new from a human interchange.

Anna Freud's impact on me was telling: she exuded such a regal aura that after our meeting, I started to leave with my back to her door. At the conclusion of the generous amount of time she willingly gave me, I headed straight for a local tea shop where I carefully wrote down everything I could remember her having said that morning. My diarylike entries take up seventeen large pages of notes. No matter how often I go over the detailed records of my interviews, with her or others, I still find they prompt fresh memories.

My interview with Anna Freud was entirely about intellectual business—books and ideas. As part of the ritual of my visit, I had presented her with a copy of my recently accepted Ph.D. thesis; it would, she said, interest her, and she undertook to make sure it later went to the archives of her clinic library across the street. In making the presentation, I acted on Helene Deutsch's recommendation; unlike Helene, however, who at least made note of my extensive bibliography and read some parts of my dissertation, I never had any reason to think that Anna Freud looked through what I had written.

Although I had started off with Anna Freud pretty tongue-tied, we succeeded in covering many issues connected with the history of psychoanalysis. Because its early leaders were already dying off, she volunteered that it would be "easier and easier" to write about the movement's past. It cannot have helped me relax, now that I reflect back on it, that Helene Deutsch was herself so in awe of Freud, and had such a tangled emotional relationship with his youngest child Anna. One issue I had worried about beforehand was how to properly refer to Freud in Anna's presence; certainly not "Mr. Freud," Helene had immediately countered, but only "Professor." Though I stumbled several times on the issue, I got by mainly with using "your father."

Before the interview, I had learned some of the jargon appropriate to that tiny subculture. While Helene Deutsch referred to Anna Freud as "Anna," at least in conversations with me, the in-group reverentially spoke of her as "Miss Freud." Freud himself had been known as "Professor"; even long after his death, those who had personally known him referred to him in this way. Addressing them as "Miss Freud" or "Professor" was an essential part of the required protocol. Even one of Freud's nieces, whom I interviewed in California because she had lived with his family during a pre–World War I summer holiday, as well as in Vienna during the winter of 1921–22, once referred to him in talking with me as "Professor Freud." One might have thought she would think of him as "Uncle," but she had like everyone else in the family come to adopt the more distant and elaborate form of address. Even Freud's wife, when in the company of others, referred to him as Professor Freud.

The irony was that the title people made such a fuss about was actually a second-class academic rank. Although professorships in Europe are rarer than on this side of the Atlantic, Freud had only attained the position of professor "extraordinarius," which meant the opposite of what it might sound like. The post itself was a typical old Austrian invention, virtually for sale. It entailed no university duties, but did give Freud the right to lecture, provided he had a bit of an audience; he continued to lecture until his sickness. (In 1920 he was given the higher title of "Professor Ordinarius," but still was not a regular academic member of the faculty.) His appointment was without salary, but possessed financial value in that it allowed him to charge higher fees to patients; therefore, no one blinked at the many attempts to pressure the Ministry of Public Instruction to grant titles which it alone could confer. In Freud's case, two of his former patients, both women, worked on his behalf; their donation of a certain painting to a public gallery ensured Freud's becoming a professor "extraordinarius" in 1902. There is some dispute whether Freud would have been rewarded sooner had he earlier set in motion such forces in his behalf.

It is no coincidence, I think, that at precisely this point in Freud's career, the fateful year 1902, he felt secure enough to start assembling a following. His status was increasing in the outside world, on a par with his traditionalistic patriarchal standing within the family. None of his relatives ever considered him an ordinary human being; what he was concerned with, or if he were writing again, would be communicated in awed whispers. Freud's own mother had apparently been the first to put him on a pedestal, and his wife did too. And for all the differences between Anna and her mother, she inherited her mother's reverence for Freud.

It was important that Anna Freud and I talk about individuals in the history of analysis, especially those who were still alive and whom I intended to meet. James Strachey was, she commented, "very English"; I had already spoken to him over the telephone, and she and I understood how peculiar the English can seem. (Strachey had told me not to expect too much when I saw him, and warned me that his home outside London was "impossible to find, everyone thinks so." He was important enough for me to meet that I was not put off by any of his attempts at discouragement.) Anna somehow thought that James's wife Alix, who also had been an early analyst and, like Strachey himself, a former patient of Freud's, was a physician. Actually Alix, who had played an important role in helping her husband translate Freud into English, was not medically trained; although I did not correct Anna on this point, her mistake definitely registered with me.

I also wanted Anna to help me understand such puzzling historical figures as Ernest Jones. At that time, I was proposing to write an account of the history of analysis by means of a country-by-country approach. For instance, the United States and England had responded differently to Freud's ideas, not only popularly but professionally as well; and the way his work was received in various continental countries also made an interesting study in the comparative national reception of psychoanalytic doctrine.

It was not hard for me to tell from the quality of Anna Freud's responses whom she thought especially well of, was guardedly neutral about, or held in disdain. Later that summer I came upon written evidence about how she had come to despise Theodor Reik. Although it was naive of me at the time of our first interview, I was struck by how cautious she was about Jones's work on Freud, even though he had dedicated his biography to her.* I soon came to

---

*Jones was much hated in London. As Anna had written about his funeral eulogy for her father: "It is strange how Jones could create something so beautiful and how little one notes those good feelings in him as a person" (quoted in Young-Bruehl, *Anna Freud*, p. 484).

believe that nothing written about her father, no matter how roman-
ticized, could ever seem flattering enough.

Yet, she was enthusiastic about Dr. Heinz Kohut of Chicago, who
as a Viennese, she felt, would be especially helpful for my purposes.
I had met him informally previously, and we had gotten on splen-
didly; he gave me reprints of his on music and literature. Kohut was a
wonderfully cultured and interesting European. In later years, he
founded his own school of thought—"self psychology"—to deal
with so-called narcissistic personality disorders, which prompted
Anna to deem him "antipsychoanalytic."[3] That single word, for her
and others, was the equivalent of casting someone into damnation.

Anna was interested in learning who was responsible for my
personal education about analysis. As a student of the life of the
mind, I considered myself in this area of history as essentially self-
taught. I mentioned Erik H. Erikson, whom I knew she had trained
and from whom I had learned an immense amount.[4] As I expected,
she was stand-offish at the mention of his name; Erikson had too
many original ideas to be popular with her, even though he had just
dedicated one of his books to her.

I think she anticipated that I would mention analysts at the Boston Psychoanalytic Society, which she ranked as "the best." I did
not then realize, although perhaps I should have, how close she was
with Grete Bibring. (When Grete's husband, who had been suffering
for years with Parkinson's disease, committed suicide, Grete wrote
about it movingly to Anna. Not long thereafter, Grete asked Anna to
destroy the letter, for the doctors had disguised the suicide on the
death certificate. Somehow Anna decided to save it.) And Anna not
only had analyzed several Boston analysts over past summers, but a
Boston student of hers had married one of Dorothy Burlingham's
children, who was also a former patient of Anna's.

When I rather off-handedly commented that one did not think of
members of the Boston Psychoanalytic Society when looking for
intellectual guidance, I am afraid it hurt her feelings, for I detected
her gulp. It must be remembered that Anna was still committed to
her father's idea that separate psychoanalytic institutes, outside and
independent of universities, were capable of continuing the tradition
of thought which psychoanalysis involved. It therefore escaped her

that the society, bereft of its original inspired leaders, was now down-at-the-heels.

I left the house with the feeling that despite how well my interview appeared to have gone, it had been more or less an official state visit. Anna had shown no specific interest in me outside of the details of how I had come to be there in the first place. One London analyst from old Vienna, whom I later interviewed, was positively alarmed at first when I told him that Anna had not got around to showing me Freud's ground-floor study, with all the antique statuary from his Viennese office. Taking her guests through that part of the house was such an integral feature of how she treated visitors that he feared that the time she and I had spent on the history of ideas—coupled with the absence of a guided tour—might mean that I had been received under a cloud of suspicion. On the contrary, as we shall see, Anna Freud was pleased enough with me, although my own earlier convictions were now to undergo revision.

5

The Hampstead Clinic

My interview with Anna Freud had centered on the kinds of questions I had come prepared to ask. Her answers, however, served to create new queries in my mind. The single most notable exception to the agenda I had set was Anna's sudden insistence on speaking on behalf of the practice of "lay" (nonmedical) analysis. The fact that I had converted to her point of view long before my arrival at Maresfield Gardens had no effect on her apparent need to give me a little lecture. This may explain why I left with the feeling that she had reacted to me too much in terms of what she had expected of a stereotypical American.

Since Anna thought that all Americans needed special instruction in the legitimacy of lay analysis, she just ignored what I as an individual might think. For years Freud had struggled in vain to convince his loyal American followers that analysis should not be confined to medicine. Aside from Anna's relationship with her father, the only training she had had when she began to practice in the early 1920s was as a nursery-school teacher; Freud therefore felt the need to protect her professionally. Although he had a good measure of success elsewhere, in Britain and France, for example, in managing to establish that analysts do not need to be medically qualified, by the mid-1960s the Americans had continued to stymie him. In those days, doctors in the States still, as from the outset of the American response to Freud, had a special monopoly on the practice of analysis.

On the afternoon of my first visit, an American professor of law at Yale was to speak at Anna's clinic on the problem of psychoanalysis and jurisprudence. Anna told me how proud she was that he had been formally accepted for training as an analyst in New Haven, Connecticut. It was then so unusual for a social scientist to be granted such first-class citizenship, instead of being considered just a research candidate, that it took me a while to absorb the news. To this day, Anna Freud exerts a special influence among the New Haven psychoanalytic community; doubtless her wishes about this particular lawyer played an important role in his being accepted.

I knew she had been going lately to teach on family law and child custody matters at Yale Law School; and she had proudly shown me her protégé's new legal casebook. Although it never crossed my mind at the time, I should have been more concerned about my Harvard appointment; I had even come naively prepared with an offer for her to lecture there again. Not only had she once had an unhappy teaching experience at Radcliffe College, but in 1936 Jung and not Freud had received an honorary degree from Harvard. Since this slight bothered Freud himself, it is a safe guess that Anna was also resentful.

Anna invited me to attend that day's presentation by the Yale professor. I was also welcome, she told me, at any other conferences that took place that summer. The conferences, which usually would be of a clinical nature, were all held diagonally across the street at #21 Maresfield Gardens. Since my time was pretty much my own, I leapt at the chance to see cases presented by analysts. As at the Massachusetts Mental Health Center in Boston, I wanted to find out more about how psychoanalytic ideas were used in practice.

Anna Freud and Dorothy Burlingham had co-founded the Hampstead Child-Therapy Clinic in 1947, and had started a training course independent of anything at the British Psychoanalytic Society. Up to the time of her death, Anna was bitter that the International Psychoanalytic Association had failed to recognize her Hampstead Clinic as a separate affiliate organization. She was frustrated in having failed to establish her clinic, alongside the British Psychoanalytic Society, as competent to certify child analysts.

The history of the Hampstead facility was that in 1951 Anna and Dorothy had bought #12 Maresfield Gardens to house a clinic, and in 1956 they opened the additional premises at #21 Maresfield Gardens. By 1965, Anna and Dorothy headed a relatively small staff who specialized in the strictly psychoanalytic treatment of children, between the ages of four and seven, who had been referred there. In the course of analyses that went on for years, she got to see older children as well.

The children were seen individually five times a week for fifty-minute sessions over an extended period of time. Often the patients came from working-class backgrounds; I found it surprising that despite how culturally disadvantaged such children are apt to be, they were all expected to benefit from the effects of long-term treatment that relied on verbalized interpretations to produce insight and self-awareness.

The origins of the clinic were inseparable from the friendship between Anna and Dorothy. Dorothy's four children were all long-standing patients of Anna's, who was said to have "reared" them from early on. Later I concluded that in terms of her own family dynamics, Anna had emotionally identified with her maiden-aunt Minna, who became Freud's intellectual companion and card partner. Minna had originally moved in with the Freud household to help raise her sister's children. Minna's fiancé, a friend of Freud's, had died before they could be married. According to everyone I talked to who knew her, Minna appeared to be a classic old maid, a sharp-tongued spinster who looked like a governess and played a key role in the child-rearing. Erik Erikson's wife remembered that during a visit, when she was in an advanced stage of pregnancy, she had plopped down on a feather quilt, only to be criticized by Minna for not knowing how to treat feathers better than that.

It has been difficult for me to imagine someone so domestically straight-laced as the *femme fatale* in Freud's own life, but many of my contemporaries have connected Minna to sex rather than to cards. Their relationship remains tantalizingly complex. Anna thought that her father had dictated one of his early translations to Minna, at a time when Freud's wife would have been directly concerned with household matters or the children. And Freud's eldest son Martin, who was himself such a ladies man that although married and a father also loved one of Freud's own patients, once wrote of Minna: "I knew Aunt Minna for the best part of my life, and I knew her very well; but I have never had any realization that she had legs."[1]

Anna Freud's own self-confessions would appear to have surfaced in *The Ego and the Mechanisms of Defense*, for it was not atypical of the early analysts to shape case material to disguise their own auto-biographies. Even Freud had used incidents from his life in this way, although it has often taken a good deal of scholarly sleuthing to establish the autobiographical nature of some of his clinical illustrations. In what is generally acknowledged as Freud's greatest work, *The Interpretation of Dreams*, he was explicitly relying on his own dreams to establish general principles for science.

In Anna's book, she seems to have chosen to talk about herself in a chapter titled "A Form of Altruism." She was purporting to describe the psychology of a "young governess" in analysis, as if such a person would have been likely in those days to seek out such an unusual form of treatment. "What chiefly struck one about her as an adult was her unassuming character and the modesty of the demands which she made on life. When she came to be analyzed, she was unmarried and childless and her dress was shabby and inconspicuous." By 1965 Anna's way of dressing was so "shabby" as to be almost outlandish, but I have no doubt she still thought of herself as being unassuming and modest.

When she had been first challenged by Melanie Klein in the 1920s, Anna had had to do little to fight back; as her father's favorite she could count on his help and that of his allies. Even during World War II, when the British Psychoanalytic Society debated whether Klein's ideas should be considered heretical in contrast to Freudian principles, Anna had stayed pretty much in the background.

As she wrote about her "young governess," "she showed little sign of envy or ambition and would compete with other people only if she were forced to do so by external circumstances." In keeping with a psychoanalyst's suspicion of all surface appearances, Anna proposed that such an adult personality structure might look like it had been built on a contrary set of early childhood characteristics. As Anna wrote:

One's first impression was that, as so often happens, she had developed in exactly the opposite direction from what her childhood would have led one to expect and that her wishes had been repressed and replaced in consciousness by reaction formations (unobtrusiveness instead of a craving for admiration and unassumingness instead of ambition).[2]

Such an interpretation would involve the hypothesis that sexual feelings had also been subdued, and were therefore a source of the other adult qualities of flatness and lack of color: "One would have expected to find that the repression was caused by a prohibition of sexuality, extending from her exhibitionistic impulses and the desire for children to the whole of her instinctual life."

Instead of interpreting herself in terms of the repressions long associated with the neuroses, Anna offered a view of her life that was more generous than any outsider might have observed. She did not choose to see herself as the product of the kind of garden-variety repressed desires that her father had made famous, and she rejected the idea that she could be categorized as a frustrated old maid; regardless of how her "young governess" might have appeared, "there were features to her behavior at the time when I knew her which contradicted this impression."

Anna was implicitly proposing a variation on Freud's own view of the Christian ideal of altruism. He had frontally challenged a variety of ethical maxims from the Christian tradition, and left serious doubt that there could be such a phenomenon as genuine selflessness; at times he had interpreted the love of mankind, and humanitarianism, as a sublimation of homosexual impulses. Yet here Anna was proposing that her own life could be characterized as being of a special altruistic sort. The concept of the repression of early childhood wishes would not do to account for the "young governess":

When her life was examined in more detail, it was clear that her original wishes were affirmed in a manner which seemed scarcely possible if repression had taken place. The repudiation of her sexuality did not prevent her from taking an affectionate interest in the love-life of her women friends and colleagues. She was an enthusiastic matchmaker and many love-affairs were confided to her. Although she took no trouble about her own dress, she displayed a lively interest in her friends' clothes.[3]

As a practicing analyst Anna Freud inevitably became intimately acquainted with the love lives of her patients; and she, like her father, would intervene as a matchmaker. Anna's involvement in raising Dorothy's children, and her concern for her other patients, were especially gratifying for her in a way that went beyond what one would expect merely as the outcome of repressed desires. Anna can be understood to have felt that hers had been a fulfilled life:

> Childless herself, she was devoted to other people's children, as was indicated by her choice of a profession. She might be said to display an unusual degree of concern about her friends' having pretty clothes, being admired and having children. Similarly, in spite of her own retiring behavior, she was ambitious for the men whom she loved and followed with the utmost interest. It looked as if her own life had been emptied of interests and wishes; up to the time of her analysis it was almost entirely uneventful. Instead of exerting herself to achieve any aims of her own, she expended all her energy in sympathizing with the experiences of people she cared for. She lived in the lives of other people, instead of having any experience of her own.[4]

There is, of course, no way to confirm that this case of a "young governess" was Anna's autobiographical self-conception; a niece of hers, who once made a special study of all of Anna's psychological writings, agreed with me that this clinical snapshot was indeed Anna's own self-confession. On the other hand, another niece told me that—unlikely as it might sound, if only because of the expenses involved—she herself had once had a governess who had been analyzed.

It was said that at one time every bachelor in Freud's circle had tried to marry Anna. Although Freud's extensive correspondence with his students has only partially been published, we do know from a fragment of one of Freud's letters to Jones that in 1914, while Anna was on a trip to England, Freud actively intervened to ensure that Jones left Anna alone. (Freud had just finished analyzing Jones's common-law wife, with the result that she broke off with Jones. Freud feared that Jones might seek some form of revenge by taking up with Freud's youngest child, about whom he naturally felt most protective.) Freud toyed with the idea that both Otto Rank and Sandor Ferenczi might make suitable husbands for Anna. Also, during the analyses of his single male patients, it was common for Freud to suggest that they were thinking about the possibility of marrying Anna.

In the era during which Anna grew up, the variety of occupations for a woman were more limited than today; so, too, were her choices of available men. The few males Anna became involved with (such as Siegfried Bernfeld and Hans Lampl) were those she met through either her father or older brothers. A close friend of Anna's, Eva Rosenfeld, told me that Anna had confided to her a hopeless love for Max Eitingon, a married analyst in Berlin, who was immensely rich and absolutely devoted to Freud. Little is known about Eitingon, since he wrote hardly anything. He was, however, important in establishing international training standards for future psychoanalysts. After the stock market crash in 1929, he lost most of his money and moved to Palestine, where he died in 1943. Then in 1988, a controversy arose about whether Eitingon had once been a Soviet secret agent for Josef Stalin.[5] Within psychoanalysis, Eitingon had functioned as the perfect *apparatchiki*—man of the apparatus—and a benefactor of Freud's cause. Until 1988, in a movement full of lively people, Eitingon stood out for his lack of distinctiveness, except for his obsessional conscientiousness; in one of his bureaucratic capacities he would write letters to himself under another title, and then answer himself.

Dorothy Burlingham, who with Anna Freud founded the Hampstead Clinic, had originally moved from the States to Vienna in order to get away from her husband. Her grandfather, Charles Louis Tiffany, had built the family fortune, and her father became famous for the glass he made. Her husband, Robert, was in medicine, and was from a wealthy family that traced its ancestors to the *Mayflower* Pilgrims. Robert was recurrently ill; a diagnosis of manic-depressive psychosis has been offered by Dorothy's biographer, who also was her grandson. Robert continued to function in his medical career, although he shifted from surgery to medical research which better suited him given his breakdowns. Loyal friends and relatives would rally around him, taking him in as he got over his depressions.

Dorothy however had left Robert shortly before the birth of their fourth child. The Burlingham family thought she had behaved selfishly, abandoning a man who desperately needed her support. Dorothy was to find in psychoanalysis a new form of morality which could be used to justify her decision. Her eldest son was angry about the separation from his father, and she later claimed that her reason for going to Vienna was because that child had become unmanageable. Robert Burlingham came over to Vienna for a consultation with Freud, who was favorably impressed by him and made a rather positive diagnosis. But the Burlinghams thought that it was Dorothy who had first driven Robert over the edge, and then deprived him of his children. Freud was a participant in the family tragedy to the extent that he reinforced the barrier between Dorothy and Robert. Although Robert was well for extended periods, and also sought the personal help of analysis, he committed suicide in 1938 by throwing himself out a fourteen-story window. He had been sleepless for nine nights, and refused to take a prescribed sleeping pill.[6]

The Burlingham children, who of course missed their father from the time they had first gone abroad, were being raised in Vienna according to then-promising psychoanalytic principles. They were all treated by Anna Freud and they attended a small private institution, set up by Dorothy and Eva Rosenfeld, for children in analysis or whose parents were in Vienna being analyzed. Dorothy and Anna then arranged to hire two young male teachers, Erik H. Erikson and Peter Blos, who later went on to be prominent analysts themselves. Dorothy subsequently said that she thought the school had been a "mistake."[7] Despite the talents of her children, they did not seem adequately prepared for the outside world.

Dorothy's confidence in her own judgment was immense. She and Anna shared in the parenting, a situation that could be overpowering for the children themselves. It will be recalled that one of Dorothy's children killed herself in 1975 while staying at #20 Maresfield Gardens. And Dorothy's oldest boy, still troubled and continuing to smoke and drink despite poor physical health, died in 1970 of an asthma-induced heart attack.

The entire profession of child analysis, whose positive results the Burlingham children were once held to exemplify, suffered from the therapists' own illusion that professionals can be trained to raise children in a way superior to the efforts of biological parents. Even when they relied on the help of parents, Anna and others like her (Bruno Bettelheim, for instance) have too often regarded them as unavoidable intrusions.

During World War II Anna and Dorothy had created a nursery as a home for normal young children whose family life had been disrupted by the London bombing. (At this point Dorothy's own children were all back in the States.) Their published findings, and in particular what they had to say about the therapeutic role of mother substitutes, was for its time a breakthrough. For by tracing the pattern of a child's emotional development to his or her success-ful bonding with a mother figure, Anna and Dorothy moved Freud-ian thinking into a new phase: symptoms that arose in children would now be interpreted in terms of lost loved ones. If emotional problems could be alleviated once the children were reattached to maternal substitutes, then their earlier problems—and the regres-sions that surfaced—were not solely the result of their primitive impulses. These insights helped promote an emphasis on ego psy-chology, as opposed to the earlier psychoanalytic concentration on the so-called instinctual drives.

The women at the nursery were able to function as surrogate mothers. Once the new ties were established, "the children began to develop in leaps and bounds." Although the point may seem ob-vious, it was by no means common sense then, or now, to recognize all the hidden sources of apparent symptomatology in children. Although Anna and Dorothy did not contrast their theoretical posi-tion to Freud's own convictions, they were able to conclude that "the infant's emotional relationship to its father begins later in life than to its mother. . . ."[8]

My own belief is that Anna Freud's writings from those war-year experiences, and her concrete descriptions of the reactions of small children to the stress of wartime separations, represent her finest single contribution to modern psychology. One can only conjecture that it was Anna's own experience of maternal deprivation—which may have helped turn her toward her father, his profession, and way of thinking—that may have also played a role in her special insights. Dorothy's own mother had died when she was only twelve.

However much Anna had, during Freud's lifetime, surrendered herself to her father, once he was gone she in some sense took his place. It is true that Dorothy's family resented how Dorothy had subjugated herself to Anna's new position. Yet, neither Dorothy nor Anna would have been disturbed, I think, that after their deaths the Hampstead Clinic was renamed the Anna Freud Clinic.

By the time I visited in 1965, Anna and Dorothy, intimate friends for forty years, had built a successful training center for the treatment of young children. Given the influence of the rival ideas of Melanie Klein at the British Psychoanalytic Society, Anna had been determined to have her own separate group. How alien Klein's work always remained to Anna was implicit in some of her comments to me.

For instance, Klein puristically insisted that she was more Freudian than Freud's daughter Anna; and Klein proposed to analyze children by making only a few modifications to Freud's own recommended technique for adults. Thus, Klein advocated so-called deep interpretations which would confront unconscious drives. At one point, she recommended that every child undergo an analysis, based on the principle of universal public education. She also proposed that all patients, including children, need prophylactically to have their so-called psychoses "cured." Klein represents a messianic aspect of the psychoanalytic movement, approaching patients as if they were laboratory guinea pigs. One eminent Kleinian analyst I met in London that summer thought that as a matter of principle, all analyses should last for ten years. When I gently asked what could justify such an intense therapeutic invasion of another human life, I got a one-word response: "Research." At that instant, my mind closed shut against therapists who abuse their power in the guise of helping children. Yet despite my own negative initial reaction to such Kleinian detachment, I have since met child therapists who have been genuinely inspired by Klein's teachings and who have used them to explore the inner worlds of deeply troubled youngsters they have treated.

However ambitiously Anna and Dorothy had behaved about the Burlingham children, in principle the Viennese approach had limited therapeutic objectives. Unlike Klein, Anna was more apt to rely therapeutically on the existing family situation. She was working along the lines that her predecessor in Viennese child analysis, Hermine von Hug-Hellmuth, had laid out—although Hug-Hellmuth's work has rarely been accorded its proper place. Hug-Hellmuth proposed that an educative relationship was needed between the therapist and patient.[9] Along these lines, in the 1920s Freud wrote to a relative in England that Anna had "become a paedagogic analyst." Freud also commented to that same relative that "Anna is treating naughty American children,"[10] which referred to her work with the Burlinghams.

In the mid-1960s, Klein's ideas had not yet entered the mainstream of American psychoanalytic thinking, so I did not realize until that summer just how heretical Freud viewed Klein's ideas. If Freud was horrified at the implications of Klein's approach, and appalled at the criticism she leveled at Anna, he was delighted that Anna had found such a good friend in Dorothy, and relieved that her financial situation would now be secure. Freud had described Dorothy as "a quite congenial woman, an unhappy virgin." By "virgin" he presumably was alluding to her asceticism. According to another of Freud's letters, what had been established between the two households, his and the Burlinghams, was "a symbiosis with an American family (husbandless), whose children my daughter is bringing up analytically with a firm hand. . . ."[11]

Although Anna's allies at the Hampstead Clinic came and went— and a few stayed through thick and thin—most were clearly subordinate to her. No matter how dissatisfied some of the leaders of the British Psychoanalytic Society might have been over Melanie Klein's position there, few of Klein's critics chose to join Anna's forces at the Hampstead Clinic. Anna had withdrawn from the Training Committee of the British society, and an arrangement had been worked out allowing her own people to enjoy an existence apart from Kleinian teaching. Some of those who did go so far as to join Anna at Hampstead, like Willi Hoffer, were chafing under her leadership. Of those who gathered around Anna, none could rival the special importance of Dorothy. By the time I first saw her she had some publications of her own and a handful of pupils she had trained in England. And despite my interest in the history of ideas, my overwhelming first impression of Dorothy was that, although she had come from such a rich and socially prominent family, she dressed in a noticeably unfashionable, almost mannish, manner.

Dorothy was so close to Anna personally that I concluded she might not be forthcoming enough to warrant my risking an interview. But the real reason for my failure to meet her on a one-to-one basis was that, as the summer wore on and I happened to read some of Dorothy's letters to Freud's biographer Jones, I determined that she was not interesting enough to be worth the extra effort. People express themselves in letters by different means. I was mildly appalled at the flatness of what she wrote, the lack of individuality and color to her own Freud anecdotes. I have little doubt now that I made a mistake in not making a special point of seeing Dorothy. I later learned that just as Anna had exaggerated, in his lifetime, Freud's own likes and dislikes, so Dorothy could be more stubborn and ideologically intransigent than Anna.

Years afterwards, when I was writing my biography of Helene Deutsch, I came across a passage in a 1935 letter from Felix to Helene that confirmed my earlier judgment about Dorothy. Felix was then Dorothy's physician as well as Anna's. At the time Felix was writing Helene, Dorothy's analysis with Freud was temporarily interrupted—although it would soon be resumed and continue until Freud's death. Felix observed that her emotional transference to Freud, despite the stated objective of overcoming it in the course of analysis, remained undissolved. As Felix wrote to Helene, who was then living in Cambridge, Massachusetts: "I find she is not in the best psychic condition—the analysis is finished, and the transference is unsolved. She is now having me treat her organically—a feeble substitute." Felix went on to make remarkably insightful predictions. Dorothy was, he held, "a poor shadow creature: can't live without the light which Professor infuses into her. It will be no different with the children."[12] Felix's remarks confirmed my belief that Dorothy would so idealize Anna that I could not have expected much in the way of a fresh perspective toward the history of psychoanalysis.

Thanks to Anna Freud's invitation, extended during the course of our first interview, I had the chance to see her perform extemporaneously about cases at the Hampstead Clinic. At precisely the appointed time, she and Dorothy would enter the room, usually together, and sit side-by-side in the front row of the small auditorium, which also served as a library. Their uncanny closeness reminded one that Dorothy herself was an expert on the subject of twins—she had older twin sisters—and that Anna used to refer to herself and psychoanalysis as twins, born in 1895. The way both Anna and Dorothy dressed was noticeably not "smart." And I was told the story that after the singer Yvette Guilbert's concerts in Vienna—the only music Freud could tolerate in the 1920s—the two women would arrive separately at a restaurant, but would always be seated together, with another of their analytic friends.

Meetings in London began so punctually that it was eerie. As I had heard, Anna—like her father—had a remarkable ability to speak sequentially and with clarity. Her mild accent was no impediment to understanding her, and she would lead off the discussion after each formal case presentation was completed. I remember her speaking only in complete sentences, with no noticeable pauses or hesitations. Her comments were carefully spaced, well-rounded, and balanced, directed toward establishing some general lesson. She always found something instructive to draw from the general discussion of the case presentation just made. Evidently she preferred to speak without notes, just as her father had done; he held that a prepared text interfered with the ability of the audience to identify with the speaker. Anna's thorough devotion to her father's "cause" facilitated her confidence and ease in extemporaneous exposition.

After sitting in on about a month's worth of clinical cases, I was not as favorably impressed as one might have expected with the facility Anna headed. Although it was long before I became a father, I felt then that I would never want any of my children treated at such a place. It was, for my taste, too pedagogic, a musty atmosphere of old-fashioned nursery school teachers talking with barely suppressed prurience about the implications of "infantile sexuality."

In 1965 the workers at the clinic were developing a diagnostic profile using index cards, which struck me as appallingly beside the point, considering the rich diversity of the clinical material presented by young children. Anna Freud and her disciples were so committed to the idea of indexing each case that they evolved manuals for that purpose. It was as if they forgot the significance of the artistic and humanistic side of any therapeutic use of psycho-analysis; they labored in the belief that they had a securely established science.

Anna took this new indexing project very seriously and was its guiding spirit; she was cooperating with a staff in a way that would have been inconceivable for her father. When I asked someone who had known Freud, and had also participated at the Hampstead Clinic, whether "Professor" could ever have run such an establishment, the response was a surprised smile and an implied indication that I had failed to appreciate the chasm between Freud and his daughter.

One did not have the impression at the Hampstead Clinic of a free and open exchange of ideas about the children in treatment. Despite its aura of being devoted to the dispassionate search for new knowledge, I felt that Anna and the staff presented themselves as teachers, as opposed to either healers or inquiring scientists. I remember being startled by the question put to me by another visitor there, from Scandinavia: "Are you a Freudian?" she asked me. As an American I already took for granted Freud's immense stature in intellectual history; yet to a neutral outside observer, the peculiar ideology of the Hampstead Clinic stood out in stark relief. A cultlike atmosphere was pervasive. People and problems were being classified and codified, as if the truth were already known.

These clinicians, almost all nonmedical, were well meaning, earnest, and they knew how to be fully hospitable to me. But by my standards they did not seem to be enough at sea, or trying to reach for the uniqueness that should, I think, characterize any genuine therapeutic experience. That same summer I also interviewed Dr. Donald W. Winnicott, an analyst who had first been a pediatrician; he thought the American response to Anna Freud's ideas could be comically uncritical and naive. No matter how theoretical Winnicott himself sometimes appeared, he always imparted a sense of wonder at what he did not know. Doubts and questions have to be a part of the trust that makes for true conviction. The Hampstead Clinic seemed to me too coldly rationalistic in its inherent sectarianism.

Anna had considered Dorothy's daughter Mabbie the "most successful" of ten early cases she wrote up in the 1920s. Anna's active intervention went beyond merely analyzing the Burlinghams; for example, on behalf of the analysis, Anna had shaken Mabbie's confidence in her nanny. Even without knowing of Mabbie's subsequent suicide, it is disquieting to read her childhood journal. She floundered as a child in her contact with the unconscious and was beset by rationalistic inquiries about her motives: "I with my many troublys [*sic*] and unknown reasons. Everything has an unknown reason. Oh reason after reason, everything with its reasons. It nearly makes me mad."[13]

Freud himself knew enough at least to pretend to be uncertain even when he felt most sure of himself. It is not clear what attitude he would have taken toward child analysis had Anna not been so interested in pursuing it; he knew something about the moral limits on what any analyst can do, even if he did not succeed in establishing enough safeguards against the abuse of power by future practitioners. The idealistic purposes behind psychoanalysis sanctioned all kinds of special efforts, but it is almost inevitable that a gulf will exist between high aims and actual accomplishments. Despite Freud's pronounced skepticism, it was in keeping with his implied messianism that at the Hampstead Clinic they could be too much devoted to promoting what was supposedly already understood, rather than trying to learn something new from the patients and their families.

Sigmund Freud in 1921 (Courtesy of Helene Deutsch)

Freud in 1905 with his mother and his wife (Courtesy of Freud Museum)

Jacob Freud in old age
(Courtesy of Freud Museum)

Minna Bernays,
Freud's wife's sister
(Courtesy of Freud Museum)

The 1908 Oppenheimer portrait of Freud without a beard (Courtesy of Freud Museum)

Anna Freud with Lün in London,
December 6, 1938 (Courtesy of
AP/Wide World Photos)

Oliver Freud (Courtesy of
Freud Museum)

Mathilda Hollitscher, Freud, and Ernest Jones in London, 1938 (Courtesy of AP/Wide World Photos)

Esti Freud
(Courtesy of Sophie Freud)

Martin Freud (Courtesy of Tim N. Gidal)

Portrait of Sigmund Freud, by Wilhelm Krausz, 1936 (Courtesy of Freud Museum)

6

The Movement: Jones and Kleinianism

My central concern in 1965 was not child therapy but the history of ideas. The import of my inquiry did not ride on the success of psychoanalysis as a treatment or training process; in my view Freud primarily mattered as a notable aspect of Western culture. I was interested in the relationship between Nietzsche and Freud, for example, an obvious topic of concern for intellectual historians. The full implications of how disturbing a philosophy Nietzsche espoused, and the ways in which his spiritual subversiveness gets echoed throughout Freud's thinking, have rarely been spelled out. Some of Nietzsche's sayings, such as those on the sources of conscience, strikingly anticipate classical psychoanalytic doctrine; the resemblances between Nietzsche and Freud are so close as to be almost uncanny. "Conscience is not," Nietzsche once wrote, "as is supposed, 'the voice of God in man'; it is the instinct of cruelty, turning in upon itself after it can no longer release itself outwardly." Freud's favorite modern novelist was Dostoevsky, and the comparisons and contrasts between Dostoevsky and Freud also intrigued me. When I taught psychoanalysis to university students it was always in the broad context of intellectual history.[1]

It was not easy for Anna Freud, so involved with therapy and training, to see what I was up to. But Jones had, in the course of writing his biography of Freud, devoted a considerable amount of space to outlining an exposition of psychoanalytic doctrine. So Anna told me that was how she knew there were legitimate precedents for approaching her father's ideas from a historical perspective. In fact, when we were talking about some of her father's writings, she was apt to jumble the correct sequence of his works. "You are a better historian than I," she quietly exclaimed at one point. As she also put it, what she and her colleagues had to do at night, we university people could study during the day.

In our conversations, Anna had been at best lukewarm about Jones's biographical efforts; as I have already indicated, I had taken too much at face value that he had dedicated his biography to her as a "true daughter of an immortal sire." Of course, during our meetings, I was observing the psychoanalytic movement from the outside. From that point of view it appeared that Jones was a staunch defender of orthodoxy, and therefore I had thought Anna would have been enthusiastic about his work. Jones was tireless as an author and notably clear in his expository style, and Anna respected his literary capacities. I was not then privy to the personal tensions between Anna and Jones, nor to Freud's own private reservations about Jones.

According to Anna, Jones's biographical books had succeeded largely because she had allowed Jones to use her father's letters. Anna had become the head of the psychoanalytic family, so although she would consult with her brothers and sister about various issues, her opinion always carried the greatest weight. A key batch of letters that Anna Freud had at her disposal, as I have already mentioned, were the love letters between Freud and his future wife during the years of their courtship from 1882 to 1886. Anna told me that she felt that it was only in his family correspondences that Freud could relax and be himself; in his many letter-writing relationships with colleagues, there were always professional matters that had to be considered when evaluating Freud's meaning.

Obviously, Anna was the key to the success of Jones's volumes, for the documentation she had rendered all previous accounts of Freud's life less reliable. To this day, Jones is the only one who has written about Freud with the advantage of having read those early love letters. Although Anna knew how essential she was to the success of Jones's venture, I do not think she ever realized how burdensome her presence was bound to be for Jones.

She once suggested to him, for example, that her father's English in his correspondence with Jones was not always correct and might be improved upon. When Jones asked James Strachey what he thought of Anna's idea, Strachey wrote back with heavy irony that if they were in the business of making improvements upon Freud's works, he had a number of suggestions of his own to introduce. Strachey was justifiably horrified at the notion of tampering with Freud's texts, and it is a sign of her distance from the world of scholarly standards that Anna could suggest such a proposition. For Freudians who believed that the power of the truth was liberating, her suggestion had to be immensely troubling. Helene Deutsch told me she would not have believed it had I not read her portions of the relevant exchanges between Anna, Jones, and Strachey. Jones did, in fact, introduce some silent editorial corrections when he quoted Freud's letters.

The full correspondence between Freud and Jones has appeared in print only in 1993. Although we now have a small number of books of Freud's letters to go along with the Strachey *Standard Edition* of Freud's psychological works, the great bulk of Freud's correspondence remains unpublished. Freud was a truly great letter-writer. And although it was already apparent by 1965 that he was a literary stylist of enduring stature, the scope of his correspondence—and just what he could sound like when writing off the top of his head—was not yet clear.

First we had, in 1954, an edition of Freud's letters to his intimate friend Wilhelm Fliess, a Berlin physician; a complete volume of the Fliess letters came out only in 1985. A general collection of Freud's correspondence was published in 1960. Other books, containing both sides of exchanges of letters, were with his students and disciples: his correspondence with Oskar Pfister appeared in 1963; with Karl Abraham in 1965; with Arnold Zweig in 1970; with James Jackson Putnam in 1971; and with Lou Andreas-Salomé in 1972. Perhaps the high point of them all was when the Freud/Jung correspondence was published in 1974; in addition, Freud's letters to Edoardo Weiss had first come out as a book in 1970.[2]

It is a well-known fact that in 1937, Marie Bonaparte paid a German bookseller the equivalent of some $500 for Freud's letters to

Fliess. When Freud heard about it, he had been angry with Fliess's widow for having sold the letters, but she had done so out of fear that unless they went to a bookseller, the letters would not get out of the country and survive. In an effort to exert some control over the fate of his Fliess letters, Freud offered to share in Marie Bonaparte's expense; she declined, afraid of what he might want to do with them, but carefully saw to it that the correspondence was safeguarded on the continent throughout World War II. Because Freud's friendship with Fliess had spanned the critical years during which Freud created the central doctrines of psychoanalysis, their correspondence has been considered of key historical significance. It is a sign of the growth (or inflation) of Freud studies that a batch of his letters, which were published in 1990—written to a Romanian school friend and unconcerned with Freud's ultimate professional work—were able, over a decade ago, to fetch the sum of $100,000.[3]

The most important new information about Freud will come from the huge quantity of letters still to appear. The attention of experts has been focusing on the large number of Freud's professional letters, some of which—like those to Jones and to Sandor Ferenczi—have editorially been in the works for years. Although Freud's letters to his fiancée have been sealed to outsiders—except for their use by Jones—a German analyst is now in charge of their eventual publication.

It is remarkable to me that this complicated state of affairs about Freud's papers persists even today; Jones has been dead since 1958, and Anna Freud died in 1982. Yet, it is consistent with everything we know about Anna that she would be possessive of anything connected to her father. She was generally horrified by what she regarded as the invasion of her family's privacy by historians and biographers, and she was also concerned about the possible damage that could be done to the practice of psychoanalysis. For her, and someone like Helene Deutsch, the man Freud and the profession of psychoanalysis were the same thing.

At this point it would be helpful to clarify the distinctions among the various organizations—often involving the same people—that have been in charge of Freud's letters. The Freud Archives in New York is well known, if only because of Janet Malcolm's 1983 articles in *The New Yorker*. Yet the Supreme Court's unanimous 1991 decision surprisingly confused the Freud Archives with the Freud Museum in London. Masson's multimillion-dollar libel suit against Malcolm has an added piquancy, in that Malcolm—without once mentioning Masson's suit against her—made a parallel accusation about the writer Joe McGinnis in several *New Yorker* articles in 1989. Malcolm claimed that McGinnis, in his book *Fatal Vision*, had betrayed his subject, Dr. Jeffrey Macdonald, concerning MacDonald's trial for the savage murder of his family. The world of journalism was in an uproar at Malcolm's contention that all journalists are confidence men.

Orthodox analysis prefers to shun the glare of publicity that people like Masson and Malcolm arouse; the Freud Archives had quietly been established by Eissler, and became the main conduit by which Freud material wound up at the Freud Collection at the Library of Congress. The archives's status as the official donor of most of the Freud Collection has meant that the Library of Congress, although publicly funded, has had to abide by any restrictions on access that the archives has seen fit to impose. That situation remains still true today.

There is no evidence that the arbitrary dates by which items in the Freud Collection become accessible to inspection by scholars are the product of anything but Eissler's protectiveness about Freud; some material has actually been restricted until the twenty-second century. Even people who donated their own Freud letters to the archives were unable to retrieve copies from the Freud Collection without the express permission of the archives. For example, Helene Deutsch was unable to get duplicates of the few letters Freud wrote to her; but at the time she made the request in 1978, I was known to be working on her biography, and as we shall see, I had long before then become persona non grata to Anna Freud and Eissler.

It had to be an embarrassment to both Anna Freud and Eissler that Masson—whom they had selected to lead the archives—had alleged that Freud should have stuck to his original guns in tracing adult neurosis back to childhood sexual seduction. Their man Masson claimed that Freud's theory of the Oedipus complex was mistaken, a rationalization, although it had been an essential part of Freud's most famous struggles against those he deemed traitors. While Eissler has not been in power at the archives for years now, he still commands

some control—as Anna Freud's personal representative—over a siz-
able chunk of material that she gave directly to the Freud Collection.

Anna Freud did her best to prevent any further publication of
Freud letters in the foreseeable future, although she made an exception in regards to Freud's boyhood letters to his Romanian friend. It is
therefore a safe assumption that she would not be entirely happy at
the recent course of events: a new organization, the Freud Literary
Heritage Foundation, has now been set up, with Eissler in charge, to
raise funds in order to bring out complete editions of Freud's correspondence with friends, colleagues, and family members.

During her lifetime, Anna Freud felt free to pencil out anything
she chose in Freud's published correspondences; in spite of this
arbitrariness, somehow the historical fraternity has not been able to
challenge her almost-unquestioned North American public standing. I first raised the issue of the censorship of Freud's letters in a
1968 book of mine; no reviewer, even in professional journals, took
notice of what I had said.[4] Then in 1969, my book *Brother Animal:
The Story of Freud and Tausk* gave an appalling example of an
excision from a Freud letter in connection with the suicide of Victor
Tausk.[5] Since then, there has been no more such tampering with
Freud's letters. Because entire passages had been dropped without
any indication of their deletion, "complete" new editions of Freud's
letters to Abraham, Pfister, and Zweig, for example, are now necessary; for the earlier ones are all chopped-up in ways that are histo-
riographically incomprehensible.

Starting with *Brother Animal*, there was an end to the hanky-
panky with Freud's correspondence. In England, the publication of
his letters to Lou Andreas-Salomé had to be temporarily withdrawn
until the cuts concerned with Tausk's suicide (introduced in the
German edition) could be reinstated. The full text subsequently
appeared in English. By then I was on the outs with the powers-that-
be in psychoanalysis for having exposed all the dubious editorial
practices connected with Freud's correspondences.

Jones did not anticipate how the material from Freud's letters
would whet the appetite of historians. Perhaps he was just telling
Anna Freud what he knew she wanted to hear, but he wrote her that
the reason he was quoting from Freud's correspondence so freely was

in the hope that it would make his study so definitive as to impede the independent publication of Freud's various sets of letters. If the Freud Literary Heritage Foundation succeeds in publishing all of Freud's letters, it would defeat what Jones said he had been hoping for.

Jones had already retired to the countryside when he began to write Freud's biography. Thus, there is abundant documentation between him and Anna about his composing the three-volume study. It is in this context that we know she suggested that he correct some of her father's English, to make it more grammatically correct. In reality, Freud's English is telling, since he sometimes coined new words and chose special idiomatic expressions that make his unedited English both expressive and idiosyncratic.

One would have thought that for Jones to have agreed to alter any of Freud's apparent imperfections in word choice at Anna's behest would be bound in the long run to prove embarrassing. According to those I met, Freud's spoken English was said to have been splendid. From a true historical perspective, any use of English Freud made, including whatever linguistic slips he might have committed, should become its own avenue to the understanding of his mind and intentions.

Jones enjoyed a special standing in Freud's eyes, for not only had he—while living in Canada before World War I—helped introduce psychoanalysis to America, but for many years Jones almost single-handedly ran the British Psychoanalytic Society. His way of exercising power sometimes entailed his excluding people who might be considerable enough possibly to challenge his own position. I found that Jones was much hated both in London and America. One person I interviewed called him "querulous, nasty, a mean son of a bitch," and such a characterization deserves to be weighed seriously in spite of what might seem suspect because of the colorfulness of the language; that evaluation was fairly typical among those I met. An English analyst had reportedly said that Jones was "wonderful in print but equally bad in person."[6]

From Anna Freud's point of view, Jones seemed appallingly, if not presumptuously, independent. It has been said that toward Jones, Anna "displayed unfailing cordiality mingled with distrust and resentment that he never—despite his protests to the contrary—took her or her work seriously but treated her merely as an access to her father."[7] Her forebearance toward Jones endured even though, in 1926, he had been bold enough to bring Melanie Klein from Berlin to London; Klein was already a threat to Anna Freud in the area of child analysis. Jones wanted Klein to help him build up the stature of British psychoanalysis, and also to treat one of his children; in the end she saw several of them therapeutically, as well as his wife. Her presence lent a distinctive twist to the growth of psychoanalysis in Britain.

Jones was fully supportive of Klein's work and her ideas, which itself was to become a major source of tension between Jones and Freud. In one of the most tactless letters Jones ever wrote, he told Freud that the problem with Anna was that she had been insufficiently analyzed. As we shall see in Chapter 7, it was a closely guarded secret—until I made it public in 1969—that Anna's psychoanalyst was Freud himself. But one has to presume that in the 1920s, when Jones was complaining to Freud about Anna being inadequately analyzed, Jones was well enough connected either to have known or suspected that Freud had undertaken to be her analyst.

Regardless of whether Jones was aware of the family secret about Anna's analysis, the content of his letter amounted to questioning Freud's own judgment. In view of Jones's assertion—that Anna was so submerged in her inner conflicts that she was unable to function objectively within the world of psychoanalysis—it took remarkable self-restraint on Freud's part when he chose to fend off Jones by turning the tables: "Who, then," Freud rhetorically asked, "has ever been sufficiently analyzed?"[8] If that personal side of things were to be invoked, Freud challenged Jones, then Anna had been in Freud's opinion more thoroughly analyzed than Jones himself. (Jones's own analysis in Budapest had been relatively brief; it has usually been thought that Jones bore a lasting grudge against Ferenczi, who was temporarily his superior as Jones's analyst. That resentment helps explain why Jones, in his biography of Freud, publicized the charge that when Ferenczi died in 1933, he was psychotic.[9] Freud knew details of Jones's analysis straight from Ferenczi.)

Toward the end of his life, Freud was too old and ill with cancer to suffer the strain of any more heresy-hunting. Nothing in the history of Freud's school ever troubled him as much as the public controversies over Adler and Jung. In the case of Otto Rank, who also turned into a "renegade," Freud did everything he could to keep Rank in the movement. But by then the myths surrounding Freud were so enlarged, and the mythology of heresy so well-established, that Freud proved helpless in protecting a personal favorite like Rank from the enmities of those who were jealous of his special position in Freud's life. Anna Freud, and as we shall see her brother Martin as well, resented Rank's standing. The difficulties between Freud and Rank arose initially because of how Rank reacted to Freud's illness.[10] But the problem between Freud and Wilhelm Reich was strictly a theoretical one; despite Reich's special therapeutic gifts, his Marxist politics caused Freud to take a firm stand against Reich's brand of psychology.

When it came to Melanie Klein, Freud made it clear to his associates how incomprehensible and "deviant" he found her approach; that was the characteristic way Freud, and Anna after him, chose to indicate their most severe form of disapproval. When Freud disagreed with someone's ideas, he pronounced them literally unintelligible. Jung, for example, was commonly dismissed by Freud as a mystic; consequently, there was no reason to evaluate his ideas. Because of this habit of stonewalling dissenting opinion, I found it striking that Anna, despite her admitted inability to understand what the Japanese analysts were up to, refused—for political reasons—to say anything critical about them.

With regards to Jones, Freud and his family had to have been grateful to him for having helped rescue them from the Nazis in Vienna. Jones had not only flown to Vienna to see about Freud's safety, but he also managed to exert pressure on the British government to facilitate the family's move to England. Jones coordinated his efforts with those like Marie Bonaparte who were also working on Freud's behalf.

Klein, on the other hand, resented Jones for having brought the Freuds to London. Until then, the British Psychoanalytic Society had been a nurturing environment, but with Freud's arrival in 1938, Klein grew more fearful and withdrawn in reaction to the perceived threat of the Viennese. The thick of the fighting between the Kleinians and the Freudians took place during World War II.

Britain had been a difficult place for the Freuds to move to, and from Anna's point of view, no location could have been worse. Yet, Freud had admired the British and their traditions of liberties for years, and his half-brothers had emigrated there when he was a small child in Moravia. Freud knew beforehand that England would mean trouble for Anna, but given his anti-American prejudices, moving to the States would have been out of the question.

The controversy over Klein was so well-established that in the 1930s, there had been an exchange of lecturers on the subject: a Viennese, Robert Waelder, had gone to England to present a critique of Klein, and a British Kleinian, Joan Riviere, had spoken on Klein's behalf in Vienna. The British harbored such strong feelings against Waelder that by 1938, Jones made it clear that despite Waelder's position as a favorite of the Freuds in Vienna, he would not be welcome to practice in London.

Melanie Klein eventually achieved immense influence in Britain, and her ideas have since spread elsewhere. Klein's undisputed stature in London meant that Anna Freud could never expect to garner the adulation in England that she was accorded in the States. Even Anna Freud's official biographer, noting her "desire to be in control," characterized her as "an enlightened despot."[11] It was not unusual for Freud to behave autocratically in central Europe; even in England, with its more democratic ways, he was still Freud. Anna, who could not expect to attain his level of genius, nevertheless shared in his autocratic bearing.

Melanie Klein was regularly referred to as "Mrs. Klein," a formality that continued long after her death. One of her sons died in a mountaineering accident that sounded mysteriously suicidal; and her daughter, who for a time was a psychoanalyst, helped lead the struggle against Klein at the British Psychoanalytic Society. This daughter was so disaffected from her mother that whenever her name came up in our interview, she referred to her mother as "Mrs. Klein." This tremendous hostility seems to bear a psychological similarity to the inverse, but equally intense, filial piety of Anna Freud toward her father.

In that productive summer I spent in London in 1965, I managed to read through all the letters Anna Freud had written to Jones during the course of his writing the biography. Jones had adopted the practice of regularly sending her drafts as they were completed. She wanted to ensure that certain family matters were tailored to suit the sensibilities of surviving relatives; one of her cousins had threatened a law suit in defense of his side of the family. However, Anna was mainly concerned with issues connected to the politics of the movement as a whole. She thought she knew, for example, what Jones should leave out from her father's letters for the sake of promoting psychoanalysis in America; for example, disparaging references by Freud about the States ought to be omitted. And she sometimes worried that followers of Freud's former disciples might take offense at how harshly Jones was inclined to treat them. When Jones was describing the difficulties between Freud, Adler, and Jung, Anna rather reveled in the fierce so-called resistance to psychoanalysis; but she did have some second thoughts about how Jones chose to treat Rank and Ferenczi.

All of Jones's papers, including Anna's letters to him, had been stored in a large cabinet in the basement of the British Psychoanalytic Institute. Since no one had ever gone through them systematically, I did not have to sign for anything I chanced to find there; an elaborate system of prior restraints has since been instituted for those who use the Jones Archives. Inasmuch as I was the first person ever to go through these papers, the exciting experience of handling such primary documents is one I will never forget.

It seemed to me that without much reading between the lines, one could grasp Jones's frustrations at some of the constraints he felt working under Anna Freud's official auspices. Jones's ally, James Strachey, had encountered similar problems, so Strachey chose to work on his translations almost entirely from published texts; he did not consult existing original manuscripts. Had Strachey opted to base his *Standard Edition* on original documents in Freud's handwriting, or on surviving prepublication galleys, it would have entailed all sorts of additional back and forth between himself and Anna.

In recent years, with more attention being paid to Freud's original manuscripts as sources, some interesting differences have been pointed out between those texts and what ultimately appeared in

print. The bulk of the attention has been directed at efforts to challenge Strachey's translation from German into English. Bruno Bettelheim in particular raised the point that although Freud chose to
describe the workings of the mind in a deliberately simple German
vocabulary, Strachey had invented a term like "cathexis," which
Freud himself had not employed. Bettelheim believed that the English translations were falsely scientific, unlike the truly humanistic spirit behind Freud's original works. Bettelheim blamed these
Strachey translations for the medical monopoly that took over Freud's
profession in the English-speaking world after Freud's death.[12] In
fact, neither the Stracheys nor the other translators who worked on
the *Standard Edition* were physicians. And Strachey proudly told me
that although Freud at first had been somewhat doubtful about the
choice of "cathexis," he had by the end of his life incorporated that
term in one of his texts.[13]

Freud's own knowledge of different languages was considerable,
and he had some experience as a translator. Eager to get his writings
promoted, he allowed considerable latitude to those whom he ap-
proved as translators of his own works. Freud picked Strachey as a
translator while Strachey (along with his wife Alix) was in analysis
with Freud in Vienna, and there is no evidence that Freud was
anything but delighted with Strachey's work. The example of the free
hand Freud gave Strachey could be fleshed out by different figures in
other countries, and in languages besides English.

Strachey's *Standard Edition* was begun only after Freud's death.
Had a committee of people been involved, it probably never would
have been completed, but Strachey proceeded with the full support
of Anna Freud and Jones. Jones probably played the largest single
role in choosing the English equivalents for Freud's technical psychoanalytic vocabulary, and worked harmoniously with Strachey. In
the 1920s a small committee in London, of which Jones was the only
physician, met to decide on a standardized way of translating Freud's
works.

I doubt that Strachey was ever paid for all his work as a translator,
or received what was then the normal professional fee. Strachey did
his translations out of dedication to "the cause." It would seem to me
extremely unfortunate to dwell on the consequent limitations of his

splendid edition; after all, the excellent notes Strachey provided for each of Freud's papers have been translated into German editions of Freud. And the miserably inadequate way Jung's writings have been presented to the public should make us grateful for what Strachey accomplished. The inevitably interpretive nature of any translation ought not to lead to a fundamentalist quest for the so-called true Freud. It is far more important to concentrate our energies on a mature evaluation of the substance and validity of Freud's ideas themselves.

Strachey was one of the few people in England in a position to understand the difficulties Jones had encountered while working under Anna Freud's supervision. Strachey and his wife Alix had been open-minded about Klein's initial contributions, and although they were shocked that Klein seemed so uncritical about everything she had ever written, the Stracheys retained their independence from Anna. Hailing from the famous Bloomsbury set of intellectuals, both James and Alix felt culturally superior to many other British analysts.[14] Someone like Winnicott, who—unlike Strachey—was not dependent on Anna for translating work, could be far more free in discussing with me the inhibitions he thought Jones suffered because of Anna Freud's special position; Winnicott had once been in analysis with James Strachey and was receptive to Klein's innovations. When later, while Anna was still alive, I put into print how she had overseen Jones's biographical work, reading it line by line before he sent it off for publication, she reacted with public indignation.

In 1979, while writing her "Personal Memories of Ernest Jones," Anna spoke about his biography of her father and noted: "I remember a rather malicious American author asserting that this was done under my direction, and that I carefully scrutinized every page which he wrote."[15] In the typed final copy of her article about her reminiscences of Jones, which I later found among her papers at the Library of Congress, she had actually referred to me as "an American rather malicious author," highlighting her specific disapproval of me amidst her general distaste, like that of her father, for all things American. Presumably that sentence underwent editorial change at the journal in which it first appeared. The most significant point, however, is that Anna Freud could not understand—although it was evident from correspondence between Jones and James Strachey, for example—how intimidating to them both she could be.

To Anna Freud, Jones was an extremely stubborn Welshman. Although in public Freud had been known to congratulate Jones— for example, in honor of Jones's fiftieth birthday in 1929—in private, Freud "complained bitterly . . . about how little he wanted to say anything in praise of Jones. . . ." Freud once wrote that Jones's "application of my ideas has stayed on a schoolboy level." As Freud wrote in a 1927 letter to Eitingon, "I don't believe that Jones is consciously ill-intentioned; but he is a disagreeable person, who wants to display himself in ruling, angering and agitating, and for this his Welsh dishonesty ('the Liar from Wales') serves him well." Freud went on to illustrate his point by telling Eitingon that Joan Riviere had claimed to Freud that Jones "chased her into her position, congratulated her on the telephone for her theoretical propositions, and then betrayed her when he told me that he had tried unsuccessfully to tone her down." That kind of double-dealing on Jones's part was par for the course. For example, he tried to pacify Klein's irritation at his having brought Anna to London by denigrating Anna: "She is certainly a tough, and perhaps indigestible morsel. She has probably gone as far in analysis as she can and she has no pioneering originality."[16]

From Jones's point of view, once he had managed to land Anna's authorization to proceed as a biographer of Freud, she became the prime source of his material and the first audience for whom he had to write. He did not, in the course of all his three volumes, even hint at the fact that her father had analyzed her. When I later discussed Freud's analysis of Anna with her old friend Dr. Marianne Kris in New York City, she tried to suggest that I not mention it in print, since according to her, such information "would surely be misused."

In 1969, I published the fact that Freud had analyzed Anna himself. Although Anna privately sought to contest many other aspects of my work—as she sought to promote criticism of my writings—she never tried to deny that one key fact. My own nationality as an American could only occur to her in the context of her broad discontent, and that of her father as well, with American culture; this was an explicit theme in my interviews with her, as for example when she wanted to credit the influence of a few emigré analysts coming from Vienna for the entire success of Freud's ideas in America. I ran into plenty of additional anti-Americanism among British analysts that summer.[17]

Yet the United States had been a country that openly welcomed psychoanalytic ideas; the only honorary degree Freud ever received was in 1909 from Clark University in Worcester, Massachusetts; that same institution was the first to award an honorary degree to Anna herself in 1950. In our talks, Anna had raised her father's fear that analysis would take hold in America too easily and not represent real conviction but a kind of faddishness that might soon turn in another direction. At one point Anna had spoken to me rather grandly about the "two Americas" being strangely split, since Klein's ideas were then so influential in South America. To speak of the "two Americas" was Anna's way of putting the northern hemisphere in its place.

When other aspects of my later publications proved objectionable to Anna Freud, she exerted her opinion in letters behind the scenes, more than I would have anticipated. Dorothy Burlingham formally contributed to one notable critique of my 1969 Brother Animal. Throughout the 1970s, the Freud Copyrights in London—which Anna took an official part in—pursued my American publisher for having purchased the right to use pictures of Freud from photographic stock companies. We had taken that path since the Freud Copyrights stated that I could buy reproductions from them only if they first read a prepublication copy of my manuscript—which would have then likely gone, as had Brother Animal, straight to Anna. Although photographs are worth at least the proverbial thousand words, I had no intention of exposing my work to the threat of prior censorship—or to less-than-subtle pressures—for the sake of winning enough approval to secure pictures from the Freud Copyrights.

Once I had published Brother Animal, Anna Freud and at least some of her doctrinally orthodox allies deemed that I should be discouraged, if not controlled. My book was designed to redress the historiography of early psychoanalysis, and to revive an interest in Victor Tausk; to the faithfully devout, however, Brother Animal was misunderstood as an assault on Freud's character, and one which supposedly blamed Freud for Tausk's suicide.

After my publisher and I had successfully secured photographs, the Freud Copyrights tried to lay claim to financial compensation for the use of every photograph, now held by different corporate bodies, in which Freud had ever appeared. This policy in behalf of Freud's heirs contrasted with his own generosity, for he often unasked gave photographs of himself to patients and pupils. The Freud Copyrights then charged my publisher high fees (to be deducted from my royalties) for permission to quote from Freud's works in order to discourage me from using such quotes.

While Freud was alive, Anna—in her capacities as his secretary and nurse—was becoming an independent source of power; after his death, her words were regularly repeated by those who consulted her about the history of analysis. If I found her cautious in what she allowed herself to say to me, and less personally outgoing than other analysts I met at the same stage of my work, it partly had to do with the special role she knew she had to play.

As I later learned, she had explicitly denied ever having been analyzed by Nietzsche's friend Lou Andreas-Salomé. Her story was widely circulated, even though more than one person I interviewed insisted that Lou had been Anna's second analyst. From reading Freud's letters, it would appear that he himself thought Anna had been helped analytically by Lou. Tola Rank, Otto Rank's first wife, swore to me that she had been present in the Freud apartment while Lou was staying there for the purpose of analyzing Anna. But Tola did qualify her judgment when she affirmed that it might be possible for Anna "to get out of it" by arguing that such an analysis had not really been a proper one.[18] The proprieties were all oddly distorted, inasmuch as Lou and Anna were close friends. This should have in principle interfered with Lou becoming her analyst. Although one would have thought that Freud's having analyzed Anna represented the greater indiscretion, Anna herself seemed to prefer that she be indebted only to him.

7

My Discovering about Anna's Analysis

My own emancipation from the conventional pieties about Anna Freud came about gradually. A natural initial reaction to her was to see her as the living embodiment of the tradition of thought which her father had inaugurated. In that sense a special sort of respect was appropriately due her. To clinch the matter of what sort of response she should have been capable of having evoked, she was still living in the house Freud had died in, surrounded by all the furnishings and antique art objects the family had brought with them out of Vienna. Had she not been an analyst in her own right, it might not have been so awesome to have come in contact with her.

On the other hand, I had been brought up in a democratic climate, and no matter how impressed I might have been when I first met Anna Freud, it did not take me long to begin to judge her by more realistic standards. For one thing, I was a bit taken aback by her coolness toward Helene Deutsch, and by the fact that she was neither warm nor outgoing toward Erik Erikson. Erikson was not yet teaching at Harvard when I was an undergraduate there; when I first met him, I was already pretty far along in my intellectual development. So although I did not owe him any early educational debts, I did find him unusually insightful about not only the history of psychoanalysis but also human psychology in general. I disagreed with Erikson on many points, and the book and articles I subsequently wrote about him express my independent evaluation of his approach. Yet, at chance meetings in a local Cambridge coffee shop, or on a street corner where we might converse, and even in his own house at dinner or a party, I found him exceptionally intuitive. I do not think there was ever an occasion when, having mentioned something I had just learned to Erikson, he did not offer me some new way of considering what I had brought to him.

As with Helene, Anna Freud was distressingly unresponsive and noncommital about Erikson. I could only get Anna to agree about Erikson's talents when I volunteered how immediate and direct a person he was. It never occurred to me to "talk up" Helene Deutsch's talents to Anna. I assumed that it went without saying that—given the prominent role that Freud himself had assigned to Helene within the history of psychoanalysis—there was no need to try to bolster her status. Even in her early eighties, Helene was an unforgettable phenomenon, witty and smart, capable of being the life of the party—if she so chose to display herself. Since Erikson was a former student of Anna's, it seemed appropriate that I praise his notable qualities to her. But about both these people I already knew and admired, Anna Freud was less than forthcoming.

I was not prepared to find Anna in any way wanting, which may help explain why I became quickly disillusioned. In the United States, there has yet to be any widespread critical examination of her ideas, even though they have notably influenced U.S. law. As part of a multivolume set of *The Writings of Anna Freud*, a so-called revised edition of *The Ego and the Mechanisms of Defense* came out in 1966, although the text of the book itself is identical to the earlier version. In an American survey conducted in the late 1960s among psychiatrists and psychoanalysts to determine whom they considered the most outstanding representative of both professions, Anna Freud's name topped the lists for both groups. At that time, I was unaware of how derogatory the French attitude toward her was, but having lived in England that summer, and having met British analysts influenced by Klein, I was aware of their skepticism regarding Anna's contributions. Exaggerated views of anybody's stature are an invitation to subsequent debunking.

My doubts about Anna were reinforced when I interviewed an old

Viennese analyst, Dr. Robert Jokl, while I was conducting research in California in December 1965. Jokl told me that in the 1920s, Anna Freud had denied being analyzed by her father. In those days Jokl was a member of the Vienna Psychoanalytic Society and had been briefly analyzed by Freud himself. When I met him, Jokl was a practicing analyst in good standing in Los Angeles. Without reconstructing in too much detail how the matter of Anna's analysis by her father came up, Jokl told me how he had happened to meet her on a walk one night in old Vienna. She seemed depressed, and he— perhaps as a challenge—suggested that she undergo a bit of analysis. Jokl said that she simply shrugged, indicating that she had already tried that. Jokl then directly asked her, "With your father?" Her answer was, "No." It was not until Jokl and I talked that he got final assurances about the true story. Jokl, like Helene Deutsch, had a tie to Freud that did not include Anna, and she tended to resent almost anyone like that. Jokl concluded, in talking with me, that she had been capable of lying to him. I think this is an important example of Anna's capacity for being evasive, and it should bear on the matter of whether, as I was assured, she really had a second analysis with Lou Andreas-Salomé, which somehow she was bent on denying. If she could lie about being analyzed by her father, surely she could do so about a matter of less significance.

It was in the summer of 1965 that I inadvertently stumbled onto confirmation of Freud's having analyzed Anna. In April 1965, an old Italian analyst in Chicago, Edoardo Weiss, told me about Freud's having analyzed his own daughter. Weiss had been tempted to analyze one of his sons, and in writing to Freud for clinical advice, as Weiss often did, Freud mentioned that he had analyzed Anna. Freud said he thought he had succeeded with his daughter, but he was less optimistic about analyzing a son. Nonetheless, Freud did not think he had the right to forbid Weiss from proceeding. Weiss's son turned out to be uncooperative, and Weiss interpreted Freud's remarks to imply that he should not try to push the matter. Weiss knew that in terms of the politics of the psychoanalytic movement, he was venturing on dangerous ground by mentioning the analysis to me. Although he showed me copies of many of Freud's other letters to him,

Weiss would not even give me the date of the correspondence touching on the analysis of Anna.

Weiss's book containing Freud's letters to him, including the one about Anna's analysis, appeared just a year after *Brother Animal.* But even in 1965, Anna had indicated to me her intense disapproval of Weiss. Earlier, they had been on fine terms; he was the actual founder of the psychoanalytic movement in Italy and was once a member of the Vienna Psychoanalytic Society; Freud had even written a preface to one of Weiss's books. Yet by 1965 Weiss was partly aware of how Anna now felt about him. She was later able to block the publication in England of the volume of Freud's letters to Weiss, although clinically they are of great interest.[1]

Many famous quarrels in the history of psychoanalysis have hinged on the matter of proper technique. Following his disagreements with Adler and Jung, Freud felt the need to publish his own recommendations for how analysts should clinically proceed, based on where he felt he had once gone wrong. These pieces were an effort to establish what was most distinctive about his own approach. Other analysts have tended to be more rigid than Freud, but certain practices—such as the use of the couch, the length of each analytic session, and the number of sessions per week—did tend to settle into a conventional routine, which if violated meant that proper psychoanalysis was no longer being conducted.

Freud also proposed that it was critical that the analyst maintain a special sort of neutrality toward patients. This distance, which Freud thought was essential for genuine transferences to occur, would be impossible if the analyst were personally familiar with his patients. Of course, the circumstances of Freud's own practice of analysis were unique; a clinical contract with the founder of analysis was unlike a contract with anyone else in the field. I found out that Freud violated all the rules that he laid down for others: he treated some patients free of charge, even though he had stated that there had to be a financial incentive for the patient to recover; he was known to have invited patients to his home for a meal or served them food in his office, even though he had advised against an analyst's becoming too familiar with his patients; and as long as he could talk freely, and without the pain of his later illness, Freud was said to have "chattered."

Thus, Freud maintained a degree of normal human contact with his patients that orthodox historians of psychoanalysis later sought to disguise. Even the uniqueness of his own consulting room communicated aspects of his personality that one would have thought were ill advised, considering the counsel he gave to other analysts. Yet, in spite of all the liberties Freud took as a practicing analyst, it is my conviction that the sheer weight of his persona was enough to ensure that emotional transferences would continue to occur with his patients. I am not trying to justify Freud's particular form of clinical practice, but I do think it is necessary to appreciate the special circumstances under which he alone had to proceed.

It is difficult to imagine a more irregular technique than Freud's analyzing Anna. The subject came up in my interviews during that summer of 1965. Such a sensitive matter did not even cross my mind when I was speaking with Anna Freud herself, but while I was seeing Kata Levy, an old Hungarian analyst, the matter arose almost casually. Kata's brother had been an early financial benefactor of Freud's movement; he, his wife, and Kata had all been analyzed by Freud. Although Kata did not leave Hungary until late, 1954, Anna could never forget that Kata's family had supported Freud's cause in its early days.

When I met Kata, she was an old lady living on a street directly behind #20 Maresfield Gardens. Anna had put in steps so that the backyard of Kata's house was connected to the rear of her garden. Kata had been a practicing analyst in Budapest, and her husband was one of the physicians whom Freud turned to for advice. Although Kata had only published a handful of papers, Anna had written a preface to one of them. Like her father before her, Anna chose to promote the work of her favorites by adding some enthusiastic words to their writings.

At the Hampstead Clinic meetings Kata regularly sat in the same front row alongside Anna and Dorothy. In the course of interviewing Kata at her house, mainly about psychoanalysis in Hungary, we got onto the subject of how she had come to be analyzed by Freud. She said that while Freud was staying with her family in the mountains outside Budapest the summer before a momentous meeting of analysts there in September 1918, he had volunteered to analyze Kata.

Because I found her to be modest and shy, I could believe her report of how she had answered Freud: "Surely you are on vacation, Professor, and do not want to be bothered by analyzing me." But Freud surprised her by saying straightforwardly that he had begun to analyze Anna, and that he would just as soon have both of them at the same time.

Anna Freud remained such a sacrosanct figure, not only to the people immediately around her but also within the profession at large, that almost twenty years went by before the literature began any extended discussion about the significance of her analysis by her own father. Even then, the matter was handled with kid gloves.[2] In terms of the formal rules of psychoanalytic technique, Anna's analysis by Freud violated almost every taboo; spiritually it was seemingly incomprehensible, since it had to be such an intrusion on her individuality. I found that critics of Freud who knew about this skeleton in the family closet chose to consider Anna a victim of her father's grandiosity. Kurt Eissler offered a unique response to my revelation about Anna's analysis; in the course of assaulting *Brother Animal*, he called Anna's analysis by her father "well known,"[3] although he could not cite a single published reference to the subject.

Other evidence has surfaced that different analysts have tried clinically to observe their children, and even to treat them analytically; for example, Melanie Klein, A. A. Brill, and Ernst Kris all analyzed children of their own. But in Anna's case she spent approximately four years in analysis with Freud. Entirely aside from violating the supposed ideal of the analyst remaining anonymous and neutral, such a procedure represented an invasion of Anna's integrity. She was revealing not only her free associations but also her dreams and intimate fantasies. Even if she had helped initiate the idea that her father analyze her, Freud was the adult and must therefore bear the ultimate responsibility for her surrender.

Putting the best face on what happened, I think Freud was trying to teach Anna as best he could; at the same time he had to be afraid of the harm any other analyst might inflict on her. He knew better than anyone how complicated were the emotional relationships between other analysts and himself, and how that might influence the way they approached Anna. Freud also understood how clumsy his disciples could be in implementing his ideas.

Once we face up to the fact that Freud allowed himself such an enormous liberty, it leads to further vexing questions about his life. Did he ever have an affair with his sister-in-law Minna, which traditional Jewish religion would have seen as incest? As he once wrote in a letter, which remains enigmatic: "I stand for an infinitely freer sexual life, although I myself have made very little use of such freedom. Only so far as I considered myself entitled to."[4] Although I still choose to think of Freud as a self-denying puritan, others continue to raise the possibility of still further transgressions against traditional moral standards within that tightly knit family. For example, there is the question of whether Anna and Dorothy were more than the closest of old friends. There is little doubt in my mind that both Freud and Anna saw themselves as a part of a small elite, beyond the everyday standards of good and evil which might apply to lesser mortals. Analysis itself was seen as a technique suitable for superior beings, and Freud hoped to evolve out of his work a higher form of ethical existence.

In that summer of 1965 I was still naively feeling my way into this research. I looked up to Anna Freud with the reverence commonly shared by others; the seditious questions that later came to my mind scarcely had begun to occur to me. But the more I proceeded with my various interviews, the greater independence I felt—especially after I had a chance to study Jones's papers and saw what had gone on behind the scenes while he was writing his biography of Freud.

Even though I immediately knew that I had slightly annoyed Anna Freud when I asked for a second interview with her in July 1965, I went ahead with it for the sake of my work. She could not think of refusing me, for I was proceeding with the encouragement of key people at her clinic; yet I knew that I had displeased her by making an additional demand on her time. The lightning speed at which her supposed interest and kindliness could evaporate taught me something unforgettable about the shallowness of Viennese *schmaltz*, and how charm can be used to maintain one's distance. From an American's point of view, raised to admire straightshooters, the Viennese courtliness masked so many surprises as to make them appear sneaky.

The first time I had met with Anna, we had only briefly discussed the forthcoming publication of a book her father had collaborated on with William C. Bullitt about President Woodrow Wilson.[5] It was, she said, very "disturbing" that a president could be so "ill," and yet these words were spoken with a half-smile, as if she also enjoyed the idea of such a diagnosis of Wilson. For a variety of reasons Freud had especially hated this particular American president: for Wilson's hypocrisy, his religiosity, and the mortal damage the Treaty of Versailles had inflicted on the Hapsburg Empire.

In London I came across much informal talk about the Freud-Bullitt manuscript. Given the nature of my own plans for a book on the political and social implications of Freud's thought, it was vital that I learn more about the Freud-Bullitt study, which I had not yet seen. There was as yet no hint about any alleged inauthenticity, but a controversy erupted after the book's publication in 1966, when it was generally judged to have been a partisan assault on Wilson's character. The volume came to be referred to within the profession as the Bullitt-Freud book, for reversing the order of the names on the original cover helped to downplay Freud's co-responsibility.[6] Alone among Freud's texts it has been allowed to remain out of print.

A staff member at the Hampstead Clinic, who had been helpful in showing me around, offered to be my intermediary with "Miss Freud," and that was how my second appointment was set up. (People who had known Anna Freud for years as members of her extended family would not have dreamt of spontaneously dropping in on her, even over the summer holidays; they would always call in advance to make an appointment to see her.) Anna had planned for only one interview with me, and I think she considered it presumptuous—and all too American—for me to request a second. But the members of her own staff whom I consulted encouraged me to persevere.

I had innocently thought our first meeting had impressed her, and I had scarcely begun to have the thoughts that, when ultimately expressed in print, would prove so offensive to her. This time Anna's pet chow took part in the interview, as she momentarily played with it rather than address herself to me. In Vienna, Anna was known for having had an undisciplined German shepherd; and some of her early theories about child-rearing did have an anarchistic-sounding bias. For example, she once wrote that she considered "the question . . . unanswered as to what would happen if the adults round a child refrained from interfering with him in any way."[7]

Freud himself had taken to chows after first getting cancer, when he was withdrawing from his more usual human contact. His wife, perhaps as a remnant of the traditional Jewish prejudice against such animals that was common in Eastern Europe, objected to their presence in the household. However, a relative of Dorothy Burlingham's had been his source of supply, and there were to be several chows in the apartment. A curator of the Freud Museum later complained how, over the years, Anna's dogs helped destroy some of the oriental rugs that had originally been Freud's.

Only a few minutes into my July interview, Anna realized the legitimacy of my further inquiry and why I had needed to see her again. Almost immediately she once again became outgoing and gracious. According to her, Wilson had suffered a "psychotic" denial of reality, a "delusion" about what he had done at Versailles. At that time, there was no scholarly evidence about any of Wilson's neurological difficulties, especially toward the end of his political career.

Whatever doubts she had about the Freud-Bullitt manuscript she kept to herself. She, like Jones when he had seen the manuscript while writing his biography, told me that anyone who knew her father's work could easily detect the parts he had written. Jones had even proposed to Strachey that the book be considered for inclusion in the *Standard Edition*, but Strachey's final plans were already made. Freud's introduction, written in his own hand, specified that Bullitt, who had known Wilson, alone prepared "the Digest of Data on Wilson's childhood and youth." But "for the analytic part we are both equally responsible; it has been written by us working together."[8] At the time I talked to Anna, it was troubling to me that she seemed to show no interest in trying to verify the study. However, she and her family accepted their full share of the book's royalties.

It is telling that Freud had never shown Anna any portion of the manuscript, either at the time of its composition or upon its completion. It was written with Bullitt over a period of years, from the late 1920s until 1932. It was widely known in 1965 that Bullitt had played a role, as American ambassador to France, in helping to protect the Freuds in Vienna after the Nazis marched in. Many knew that Bullitt also had been a patient of Freud's. Once the book was out and the reviews were almost uniformly unflattering, it did not sell well and orthodox analysts did what they could to downplay Freud's association with it.

The Freud-Bullitt collaboration, and Anna's unique role at the time of its publication, points to how historians writing after Freud's death found it easy to misunderstand the position she held during Freud's lifetime. It was in the interest of her own disciples to exaggerate her earlier standing in the history of psychoanalysis. The sicker and more frail Freud became, the more her stature grew; she assumed increasing responsibility for his health, although she had her rivals among Freud's pupils even in that area. Freud was obviously proud of her many achievements, but he could refer to her irreverently as "St. Anna"; he told her that he considered her personally "a little odd",[9] and worried how she would fare without him. It became clearer to Freud that a life of sexual asceticism was to be her fate.

The more Freud worried about what kind of existence Anna was destined to lead, the harder he sought to fortify her position within psychoanalysis. Once he was ill and found public speaking no longer possible, he sent Anna to deliver some of his last papers, and she represented him in receiving such honors as the Goethe Prize from the city of Frankfurt. (That award was worth a lot of money—10,000 German marks or about $25,000 in today's terms.)[10]

None of the politicking Freud undertook on Anna's behalf ever had to mean that he relied on her intellectually. For example, he never consulted with her about his collaborating with Bullitt on their Woodrow Wilson study. And although he sent a few pages of the Wilson manuscript to a favorite pupil like Ruth Mack Brunswick, and even offered to show the whole book to Ernst Kris, Anna herself had never been taken into Freud's confidence about that manuscript. (Ruth Brunswick was such an important figure in Freud's final years, and her standing still remains so unrecognized, that I was tantalized when Marianne Kris told me that she had a "trunk-full" of her friend Ruth's papers; doubtless they have by now disappeared into the hands of the Freud Archives in New York.) Anna was so jealous of someone like Ruth that she later claimed, in a long letter to me in 1967, that her "father had treated his cooperation with Mr. Bullitt on the Wilson book as a discreet matter which should not be discussed with anybody." Having politically betrayed Wilson's administration before the Senate committee that was considering the ratification of the Versailles Treaty, Bullitt wanted nothing to interfere with his political career which, at least for a time in the early New Deal days, was again starting to prosper. Bullitt later crossed President Roosevelt in such a blatant way, depriving him of the services of one of FDR's favorites, that Bullitt never again held office in the New Deal administration. [11] Although Bullitt later became a Republican, his political career was over.

In July 1965 Anna had expressed concern over repetitions in the book, and she wanted to know exactly what Bullitt had said to me in recent letters. Afterwards I heard from Bullitt that she had suggested some changes that she considered improvements in the text itself. In her 1967 letter to me about the book on Wilson, she wrote that she thought she "had not read the book" when she had spoken to me about it earlier. This clearly was a false memory on her part, since both times we talked together the manuscript was an important part of our discussion.

In writing to me afterwards, she claimed to have "disliked the book as soon as" she had "read it." If that were so, she had successfully disguised her reaction when talking with me. I suspect that as time went on, and other people told her how negatively they had reacted to the book, she may have altered her original response. In writing to me she said that "for a while" she "had hopes that it could be changed to a large extent," but the suggested improvements she sent to the publisher were relatively minor. When I wrote to her about the book in 1967, I was completing an epilogue to a manuscript and was looking for her help and clarifications about the Wilson study. She now was claiming: "I am unhappy about the book and I wish that the whole cooperation had never happened, or that my father had had less trust in Bullitt's use of his suggestions." Although in 1966 she had written to me that she had found the book "disappointing," not a hint of this ever came up in our discussions.

Anna felt so secure in her relationship to her father that she had had no doubts about proposing to alter what Freud had considered ready for publication. Freud had left the matter entirely up to Bullitt as to when the Wilson manuscript should finally appear. According to Bullitt's version, he had persuaded Freud, when Bullitt visited him in London in 1938, to drop some sections of the book which would have been even more contentious than what finally appeared. Either Bullitt was more persuasive than others, or else Freud felt especially indebted to him for his help in the escape from Vienna; for unlike the intransigence encountered by those who tried to convince Freud either to tone down or to withdraw his *Moses and Monotheism*, Freud seemed agreeable to giving in to Bullitt's suggestions. By 1965 Bullitt knew his health was in serious danger, which doubtless helped precipitate his decision to go ahead with publication.

Anna's willingness to propose changes of her own to the Wilson manuscript was consistent with the silent censorship she had been exercising over the publication of Freud's letters. For example nobody, as far as I can determine, has ever been able to make any rational consistent sense about what she wanted deleted from the original edition of the Freud-Fliess correspondence. When Anna decided to give Jones the love letters Freud had written to his future wife, Anna had permitted the publication of material that her father might have withheld. Some of Freud's most orthodox disciples, like Herman Nunberg for example, expressed to me their chagrin that Anna had allowed Freud's private life to be so compromised.

Before I began my interviews, I understood that there exists a principle in biography-writing to the effect that historians and the families of their subjects almost inevitably have an adversarial relationship. This palpable tension between a biographer and the surviving heirs of his subject is difficult to bear. The attitude of the Freuds, headed by Anna, was understandable, for Freud deserved his special place in history. But there is no way a biographer can hope to accomplish his or her objective if the biographer remains completely under the family's control.

If Jones had earned Anna Freud's displeasure, it was partly because he seemed too independent. Yet by July 1965, I discovered just how partisan Jones had been; he had seriously underrepresented the point of view of those who had struggled to establish their own identities by opposing some of Freud's expectations for them. At that time, and the situation has only begun to shift relatively recently, some historians still accepted the orthodox psychoanalytic version of the history of Freud's early struggles.

Even independent-minded psychoanalysts were, from my point of view, too easily intimidated by pressures from within the establishment. It was not just that analysts feared losing their referrals if they crossed Anna Freud. They dreaded the possibility of being excluded from the "movement." (Someone like Edoardo Weiss just shuddered with the knowledge of how Anna felt about him.) One established heretic, Dr. Sandor Rado in New York City, was already famous as a theorist and clinician; yet at one point he ordered me not to write something down on paper. It was terribly naive of him to try such a stunt, since his momentary anger, and the subject that had evoked his fear, would be indelibly etched in my memory, whether I recorded it on paper in Rado's presence or not. At some point in my interview with Rado, my knowledge about who had analyzed Anna Freud came up and Rado exclaimed: "You know about that!" Sharing such a secret helped establish my credentials as an insider. Only much later did I find out that Rado and Helene Deutsch had once, while both were being analyzed by Karl Abraham in Berlin, been intimate with one another. In contrast to Rado, Helene had remained organizationally loyal. When I raised the issue of Anna's analysis by her father, Helene chose tactfully to remain silent, looking off in the distance as if she had not heard what I had been saying. My willingness to put such a sensitive subject into print was an automatic historiographic reflex on my part, since it was telling about so many hypocritical aspects of the history of psychoanalytic technique. Yet, for those who wanted to defend the status quo, my impiety was unforgivable.

Once I had learned that all of the published versions of Freud's letters had been crudely censored, without even an indication that gaps in the letters existed, I realized that I had a powerful weapon that could emancipate people from the conventional wisdom about Freud. I still wonder how Anna Freud and her allies thought they could get away with publishing tendentiously edited volumes of Freud's correspondence.

I never thought that these zealots were emotionally capable of actually destroying anything Freud wrote. I suspected that they would have been too blinded by loyalty to notice if Freud had written something which, from their idealized point of view, he should have omitted. Their kind of incompetent censorship is bound to fan the flames of suspicion, and in the end is worse than allowing the most potentially damaging material to appear in its totality. A letter by one of Freud's mentors, Josef Breuer, has been sealed until the year 2102. My own educated hunch is that nothing so shocking will be found in that letter, certainly not enough to justify such a distant date.

The result of allowing doctored manuscripts to become available is that in the end, more attention is paid to what has been left out than would ever have been the case if an uncensored version had been published in the first place. By 1974, with the appearance of the Freud-Jung correspondence, the Freud family had evidently stopped its policy of expurgating Freud's letters. But that was in direct response to the previous publicity I had given to the whole issue. In reflecting back on what I was doing in 1965, it is important to remember what the state of the relevant literature was in those days.

8

"Altogether Feminine": Mathilda Freud Hollitscher

My discovery of Anna Freud's analysis was a major factor in the brouhaha over *Brother Animal*. Yet at the outset of my work, I had had no intention of correcting any myth-making about Freud. Within my own field of political science, the study of psychology was not an acceptable avenue of research and, as I explained earlier, writing about Freud was not only frowned upon but was unlikely to help my career. I stood to gain nothing by trying to find weak spots in connection with Freud, for to denigrate him would only undermine the legitimacy of my own efforts to use modern psychology within social thought as a whole. In my first interview with Anna Freud, she indicated that she realized my interests were bound to cause trouble for me, and she sympathetically agreed that the young people I was teaching in college had not yet acquired the prejudices of their elders.

As I see it, my independence within the field of political science carried over into my new study of psychology. Thus, as I arranged to see Anna Freud's only living sister, Mathilda Hollitscher, in London in November 1966, I was a bit concerned that what I had unearthed would have already rendered me unacceptable to the family. Since the summer of 1965, in addition to my university teaching, I continued to conduct interviews on the early history of psychoanalysis. In 1966, most people did not seem to realize that Freud had another surviving daughter besides Anna. Mathilda was the first-born of the six Freud children.

My notes indicate that during the summer of 1965, Eva Rosen-feld—a mutual friend of Mathilda's and Anna's—had volunteered to introduce me to Mathilda. Eva had been Anna's closest friend before Dorothy Burlingham had entered Anna's life. Anna actually ar-ranged for Eva to be analyzed by Freud. When Eva later became an analyst and then chose to be treated by Melanie Klein, a subtle permanent break occurred between her and Anna. But Eva kept up her relationship with Anna, even though Eva was one of the most outspoken people I met when it came to interviewing people about the history of psychoanalysis.

At the time Eva first suggested that I see Mathilda, I was still too scared of Anna to be willing to risk it. When I told Eva that my intellectual exchanges with Anna had not allowed time for me to be given the customary tour of the house, Eva suggested that she contact Mathilda on my behalf, for the family had agreed that Mathilda was entitled to show people around #20 Maresfield Gar-dens. Eva was herself so open-minded and generous that no matter what I decided to publish, she and I stayed on excellent terms. During the summer of 1965, however, I superstitiously decided that since I was doing well enough as it was, I preferred to maintain a low profile and restrict my contact just to Anna.

In November 1966, when I did ask Mathilda directly to see her, I must have felt that there was nothing left to risk losing. I had seen Dr. Michael Balint, Ferenczi's literary executor, both in July 1965, and again in the late fall of 1966; he was in full agreement with me about the immense distortions that Jones's biography had imposed on the historical record. Balint was regarded as a free spirit in the field, but he knew where the power lay in London and in the international psychoanalytic movement. He simply could not believe that I pro-posed to rectify Jones's errors, even though he and Jones had dis-agreed in print over Jones's biased version of Ferenczi's last days. As Balint said when it dawned on him that I would not be intimidated: "Anna Freud will destroy you!"

It is striking that Balint was so prudent about Anna and willing to conform to pressures from the psychoanalytic powers that be, espe-cially since he was neither a member of Anna's circle nor of Melanie

Klein's group. Balint was one of the so-called British Independents, or "Middle-Groupers," who within British psychoanalysis refused to align themselves with either of the opposing ideological poles. Balint's house in London was decorated to reflect his native Budapest, but impressive as his surroundings were, I found I was not imbued with as much traditionalist magic as he. Balint knew intimately how difficult it had been for Ferenczi's work to gain acceptance because of Ferenczi's personal problems with Freud. Since Anna Freud had never forgiven Ferenczi, even though he had been dead for over three decades, it had taken years for some of his most brilliant papers to be translated into English. Balint himself oversaw that work. When I knew Balint, he was thinking about the future publication of the Freud-Ferenczi correspondence, for which he needed Anna Freud's cooperation. And Balint had in his charge an important clinical diary of Ferenczi's, which finally appeared in 1988.

Even without Balint's warning to me about Anna, and despite her personal charm, she represented an enormous obstacle to historical inquiry by an outside researcher. Before Jones had undertaken the biography of Freud, she had written about his "negative attitude" toward her father.[1] If Jones, with all his loyalty, was not good enough for her, there was little hope that I could succeed in pleasing her. When I finally arranged to see her sister Mathilda, I had not yet published anything. But the more the family helped me, the more inhibited I feared I would be in ultimately writing what I truly thought.

Mathilda was eight years older than her famous sister. Although Anna was the only child to have remained in the Freud household, as well as having been the one to become a practicing analyst, Mathilda had lived around the corner from her parents in Vienna. I had been advised by other members of the family that, compared to her brother Ernst, for instance, who had lived in Berlin for many years, Mathilda would have to know a lot about the family. In Vienna she came to see her mother and father every day, as a "good daughter" in that culture was supposed to do. If only because of her age, which was then seventy-nine, Mathilda was bound to be privy to aspects of the family's history that Anna would be unaware of.

The psychoanalytic movement was like a large family, and all of

Freud's children's names were selected by him to commemorate people who had mattered to him. Anna was named for the daughter of one of Freud's revered boyhood teachers, and Mathilda had been the name of Josef Breuer's wife. In turn, Mathilda herself became such an intimate friend of Ruth and Mark Brunswick, a couple who were Freud's own patients and students, that they chose Mathilda's name for their only child. Freud's paternalism expressed itself in still other ways. In the instance of Dorothy and her husband Robert Burlingham, Freud had helped come between them. He also supported the disruption of Ruth Brunswick's first marriage to a Boston physician, but then made special efforts to set up new marital arrangements for her; at times he was like an old-fashioned rabbi, as he actively promoted the union between Ruth and Mark Brunswick.[2] Mathilda told me that Ruth had been her "dearest friend."

When I asked Mathilda if she had ever thought of becoming an analyst herself, she raised the issue of her health. She explained that she had been too ill as a youngster to have planned to study for a professional career. In Freud's letter to her written when she was twenty-one, he alludes to "the weakness . . . which those three serious illnesses in your early life left behind. . . ."[3] Mathilda had attended a girls' school in Vienna until she was eighteen. After her death in 1978, Anna somehow publicly stated that old-fashioned culture had blocked Mathilda's education; the *New York Times* quoted Anna as having said of her sister: "there was no college for girls in those days, so she got married at a young age."[4]

Freud had actually reassured Mathilda that there was no urgency about an early marriage. When she was recovering from a bout of ill health at the age of twenty-one, Freud reminded her that her mother had not married until she was twenty-five:

> I think you probably associate the present minor complaint with an old worry about which I should very much like to talk to you for once. I have guessed for a long time that in spite of all your common sense you fret because you think you are not good-looking enough and therefore might not attract a man. I have watched this with a smile, first of all because you seem quite attractive enough to me, and secondly because I know that in reality it is no longer physical beauty which decides the fate of a girl, but the impression of her whole personality.

Freud's daughter Sophie, with whom Anna in particular had difficulties when growing up, seemed to be the beauty among his girls. He went on in telling Mathilda:

> Your mirror will inform you that there is nothing common or repellent in your features, and your memory will confirm the fact that you have managed to inspire respect and sympathy in any circle of human beings. And as a result I have felt perfectly reassured about your future so far as it depends on you, and you have every reason to feel the same.

Freud thought that he himself would be no detriment to her: "That you are my daughter shouldn't do you any harm, either. I know that finding a respected name and a warm atmosphere in her home was decisive in my choice of a wife, and there are certain to be others who think as I did when I was young." Freud was trying to combat her temporary downheartedness: "The more intelligent among young men are sure to know what to look for in a wife—gentleness, cheerfulness, and the talent to make their life easier and more beautiful."[5] It would be hard to overemphasize Freud's concern and devotion as a family man.

Anna Freud's own comments about Mathilda, after her death, seemed to me a sign of her own genuine family feelings, yet she was engaging in a kind of rewriting of history. For it was not only the lack of educational alternatives that had restricted Mathilda's career possibilities. While that attitude might make Anna's career seem ahead of its time, it overlooks what Mathilda had told me about her health problems.

In any event women like Helene Deutsch and Karen Horney, both born earlier than Mathilda, had themselves gone on to become medical doctors. The success of Horney in Germany and Helene within the Austro-Hungarian Empire indicates that in principle a woman, despite what Anna Freud tried to argue, could get university training. I think it is a separate issue that Anna herself had only been educated as a primary school teacher.

Mathilda looked and walked so much like Anna that at first I was distracted, and restricted, in my interviewing. To those who knew them intimately, however, Mathilda was said to have resembled her mother's side of the family, and Anna, her father's; their brothers

Martin and Oliver supposedly looked like their mother's family, while Ernst and Sophie (who died suddenly of influenza in 1920), the last of the six siblings, took after the Freuds.

In contrast to Anna, who was used to handling a steady stream of visitors, Mathilda was not accustomed to seeing researchers. Within the family itself, however, it was Mathilda who arranged for the social gatherings; she was the one who got along well with her nephews in London. She also was in close touch with Anna and their two brothers in England (Martin and Ernst) who, though younger, were already suffering from various ailments and predeceased Mathilda. While a widow, Mathilda, whose husband had been in the importing business, managed two small apartment buildings; as a couple they had remained childless. Mathilda's brother Ernst, who came to London earlier, had prepared for her accommodations and the arrangement by which she serviced flats there. One story has it that in Vienna she had once run "a boutique specializing in handmade, hand-woven clothes."[6]

I remember uncertainly looking up from the street for the address of her apartment and seeing her somewhat nervously adjusting one of the livingroom curtains; she recognized who I must be and helpfully waved me on up. Although she had extra time, scholars had not thought to consider her potentially informative. Perhaps because Mathilda was less accustomed to being questioned, I found her able to relax and show herself as a sensitive and intelligent person in her own right. Although her husband had once been wealthy, they had at some points depended on her father for money; the world in those days was such that still she took her Viennese maid with her to London. One of Mathilda's sisters-in-law, usually none too gentle about people, described Mathilda to me as both charming and ladylike. She was also, I thought, somehow more feminine than her famous sister. Much later I came across a letter of Freud's, written to Fliess when Mathilda was eleven years old, in complete accord with my own impression of her. Freud had remarked that she was "a complete human being and of course altogether feminine."[7]

It is hard to put my finger on how I was able to distinguish between two such old women in terms of their sexual identity. However, Anna's public role was a special burden, and it ended up suppressing parts of her character. Photographs of Anna as a young woman are in striking contrast to the single-minded and one-dimensional woman she later seemed to become. Unlike my impression of Anna, I thought that Mathilda had retained a certain spontaneous warmth, more like I imagined her father to be. Informally I heard that her nephews in London also thought this to be true, and that Mathilda had played a special role in helping to keep the family together. Although Ernst Freud's wife in particular was admired for her maternal capacities, her sons seem to have regarded Mathilda as an alternative mother of their own.

Mathilda did not dress as idiosyncratically as Anna. I was told by a relative that she had always looked elegant, and that unlike her sister Anna, Mathilda never appeared dowdy. She understood, liked, and was interested in how she dressed. Only the blind partisanship of Anna Freud's official biographer could attribute the tension between Anna and her mother to the bizarre idea that Martha Freud was always dedicated "to elegant dresses, coiffures, and cosmetics."[8] An American patient of Anna's once told me how in the 1920s, she used to wipe off her lipstick before entering Anna's consulting room.[9] Mathilda did not share in Anna's drabness, but neither she nor her mother was a clotheshorse.

Regarding the issue of how the women in the family attired themselves, it is worth noting that Freud had always been careful to dress extremely correctly. (His own mother is known to have been meticulous about her clothes even in her extreme old age.) A daughter-in-law of Freud's explained to me that he wore collars that were attached to his shirts, a luxury at a time when a collar was usually separate so that it could be changed daily while the shirt itself might last for two days. Most observers said it was his wife, an exacting and thrifty housekeeper, who made sure that he purchased new suits, and who objected to his old hats.

Freud's son Martin once reminisced about an Italian walking tour he had taken with his father before World War I: "My mother, who ordered all my father's clothes, tried to reach absolute perfection, always taking the greatest care in ordinary well-cut clothes made from British cloth. Thus he appeared as respectable as he did in

Vienna in his dark suits and black ties."[10] While engaged in what the Viennese exaggeratedly called mountain climbing, Freud suffered a temporary "heatstroke" but did not lose his customary self-control. "His face was purple red, almost violet, and he seemed incapable of talking." Freud motioned toward a bottle of chianti that Martin had carried in his rucksack. Martin recorded how Freud, under that sort of stress,

> did for once abandon a number of conventions which he always strictly observed. He drank from the actual bottle instead of using the small flat aluminum beaker he carried in his waistcoat pocket. He removed his tie and unbuttoned his collar. He did not, however, go so far as to take off his coat.[11]

Only once as a child, during a family emergency, did Martin see his father appear in his nightshirt.

Freud's sense of propriety seems to have afflicted Anna more than Mathilda, but then Anna was to absorb more from identifying with her father. Unlike Mathilda, who was married, Anna had to wear the mantle of psychoanalytic statecraft. I think Anna underwent a striking change from a shy young woman to a powerful leader. Although as we have seen it was Anna who, as head of the family, controlled her father's papers, she did so with the assistance of her brother Ernst. And as we shall learn, the break-up of Martin Freud's own marriage signaled the end of his standing within, so to speak, the family "business."

Nothing could be written about Freud without it being brought to Anna Freud's attention. I had little doubt that Mathilda must have checked with Anna first about the advisability of seeing me. Or perhaps Mathilda had heard about me from Eva Rosenfeld, whom I was also interviewing. I was told that the two sisters were neither very close nor too competitive, but that would be according to the standards of the late twentieth century. However, Anna had had her difficulties growing up with her sister Sophie. By the fall of 1966, when I saw Mathilda, I had already interviewed so many other figures in the history of analysis that there may have seemed little point in denying me further access.

According to Eva Rosenfeld, Mathilda had experienced her younger sister Anna to be a difficult, deprived child. Another informant told me that Mathilda thought it was eccentric of Anna to work so terribly hard. Anna's complete absorption in her professional commitments made her self-centered, whereas Freud's sense of self had been willingly sacrificed to his creation of psychoanalysis. The cause he had founded seemed much larger than himself; it brought him in contact with many other people and stirred up issues of increasingly momentous import in both social and intellectual history. He had not only created a new means of livelihood for analysts but had also fundamentally changed the way we think about ourselves. Freud worked infinitely harder than most, but those immediately around him were less apt to feel it than they did with Anna. Maybe it was Freud's originality that made people feel he was especially entitled to be treated uniquely. Up until the end of his life, he remained interested in everything, and was fortunate in having had a fine education; however, he too was singleminded about his mission, and anything which failed to advance it—or interfered—could be pushed out of the way.

At the outset of our talks, Mathilda was careful about what she said to me, as if she assumed that it paid to be guarded lest I might have come with hostile intent. From her point of view, the literature about her father and the controversies associated with his work must have been bewildering; so much had been written which from the family's point of view was bound to seem tactless. I have recently seen a book-length manuscript about Freud's "homicidal deeds," and I have read others even more strange. The greater Freud's influence was to become, the larger was the blame that people felt justified in laying at his doorstep.

Yet as the interview wore on and Mathilda perceived my immense admiration for her father as well as the genuine curiosity I had about what he had been like, I think she felt contrite about her early suspicions. She started to show me little items from her family's history, which had been so different from my own life. Mathilda now moved about her apartment with friendly animation. She shared some cherished photographs and proudly displayed a holder for service and napkin that had come from her parent's wedding reception. It was the kind of memento her mother must have saved and passed on to her. By the end of the interview, she was offering me the names of old Viennese acquaintances and their children who now lived in America and would, she claimed, "remember much."

I assumed, perhaps wrongly, that Mathilda knew little about psychoanalysis; Anna had once complained that while their mother believed in their father, psychoanalysis was another matter. Pupils of Freud also recorded Anna's mother's skepticism. I did not expect Mathilda to impart any professional knowledge, since I knew that she, unlike Anna, had "held back" and not shared her father's analytic life. She was to be sure an intimate friend of the Brunswicks, although she joked that the modern atonal music Mark composed was hardly what she and her husband loved.

Almost as a matter of course, Mathilda had helped various of her father's foreign patients settle in Vienna; there were always complicated domestic arrangements to straighten out. Sometimes she even helped them get theatre seats. In a sense she was assisting her mother perform the role that Freud might have expected a wife to fulfill. Thus, Anna had taken over her specific duties and Mathilda undertook to fulfill her share. Mathilda even translated from French a couple of pieces by Marie Bonaparte, who had become a special favorite of Freud's in his last years.

There is, however, just so far that one can go during any interview in asking questions which might jeopardize the interviewing process itself. I knew from reading Jones's files that Mathilda had wanted to destroy the love letters her father wrote to her mother; and that, according to another of Mathilda's letters, her father had never discussed his ideas and theories with her mother. Assuming this was true, Freud's reserve could have been a response to his wife's own expressed convictions. For example, the Viennese analyst Theodor Reik once reported of Freud's wife that

> from conversations on walks on the Semmering, near Vienna, I got the decided impression that she not only had no idea of the significance and importance of psychoanalysis, but had intensive emotional resistances against the character of analytic work. On such a walk she once said, "Women have always had such troubles, but they needed

no psychoanalysis to conquer them. After the menopause they become quieter and resigned."[12]

The implication of Reik's anecdote seems to me that Martha knew
rather more about Freud's work than Mathilda implied in writing to
Jones.

In talking with Mathilda I had been careful not to ask about the
nephew who had died in 1923, a son of her deceased sister Sophie,
for when I raised the subject with Kata Levy, her eyes welled up with
tears. Sophie had been married to Max Halberstadt, the Berlin
photographer who took some of the most famous shots of Freud. His
photograph of Freud holding a cigar was hanging over the man-
tlepiece in Mathilda's living room.

After Sophie died, Mathilda had taken the boy in (his father
remained in Berlin), and she with her husband had intended to
adopt him. Freud was acutely depressed about his grandson's un-
timely death; it happened at the same time Freud was trying to
recover from his first bout with cancer. In the context of what had
come to be Freud's disappointment in his sons, he could entertain
the idea that this charming child might be worthy to be his true heir.
Although Freud's most loyal Viennese pupils could be hypersensitive
in discussing how Freud felt about his own sons, in some of his letters
to his English nephew Sam, Freud was openly disillusioned with his
sons' performances. None of them had even done well in school, in
contrast to Freud's outstanding academic achievements.

Freud's honesty within the family about his feelings about his sons
was the more striking to me in that one of his most devout followers
was known to have been so defensive as to have walked away when
someone even made mention of the issue in a social situation. As it
happened, the brother of this deceased grandson was eventually
trained to become an analyst; as Freud had analyzed Anna, so she
analyzed her own nephew, known sometimes as "Little Ernst."
Inasmuch as she also allowed him to change his name from Halberstadt to Freud, one might speculate that she was trying to give her
father a professional heir. My most memorable impression of Little
Ernst was how he could sit so strangely silent at all the meetings of
the Hampstead Clinic that I attended.

The limits I placed on myself during the interviews were more unconscious than conscious, but I could kick myself now for not having asked Mathilda more about her paternal grandmother, whom others in the family described as a tyrant. As in most aspects of Freud's autobiography, his exclusive emphasis on fathers and sons has been echoed by most of those who have written about him.

Yet Freud's inner dependency on his mother might account for many of his otherwise inexplicable anxieties.[13] A Viennese analyst once told me that he had observed Freud's mother to be "domineering." When I asked whether Freud was like this in his own circle, the analyst thought I had made a connection he had not seen before. Although it might seem obvious to look to both of Freud's parents for aspects of his character, his followers simply refused to turn the tables on their mentor by using his own concepts to understand him.

I did think to ask Mathilda about the oil portrait of her father, painted by M. Oppenheimer during the brief period when Freud was temporarily without a beard. Freud had visited his half-brother in Manchester, England, in 1908. When the barbers there had been unable to trim his beard to his satisfaction, he retained only a mustache with English handlebars. Because he always cut himself when shaving, he went back to wearing a beard, which somehow never grew in as long and large as before. An aspect of that civilization of old Vienna which has long since disappeared is that in Freud's later years, a barber came daily to trim his beard. (In the 1920s, a woman like Helene Deutsch would go out to have her hair done every day.)

The Oppenheimer painting was executed in late 1908 in honor of Mathilda's impending wedding; in 1909 she was married in a synagogue at the same hour as Freud's younger brother Alexander. I regret that I failed to ask Mathilda whether her father had attended her wedding. Freud's children grew up in so secular an environment that they were not taught the most elementary rules of traditional synagogue rituals, such as men being required to wear hats. Freud fussed a lot about the religious ceremonies that this wife's family had insisted on at his own wedding, and later he did not allow her to light candles on Friday evenings. Contrary to Jewish custom, at his death he was cremated and his ashes deposited in an ancient Greek urn given to him by Marie Bonaparte; later his wife, who unlike him had a rabbi at her funeral, arranged to have her own ashes added to his.

Paul Federn, an early Viennese analyst, had commissioned the Oppenheimer portrait. In it Freud's eyes are deeply piercing, almost melodramatic. But, it does not even look like him unless one covers up the lower half of his face; then his sharp eyes stand out recognizably. Mathilda shuddered as she told me that she always thought the painting was dreadful. She only had a vague memory that it was without a beard, because the portrait had been returned to Federn. In contrast, she liked the Halberstadt photograph over her mantle. The painting can now be seen hanging at the New York Psychoanalytic Society, where it went after Federn's death in 1950. (The painting played a special role in the analysis of Edoardo Weiss, one of Federn's patients sent to him by Freud. He was so intent on it in Federn's office, musing about how he would have preferred to have been analyzed by Freud rather than Federn, that Federn had the portrait removed from sight. Weiss expressed to me the horror he felt when Jones—in Weiss's presence at a Freud celebration in 1956—maliciously pointed to a slight tear in the painting, alleging that just prior to Federn's shooting himself to death, he had first fired at the Oppenheimer.)

Mathilda shared the typical detachment and formality befitting a lady from that old world culture. I therefore could not have dreamt of asking her about Anna's hostility toward their mother, about any guilt feelings Anna might have had, or how this could possibly be reconciled with Anna's written contention to Jones that she could not remember "a single family quarrel." Family tensions would have been expressed differently in that era than our own; the Freud household was unusually peaceful but outsiders were keenly aware that, among the ladies at least, symptoms like migraine headaches and vomiting persisted.

Mathilda did choose to discuss what she thought was a common misconception: that there had been discussions about psychoanalysis at the family dinner table. (The main meal in Vienna was at midday.) When Jung was on good terms with Freud and once came to see him, Freud's son Martin recalled how striking it was to witness the way in which Jung held forth at a Freud family meal. Although the Freuds did not do much in the way of social entertaining, and never gave parties, pupils from abroad might be invited to eat with the family, and then would usually try to make some effort at social small talk. But Martin recalled that Jung

> was an exception. He never made the slightest attempt to make polite conversation with mother or us children but pursued the debate which had been interrupted by the call to dinner. Jung on these occasions did all the talking and father with unconcealed delight did all the listening. There was little we could understand, but I know I found, as did father, his way of outlining a case fascinating. [14]

At the dinner table in his home, Freud was almost always quiet, and supposedly not at all interested in what was going on around him. According to Jones, Freud would silently point to an empty seat in order to get an explanation about the absent diner. One of Freud's American Bernays nieces was impressed with how intense he was when he concentrated. (The five Bernays children were contemporaries of Freud's children.) If Freud came in and dinner was not ready, he would not join in a family discussion but would sit and read the paper.

Once, in 1924, the celebrated Leopold and Loeb case in Chicago did come up in family conversation; that these two men were Jews who were responsible for killing an innocent boy did not pass unnoticed. Freud had been invited by their wealthy families to give expert testimony in their behalf, but he declined—despite how much money was involved. Freud was already sick by then, and his disapproval of America after his trip there in 1909 was legendary. When I tentatively asked Mathilda if Freud's illness had meant he withdrew personally, and if it had affected the family, she acknowledged that this had been so. Serious illness is almost bound to make anyone somewhat capricious if not misanthropic.

For Mathilda it was a sign of how little people understood her father that anyone could think that he would discuss psychoanalytic matters within the family circle. Others told me that Freud's wife, for example, would notice a limousine of a prominent patient like Bullitt, and seemed familiar enough with that side of Freud's affairs.

But in general those I interviewed agreed that Freud kept his clinical work unusually separate from his family life.

Had Freud behaved differently, either as a psychoanalytic observer or as an interpreter of human motives within the family, it is hard to imagine that his family's life could have ever proceeded smoothly. Not even such terms as "neurotic" were used at home, and the commonsense notion of "impatience" replaced the terms usually associated with the symptomatology connected to neurosis. For Freud to have gone about diagnosing within the family would have been terribly detrimental; the use of any such labels is bound to be off-putting. Yet, although his self-restraint was considerable, it did not stop him from having analyzed Anna in his study. By and large there was little mention of Freud's pupils or followers in the house, on the general principle, enunciated by Freud's wife, that one does not talk of the rope in the hangman's house.

With Mathilda, as with Anna, I knew I could not be searching in my questions; yet having met them both I could weigh more accurately what others told me about them. Even the letters Freud sent them, a handful of which are already in print, make more sense on rereading. Despite the relative superficiality of my contact with Mathilda, meeting her conveyed something special about the tight-knit family headed by a great man. Mathilda's American first cousin, Edward Bernays—who had helped promote Freud's work in the States as part of Bernays's career as a public relations expert—had half-seriously proposed to me that each of the surviving Freud children in London phoned each other every morning to discuss what they had done the preceding evening.

Bernays was never a favorite of Freud's, even though he did handle some of the commercial aspects of Freud's American publishing; there were translators to be chosen and royalties to keep track of and forwarded. The entire American wing of the Bernays family was viewed with some of the disdain that Freud (and Anna) reserved for the commercial New World in general. Bernays never considered himself a part of what Freud disliked most about America; but Bernays knew that Freud feared that psychoanalysis on this continent would be luridly sensationalized. Even though Bernays had the reputation of being an old pirate, I thought that he was astute as to how his European relatives felt and behaved. As an example of how involved Freud family matters could become, Edward Bernays's father—a friend of Freud's—had married Freud's sister Anna and was simultaneously Freud's wife's brother. It was not always easy to keep track of the complexities of Freud's family matters.

9

"The Black Sheep": Dr. Esti Freud

During the spring and summer of 1966, I was able to conduct entirely different kinds of interviews with Dr. Esti Freud, one of Freud's daughters-in-law who lived in a modest apartment in New York City. While her London relatives lived a more or less standard middle-class existence, in keeping with the status that psychoanalysis had gained in Great Britain, in New York Freud's loyal disciples were living in grand apartments on Park Avenue, Fifth Avenue, and Central Park West. Even though Dr. Esti Freud had been married to Freud's eldest son Martin, she was not able, once separated from her husband, to participate in the American windfall that psychoanalysis otherwise brought to the Freuds. Her last name, though, had doubtless not hurt her.

With both Anna and Mathilda I had to labor under a variety of inhibitions; they were both loyal members of the family, and to the extent that analysis was a practical business, its future partly rested on their successful promotion of Freud and the early days of his school. But with Esti Freud I could be completely at ease, and as outspoken as possible. Geography has its own way of enhancing psychological distance, and once separated from the rest of the Freuds, Esti had a special, detached perspective to bring to bear on my subject. Even Edward Bernays, who did not think of himself as undermining his cousins in London, thought that it was noteworthy that Anna Freud had built what he called "a shrine" to the memory of her father at #20 Maresfield Gardens.

Esti was still technically married to Martin Freud, who had resided in London since the rest of the family had emigrated there from Vienna in 1938. By the time I met Esti, she and Martin had been living apart for almost thirty years. It was the widow of one of Freud's most devout followers, Edward Hitschmann, who had suggested to me, once she realized that I sought a historically balanced account of Freud, that I contact Esti as someone in the family who could be expected to speak absolutely freely. Because Mrs. Hitschmann lived in Cambridge, Massachusetts, she was someone I could easily interview; she had once given music lessons to Anna Freud, had gone from Vienna to London with the Freuds, knew much about the early history of analysis, and sometimes attended meetings of the Boston Psychoanalytic Society. With a nod and a wink she indicated that I could expect to learn something unique from Esti.

Evidently, from the outset of her marriage shortly after World War I, Esti had experienced some tension with the Freuds, and after the formal marital separation, things had not surprisingly grown a good deal worse. One of her two children, a daughter, had gone with her, while her son stayed on with Martin. At one point, Esti described herself as "the black sheep of the family." She said she no longer had any contact with Anna Freud. In what may be a sign of her disaffection from the family, an interview that Kurt Eissler conducted with her has been locked up at the Library of Congress until the year 2053. Esti said she knew nothing of the restrictions Eissler had imposed on her material and was willing to let me see it.

When I asked her if my interviewing approach contrasted with Eissler's, she said we were "completely different" in how we undertook the task. From other Eissler interviews that I had a chance to read, he appeared to be less an active inquirer than an apparently passive gatherer of free associations. Eissler's 1952 interviews with Wilhelm Reich were published in 1967,[1] and Eissler was so upset with the content that a disclaimer was inserted in the original hard-cover edition of the book; he had been embarrassingly silent at a number of key points in Reich's reminiscences. Although I had not yet had any difficulties with Eissler myself, I knew of his reputation as a fierce defender of psychoanalytic orthodoxy. In 1950 he had attacked Franz

Alexander, the leader of an original center of psychoanalytic training in Chicago, for being unorthodox. And when the eminent art historian Meyer Schapiro had in 1956 published an essay on Freud's study of Leonardo, Eissler answered it with a huge book, Part I of which was titled "Polemics." It should not have been too surprising that Eissler felt it incumbent upon himself to retort to *Brother Animal*, although the length of his writings and the number of his individual attacks seem remarkable. I had only met Eissler once.[2]

At the time I saw Esti, she was earning a living as a speech therapist; in Europe she had been a lecturer at the University of Vienna in public speaking and drama interpretation. Freud had once made an ironic remark to her that she had succeeded at the university despite bearing the Freud name. Esti knew that Freud always resented the fact that he was ineligible for a regular faculty professorship. She knew Freud well enough to appreciate how much he chaffed under his marginality in Viennese university life.

As one of the Bernays nieces had pointed out, it had taken courage for Esti to take an apartment alone in New York, where she later earned a Ph.D. Because of her profession, she had a tape recorder handy and suggested we try using it. Although she had no trouble following my questions, she insisted that as a professional matter I must realize that I spoke too fast. In the end I thought that recording our interviews was almost a useless exercise; the expense of having them typed up was considerable, all the foreign names were garbled by the typist, and each few hours of interviews produced a manuscript so bulky that it was not serviceable in helping me question other people I met. I also took elaborate notes in her presence, and I think it was the physical act of writing them down, and the rewriting I did afterwards to expand them, which was the best tool for helping me recall the points she made. Nonetheless, I soon bought a tape recorder of my own, only to find that my next interviewee (an American former patient of Freud's) refused to let me use it. Europeans, I thought, would have been even more wary of any such mechanical device.

"She's much too pretty for our family!" Freud had remarked, loud enough for Esti to hear, when she was first introduced to the family in 1918. Esti remained uncertain whether his comment had been intended to be a real compliment, or was even meant for her to hear. She considered herself then an artist, and had already "given her own evenings as a performer." As she put it to me, she was "not at all a home girl." She implied that this in itself was enough to cause trouble for her with the Freuds.

Although Esti never mentioned the point, and I am not at all sure that while I saw her I understood it myself, Freud did seem to follow a pattern that indicates he was especially fascinated by beautiful and narcissistic women. He had not chosen to marry one of them himself, for he thought such women were not easy to live with. Yet among his students, there were so many attractive women that it begins to look like more than a matter of chance. As a niece of Freud's pointed out to me, his own mother had been vain; when she was ninety, for example, she had her furniture reupholstered.

Esti seemed to think that Freud had a special appreciation for women, and she was concerned that I fully understand the degree of antifeminism that had been the cultural norm during Freud's time, and which he could hardly have avoided. She was distancing herself from the feminism of the 1960s which was being so rough on Freud, and she thought that a knowledge of other thinkers of Freud's era would help put some of his own views into a social context. She herself found it easy to identify with all the emancipated young women in the stories and plays of Arthur Schnitzler. He dealt with themes of "the casual, sexual use of 'the sweet young thing,'" and "exposed the frustrations and even desperation of other women, both young and middle-aged, victimized sometimes by their families but most often by their fathers and husbands."[3] Freud once wrote Schnitzler that they shared so many viewpoints that Freud considered him his "double."[4]

Esti and Martin first met at a party in 1916. They were married on December 7, 1919, which was also Martin's birthday. (Unfortunately, I again neglected to ask Esti if Freud had attended their wedding, for he could have a curious attitude toward such occasions. I only know for sure that he was present at the weddings of his former patients the Brunswicks and that of Loe Kann, Jones's former common-law wife.) Martin had served in the Austro-Hungarian army during World War I, and was a prisoner-of-war at the end; despite Esti's urgings, Freud had refused—rather "heartlessly," she thought—to try to use his international connections to help Martin. Freud did, however, send Martin some money from funds he had kept abroad. In connection with Martin's proposed marriage, Esti remembered Minna having skeptically remarked that he was taking himself "from one imprisonment to another." But according to Esti, Martha Freud was much less sharp and bitter-tongued; still, she used to say that you love a house twice: the day you buy it and the day you sell it.

Like others, Esti could never mention Martha without also alluding to her sister Minna. Esti felt that Minna was much more aggressive than Martha and "very spinsterish." To Esti, Minna was a decidedly "unpleasant woman" who had made life hard for Esti within the family. Minna was an expert in making the kind of "catty" remarks that Esti thought only women can say about each other; Minna seemed to have specialized in nasty comments about Esti's clothes. In contrast, "Mama," Freud's wife, "was much too fine ever to do that." When I asked what Minna could have provided for Freud, Esti's unhesitating answer was Minna's cardplaying; Freud's wife was never his card partner. Minna had "made a play" for Freud, "there was no doubt of that." But Esti thought it was a tribute to her mother-in-law's "great-heartedness" that she kept Minna in the household in spite of everything.

When I inquired whether Minna was more the intellectual than her sister Martha, Esti would only concede that Minna had "played" at being such. Before coming to the Freuds she had been a governess for rich young girls. Yet, however badly Esti felt toward Minna, she had never seen any quarrels between the two sisters. When I asked what sort of effect Minna's presence had had on the children in the family, Esti thought that it had not been a good one. When Esti first came into the family, it struck her how often Martin would speak about his Tante ("Aunt") Minna. Esti said she cared for her mother-in-law, not for Minna, and Esti thought that therefore Minna's standing within the household had been lowered. Esti also suggested that her attitude toward Minna had been partly responsible for Minna's being so hostile to Esti.

This sort of double-maternal authority—Martha plus Minna—was the model, conscious or unconscious, for the subsequent ar-

rangement by which Dorothy Burlingham and Anna Freud ran the
Burlingham household. Esti was right, I thought, in proposing that
her failure to be "a home girl" helped account for her inability to fit
in with the Freud family. Freud's remark that she was "too pretty" was
his way of welcoming her. I thought that she still retained, when I
saw her, a kind of stylish glamour.

Esti seemed to be a complicated person who had had a hard life;
she originally had come from a wealthy Viennese family. Her grandfather had been very rich and she said it was considered a bad
marriage for her. She grew up in an era when a young woman's
reading matter could be inspected by her father; Esti's father thought
it unwise of her to be reading one of Freud's works, and no way to get
a decent husband. She considered herself more liberated than the
Freuds expected women to be. Like Freud, her lawyer father had an
office adjoining the family apartment. He did not, however, belong
to the Jewish lodge B'nai B'rith that Freud joined; instead, her father
was a member of "a very modern, elegant assimilated club." (B'nai
B'rith in Vienna was far more formal an organization than it was to
become in America.) Esti's sense of freedom, acquired from her
upbringing, allowed her to challenge accepted modes of dress. For
example, she decided that maternity clothes were unnecessary because they encouraged an attitude of hiding one's condition. Her
behavior incited some of the Freud family criticism she ran into, as if
she were dressing like a woman carrying an illegitimate baby. When
she had her first child she experienced no special problems with the
pregnancy and "took no notice" of it. Evidently Freud had spoken in
her defense, asking: "Why shouldn't she be feeling well? To be
pregnant is a normal state in a young woman." Esti thought that as a
matter of principle, Freud regarded the members of his family as
healthy, and without neuroses.

As a psychoanalyst, Freud wrote nothing on the problems associated with pregnancy. At least one prominent female psychoanalyst
was convinced that Freud had no understanding of, and had a
negative reaction to, pregnancy.[5] How women feel when they are
pregnant would become a subject of psychoanalytic writings in the
1920s,[6] as well as after Freud's death. At the time I was interviewing
Esti, prominent feminists were assaulting Freud for his chauvinism; I

had asked Esti straight-forwardly whether Freud had treated women as equals, and in his defense, she related the anecdote about his reaction to her first pregnancy. Esti also surmised that Freud had been relieved that she was Jewish, for Martin, she held, had a taste for non-Jewish women. Although Martin's son later married a Gentile, none of Freud's own children ever did so. Even though Esti thought that on this score at least she had been a relief to Freud, she still considered herself to have been a "wild" daughter-in-law who could not tolerate criticism.

The failure of Esti's marriage was still an obvious source of pain to her. A marital collapse, like hers which took place in 1938, was far more rare than today, and it left Esti skeptical about the inevitable fate of romantic love. She seemed embittered about her personal history, and yet part of what was touching about Esti was her dignity and capacity for self-criticism. She later told me, without any resentment, that she had not slept the night after our first interview, because talking with me had stirred up so many unsettling feelings.

When we spoke about Martin having suffered as the oldest son of a great man, Esti agreed with the general view of the characteristic difficulties of such a role, then paused to add, "And with me as a wife he hardly had any chance at all." Although she never went out of her way to say nice things about Martin, it was clear that she thought that she had failed him as a wife. Esti had a certain acid, tough quality to her, which is why I found her generosity to me as an outsider all the more moving.

In her apartment she had a particularly touching photograph of Freud in his last days in London. I was always on the lookout for new pictures of Freud. As the years passed after he got cancer, his jaw was surgically narrowed. Because his initial medical treatment was poor, more radical surgery was soon necessary;[7] but Freud, as a physician, did not make the easiest of patients to get to the right specialist. By the end of his life Freud's eyes and face were etched with pain and suffering.

Esti was one of the few people I met sensitive enough to understand the full impact of Freud's medical condition on the last years of his life. He was terribly sick and very old and wanted to be left alone. Before his illness he had been more outgoing, but now everything grew more restricted for him. Other people with the same affliction, but different personalities, may have still appeared in public, but Freud considered time a precious commodity and he still wanted to write.

According to Esti, neither Martin nor Anna fully comprehended the dangerous political situation Vienna was in by the 1930s, but Esti possessed a rare understanding of Freud's special reluctance to leave for abroad. He had been treated for years by his Viennese physicians and was afraid that no one else was as competent to take care of him. Although Freud was world-famous by the time he arrived in London, that special standing did not help him; on the contrary, the London doctors were intimidated by their new patient and they were excessively slow to recommend surgery. Freud's Viennese physician was once flown to London for a special diagnostic visit.

The unusual photograph of Freud that Esti had in her apartment had been sent to her by Martin after they had separated. The fact that Martin, who had taken the photo, had forwarded it to her, implied something about the relationship he thought Esti had with his father. Freud had battled the ravages of cancer for sixteen years, but by September 1939, when Martin took Freud's picture, the end had to be near. He was by then no longer able to see patients. Minna had once proudly said of Freud that any ordinary man would have killed himself earlier.

No one with any feelings for Freud could fail to be touched by the picture in London with his head propped against a pillow. At my initiative Esti agreed to have a copy of the photograph made for me, at my expense. And yet she arranged for a level of copying that startled me with its low quality, especially in contrast to how moving the original was: the bill came to seventy cents. Esti's cheapness, I thought, highlighted her fragility of self.

Mathilda later told Esti's daughter that the problem with Martin was that he had not loved his own mother, his wife, his sisters, or his children, but had only loved himself. Mathilda was someone whose judgment about people I would be inclined to take seriously, and Martin did have the kind of glamour that led people to stare at him as he passed on the street. Mathilda's observation about Martin was counterposed by that of Freud's sister-in-law Sophie, the widow of his younger brother Alexander, who once said to me about Esti that "her heart is only for herself."

The psychoanalyst Erich Fromm had tried to establish long ago that selfishness and self-love are not at all the same thing, or even similar, and may at bottom represent psychological opposites. As Martin's daughter wrote of her father after the deaths of both her parents, "perhaps, after all, he too did not love himself very well."[8] Esti and Martin were perhaps too similar, for she also seemed to me to have lacked some element of basic self-regard. Her bothering about a seventy-cent charge for reproducing that touching photograph was unforgettable.

Money was an issue that one would have expected a single mother like Esti to know about, yet she seemed to have no idea about how relatively well off Freud was when he died. No doubt it had been in Martin's interest to have minimized the extent of the family's wealth, but she had thought that after the post–World War I inflation Freud had always been poor. Throughout our interviews, Esti always referred to Freud's wife Martha as "Mama," and to Freud himself as "Papa." I necessarily fell in with that way of referring to them both.

According to Esti, Freud's younger brother Alexander, who moved to Toronto, had been "the financial genius of the family" and "the only one who died wealthy." Freud's net estate of £16,000 may not have been a fortune, but the Freuds in London were not as poor as they may have wanted Esti in New York City to believe. I have always doubted whether Freud himself ever realized how financially secure he had become; the poverty of his youth probably had a lasting effect on him. When he wrote in letters about the possibility of his being awarded the Nobel Prize, he suggested that it was really only the money that would matter to him. Esti thought that his failure to win that prize was "a big disappointment to him," and I suspect that she was right.

Esti did remember having seen a copy of Freud's will, which she mistakenly thought had already been published, and she remembered having read it. Freud's London solicitor may have sent her the will since her daughter was still so young. From Esti's point of view, the most striking thing about Freud's estate was that her two children were beneficiaries of his having left the future royalties on his books to his grandchildren. Freud must have had some idea of how well his work would ultimately sell. Although Mathilda, like Anna, had been excluded on the basis of her childlessness, Mathilda managed to get on better with her nephews.

Esti spoke highly of Mathilda as being gifted in her own right. Mathilda, who played no special role in defending psychoanalysis, had helped take over "the social side" of Freud's life. When I asked why "Mama" had not been able to do so, Esti stressed that Mama was already old and apt to be very tired. It was therefore natural that Mathilda give the parties for her nephews. At the time of my interviews it was not yet clear how talented a family Ernst, Freud's youngest son, was to have; his son Lucien went on to achieve considerable acclaim as a portrait painter, and Clement became a television personality on talk shows, as well as a Liberal member of the House of Commons.

If anyone knew how much money Freud had it would have been Martin, although in marriages in those days such matters were less likely to be shared than would be the case today. Since Freud had his own special publishing house in Vienna, there were always questions of finance that Martin could help out on. Those in charge of the press were always tempted, out of grandiosity, to print up too many copies of Freud's own books. Even today, first editions of Freud's writings from the 1920s and 1930s are not worth much money; the psychoanalytic press ran off so many copies of everything that the supply always exceeded the demand, and one edition of Freud's collected works was too lavishly bound to be a commercial success. Money from wealthy donors regularly subsidized the deficits that Freud's press ran up, and Martin was put in charge of collecting such funds.

After World War I, psychoanalytic patients in Vienna often came from abroad. By the 1920s the best-paying clients were Americans, and Freud's practice was largely confined to them. Following World War I, inflation had eroded the value of the Austrian currency, so Freud regularly requested payment in foreign exchange; Esti patiently explained to me that unlike in the New World, it had not been customary then easily to adjust fees higher. The Dutch were also a lucrative source of income; and Freud sent referrals to his followers partly on the basis of who were his current favorites, but also with an eye to helping sustain his group as a whole. One source of Freud's power as a leader, and some thought a corrupting influence as well, was his ability to steer patients in the direction of certain analysts rather than others.

Aside from their psychoanalytic fees, foreigners living in Vienna had to be able to convert their money into Austrian currency in order to manage their day-to-day affairs. After the 1929 stock market crash, Martin—originally trained as a lawyer, but having also worked as a banker—was forced more than ever to rely on whatever family patronage his father could provide. (Freud even sent "allowances" to both his Halberstadt and Hollitscher sons-in-law.) Freud's students also had financial problems which Martin could help with. For example, when Helene and Felix Deutsch emigrated to America in 1935, Martin was put in charge of settling their affairs; they had an apartment to dispose of, furnishings that they chose not to take with them, and investments in Switzerland. Esti had hastened to point out to me that the Deutsch's son had been named for Martin; but as we have seen, Helene stoutly maintained that the choice of her son's name was made without special concern for Freud's eldest son. (Felix Deutsch had actually known Martin Freud in a Zionist organization.) It is impossible to overemphasize how tiny and cohesive the early Freudian group was. Felix Deutsch, for example, became the personal physician for both Martin and Esti, in addition to Anna Freud and Dorothy Burlingham.

After Vienna had been hit by such a terrible wave of inflation, the decision was made to keep Freud's earnings in foreign bank accounts, even after this was forbidden by Austrian regulations. By the 1930s it was customary for many middle-class Viennese to try to maintain assets outside the country. Switzerland—where the interest rates were, as now, almost nothing—seemed a safe financial haven. When in 1938, after the Nazis had marched into Vienna, the Gestapo subjected Anna to a day's worth of questioning, it is almost certain that they interrogated her about Freud's complicated finances. There is no doubt in my mind that Freud, like anyone else then with self-preservative impulses, had agreed to arrangements involving questionable legalities.

Martin was also called upon to intervene on behalf of Ruth Brunswick. In the 1930s it had not been proper for a foreigner like Ruth to earn money off patients, and Esti said that there was some problem with the local police. Martin explained that Ruth was working only under Freud's supervision for purposes of training, which was untrue. Earlier, Martin had drawn up the marriage papers for the Brunswicks.

One of the reasons that I trusted Esti's account of things was that she had explicitly warned me to expect only her personal version of what had happened. She also advised me on certain points to consult with others in the family who would be better informed. Her modesty made me more confident about what she told me. Sometimes she referred to the book Martin had published about his father, entitled *Glory Reflected*. Martin had also written a novel which Esti thought was both good and autobiographical; as a youngster he had composed poetry.

Esti insisted that Martin had chosen to leave out of his publications the role she played in successfully dissuading the Gestapo from taking Martin away for questioning. She was contemptuous about how he had handled himself in the crisis: "all the stupidities came out." First he had had too much money on hand in an office desk, which he should not have had around for the Nazis to find; and then he tried to bribe an officer within clear sight of other Germans. As Freud wrote to Minna, "almost everything that had to be done, Anna took care of. The men like Robert [Hollitscher] and Martin were useless, semi-idiotic. . . ."[9]

When the Nazis entered Vienna, they were regarded as hoodlums. They looted Freud's safe and demanded an exit tax—really a ransom—to ensure safe passage for the Freud entourage. Marie Bonaparte advanced Freud the money, and he was able to repay her once he had safely arrived in England. The Princess Marie also loaned Esti some money, which was later repaid, while she was trying to get out of Europe; first Esti lived with her daughter in Nice, where Freud's son Oliver was then staying with his family, and then Esti and her daughter managed to get to the States via Morocco.

Although we know that Freud succeeded in getting all of his possessions out of Vienna, some of his unsold books at the press could not be salvaged. The Nazis had started to burn Freud's writings in Berlin by 1933. At the time, Freud had ironically remarked with his own particularly grim humor: "What progress we are making. In the Middle Ages they would have burnt me; nowadays they are content with burning my books."[10] No one, including Freud, anticipated the rise of the extermination camps. Esti made it plain that in retrospect, the Nazi rise to power might look like an easier problem to handle than it was at the time, but for most people, it was not so easy to get out. At first the threat seemed minimal, especially for Jewish Austrians who thought they were in a totally different situation from the Germans. It soon proved difficult for everyone to survive, as the possibilities of escaping became more limited than anyone had expected.

The one central mistake that Freud made at this time, in collaboration with his brother Alexander, concerned the fate of their four sisters in Vienna; according to Esti, Rosa Graf was Freud's favorite. To have brought them to England and then tried to support them seemed beyond Freud's means, and the threat to the sisters apparently did not seem so ominous. Yet none of them survived the war. Once the Freuds were safely out, they realized they had made a shortsighted decision, but by then, even though some of Freud's influential friends tried to pull the appropriate strings, it was already too late.

Whatever I may have failed to learn from Esti, her story did fit the pattern of someone who had been badly treated as a wife; I will discuss the full details of her husband's behavior toward her in the next chapter. It seems fitting that it was Esti who gave me the first plausible picture of Freud's wife Martha, who died in 1951 at age ninety. Esti had become the senior daughter-in-law by virtue of her marriage to Martin. While I found that Freud's students tended to make fun of Martha as a pedantic housewife, Esti admired her as calm and dignified. It is true that in time Martha came to the dinner table with a pitcher of hot water and a special napkin, so that if anyone made a stain on the tablecloth she could quickly get rid of it.

She carefully bundled up her linen, just as Anna later put her own psychoanalytic correspondence in extraordinarily tidy order. Martha's annoyance with the ashes from Freud's constant cigar-smoking was commented upon among Freud's followers; but Esti maintained that Freud did not make a mess with the ashes, only that there was the constant smell of his smoking. Esti did not know who in the family was responsible for Martha being depreciated and put in the background.

It was through Esti that I gained some sense of Martha's pride. Esti swept away my thought that Martha's self-composure might have been the result of inhibitions, and instead proposed that beneath Martha's careful exterior lay a rich personality. Unfortunately, not much material in Martha's handwriting has survived—so little, in fact, that staff members at the Freud Museum wonder if she destroyed anything before her death. The handful of her letters that we do have indicate a remarkable degree of classic old Viennese tact.

When she married Freud he had little in the way of medical prospects, and therefore she must have had spirit. Her family came from a distinctly higher social status than his own. In 1908 he had written his daughter Mathilda that "finding a respected name and a warm atmosphere in her home was decisive in my choice of a wife. . . ." Martha always said that her family was shocked that she should marry someone without fortune or future. According to Esti, Martha never betrayed her feelings about being slighted by Freud's disciples—and by Anna. Yet, Martha could be noticeably ironic about her relationship to psychoanalysis; when one of Freud's pupils offered an elaborate explanation at the Freud home of a notorious public slip of the tongue committed by one of the Viennese analysts, she wryly commented: "We never hear about such things."

Esti would not rule out the possibility that Martha's sister Minna had had more than a platonic relationship with Freud; it had not been shocking to Esti that I brought the matter up, and it was as if she had more or less anticipated the subject. She thought that perhaps Freud's sister-in-law Sophie, Alexander's widow, knew the truth, but she could tell me nothing decisive one way or the other. Still, the implications of such a liaison were not the sides to Freud that were most in evidence during Esti's own experience.

What she did see was the puritanism in Freud's behavior, how very correct he could be expected to be.* Freud was always perfectly dressed, and Esti attributed this fastidiousness to how much Martha did for him. A disciple of Freud's once saw that Martha had put toothpaste on Freud's toothbrush, joking: "If I had had such a wife, I too could have written those books." According to Esti, it was definitely not the custom of the time for a wife to extend herself as Martha had; Esti's own mother would not have dreamt of doing the things for her father that "Mama" did for Freud. It was not just a matter of her picking out the proper clothes for him to buy—even though every one of his handkerchiefs was chosen by her. But the intimacy between Martha and Minna was more than Esti was prepared for; she was surprised to find how hurt Martha had been after World War II when Esti had neglected to inquire about Minna's last days. Esti believed that Freud had discussed his patients with both Martha and Minna.

Eva Rosenfeld reported to me that when, in the course of her analysis, the possibility of an affair between Freud and Minna came up, Freud had seemed offended at her disbelief in such a past irregularity. Eva thought he was partly miffed in Minna's behalf. Martha and Minna were described to me by Eva as "such a pair of Siamese twins." When the children were growing up they were jealous of the intimacy between the two women. (The Burlingham children, in turn, were resentful of their mother's preoccupation with Anna.) The closeness between Martha and Minna was hard for the Freud children to take, and different from an oedipal triangle which Freud's theory makes so much of. Instead of their having to struggle against a parental rival of the same sex, the Freud children were confronted by an alliance of two women who seemed able harmoniously to share the same man.

None of this information seems to square with the idea that Freud actually had an affair with Minna. One version has it that a child was conceived, but that Minna had had an abortion.[11] It has even been

---

*Esti's daughter discussed with Anna at the end of her life an instance of lesbianism within the family, and Anna's obvious disapproval at the news does count, I think, against there having been more than an intimate friendship between Anna and Dorothy Burlingham.

proposed in a manuscript I read that Freud consumed the infant cannibalistically. All such efforts to reconstruct the links between Freud and Minna rest on hypotheses derived from ingenious readings between the lines of his own psychological writings.

One long-standing basis for the rumors about Freud and Minna is that she once consulted with Jung about Freud's emotional involvement with her; such a tie was not the same as a physical relationship, and since Jung himself, although a married man, regularly sustained relationships with other women, he knew the difference between a fantasied involvement and a realistic one. If an affair between Freud and Minna did take place, then the whole story of the involvement between Martha and Minna would be that much more sophisticated and interesting.

In 1989, more than two decades after I interviewed Esti, the correspondence between Freud and his sister-in-law Minna was at last opened. The historian who "hurried" to be the first to inspect these letters at the Library of Congress concluded, as he had anticipated, that no evidence for physical intimacy could be established.[12] But two aspects of what I consider to be an unnecessary attempt to defend Freud's character left reasonable doubts: first, the fact that Jung had been a witness to the story does not mean, except to those unthinkingly partisan toward Freud, that the affair has to be inherently implausible because of the supposed unreliability of Jung as a source. And second, there was a gap in the letters between the years 1893 and 1910; the numbers on all the letters between Freud and Minna, key evidence for the disappearance of documents, would not have been made by museum officials.

The mystery is compounded when one realizes that the records at the Freud Museum in London, where the letters were kept before being abruptly transferred to the Library of Congress in Washington, indicate that correspondence for the year 1898 once existed. If an affair between Freud and Minna did take place, the years between 1893 and 1910 would be crucial, for it was during the 1890s when Freud was first developing psychoanalysis that he said that his two chief sources of support were his friend Fliess and Minna herself;[13] and Jung first arrived in Freud's circle in 1907, which is when he reported that Minna had consulted with him about Freud's relationship to her.

Once it was disclosed that there were missing letters, one had to decide on a possible culprit. As I already indicated, I thought that Anna Freud was emotionally incapable of destroying precious materials; nor do I think she would have—even if something compromising might appear—perceived anything in a way which was detrimental to her father's reputation. During the renovations at #20 Maresfield Gardens, when the house was being converted into a museum, all the documents temporarily went to the vault of the Freud solicitor. Confidants of Anna Freud also would have had access to Freud letters after her death.

Although in 1989 it might have looked like Freud's letters to Minna had finally been unrestricted, there are still more letters between them which are part of the Freud Collection at the Library of Congress, and which remain indefinitely inaccessible to scholarly inspection. These letters must cover the period 1893 to 1910, or at any rate were significant enough to be separated from the others which have been made public. Such selective secrecy is bound to fan the flames of suspicion, and it may be that many years will pass before we have any more firm documentary evidence. In the meantime, we have to rely on inferences that can be made from the information we already have at hand. I am hoping that these interviews may clarify the matter.

10

Like a Cuckoo Clock

The whole household revolved around Freud's work, and he was a man with predictable rituals. Although in his youth he evidently was different, in his old age anything unexpected or out of the ordinary was apt to rouse anxiety and discomfort. This need for control extended from the most insignificant detail—the use of a particular coffee-cup, for example—to the most important part of his life, his starting to write again. Each activity, which cup he favored or his having embarked on composing a book or an article, would be avidly reported within the family. Oddly enough, his constant sending of letters, although from posterity's point of view a highly significant part of his writing, was not viewed as such within the family but simply taken for granted as a given.

Punctuality was integral to a patient's therapeutic contract with Freud. He could tolerate it if someone he already knew was not on time, and he would spend the spare moments writing checks or composing a brief note. But if a new patient was tardy, Freud considered it an affront. Esti recalled how her father had pleaded with her to set up a consultation with Freud for a schizophrenic relative. She still remembered her anguish as the minutes ticked by when the relative was due. The prospective patient failed in the end to show up, Freud's allotted time was wasted, and Esti thought it had permanently damaged her in Freud's eyes. According to Freud's son Oliver, in that late period of his life Freud confined himself to only two or three consultations a week.

In between patients Freud would emerge from his office and walk through the adjoining family apartment. One of his nieces said he reminded her of the little man in some cuckoo clocks who comes out when the weather is good; Freud was that predictable in his conduct. It is this aspect of his character, during the period of his life about which I could get first-hand accounts, that has left me dubious about his ever being able successfully to carry on a love affair with Minna. It is true that he used to travel with her on holidays, but those vacations were as scheduled as every other aspect of his tightly controlled behavior. He saw his patients for a fifty-minute hour, and then would take ten minutes off to refresh himself. In contrast, many analysts today do not seem to need that extra breathing space, but the profession he created does depend on a high degree of regularity and conscientiousness. Within the Freud household meals were served on the precise stroke of the accustomed hour. Freud's way of living was representative of an entire Viennese middle-class culture which no longer exists; but even then, Freud's conduct struck younger people, such as Esti, as unusual. In London, Martha Freud once gave a young analyst, Melanie Klein's daughter, "little pieces of motherly advice. She told me how important it was to water flowers every day at the same time."[1]

The Victorian emphasis on regularity must have had an effect on the idea of a specified analytic hour that would last for fifty minutes. The fact that Freud never offered a theoretical rationale for the therapeutic advantage of a fifty-minute hour has encouraged subsequent analysts to experiment with his example. A handful of Lacanians appear to be the most extensive revisionists in this regard, since they function either without appointments or with sessions lasting only a few minutes.

Freud himself was so patriarchally in charge of those around him that he was hard to challenge. He convinced Esti not to choose for his grandchildren the pediatrician she had had as a child, for he objected to the man's having published some premature scientific findings which had not been validated. (Evidently a medical foul-up caused by a local physician had damaged Mathilda Hollitscher as a young woman.) Esti told me, drawing a deep breath, that she would not have dared to oppose Freud's will, despite her appreciation of her own pediatrician.

Freud had wanted Esti to name her son "Anton" after Anton von Freund, a recently deceased Hungarian benefactor of his, who was also Kata Levy's brother. Esti yielded and the boy came to be known as "Tony," although also by his middle name "Walter." Esti's second child, a girl, was named Miriam Sophie, the middle name being for Freud's daughter Sophie who died in 1919. This child became known by her middle name, the one that mattered to Freud. Unlike Martin's children, both of whose names fitted Freud's own needs, less was evidently expected of Freud's youngest son, Ernst, whose three sons were named for archangels.

As Martin's wife, Esti was subject to special demands which made her life difficult. When her boy was three or four months old, and too young to sit up, Freud had chastised her for "cuddling him too much." Freud thought that excessive parental tenderness was harmful because it supposedly accelerates sexual maturation. Another way of looking at it would be that Freud was suspicious, like behavioristic psychologists in that time, of mother love. John Broadus Watson also had advocated displaying a minimum amount of affection toward one's children. In a 1917 article on "Mother Love" for the *Saturday Evening Post*, a professor of psychology had argued that both Freud and Watson questioned the value of parental love:

> Though Watson and Freud were agreed on little else, he noted, "Freud makes central in his system the family romance in which the too strong attachment of daughter to father or son to mother gives rise to complexes and neurotic troubles, and in which sex relations play the leading part," while "Watson pronounces all mother love as damaging and looks forward to the day when children will be brought up (unparented) more or less officially and objectively."[2]

Anna Freud's later defense of so-called psychological parenthood as opposed to biological parenting was an extension of this particular aspect of Freud's teaching. She thought that a child's need for continuity was so great that courts ought not to divide children between warring adults. The custodian of the child should have complete power, even at the expense of the "natural" rights of biological parents. She not only was opposed to joint custody arrangements, but even attacked court-mandated visiting rights for the noncustodial parent. This theory justified Dorothy Burlingham's reactions to her husband Robert. "Children of divorce," according to Anna Freud's recommendations, "would be assigned to the custody of a psychological parent who would be relieved of any obligation to permit contact with the noncustodial parent."[3]

The psychologist who wrote that 1917 article was prescient in seeing similarities between Freud and Watson, since psychoanalysis also held out the prospect of idealized experts who knew all about child-rearing. But he felt that Watson's conclusion was "more baseless still" than Freud's. Watson's "warning that mothers should not fondle their children because some mothers overdo it, fails to recognize the many cases of neglect of children or the records of societies for the prevention of cruelty to children. Apparently he would found a society for the prevention of tenderness to children. . . ."[4] Behavioristic psychology, from Watson to B. F. Skinner, would seem directly opposed to the psychoanalytic way of thinking, since it holds that instinct is less important than the experience of training. Watson's behaviorism also excluded the idea of consciousness, not to mention Freud's concept of the unconscious. Still, for all the differences between Watson and Freud, Freud's views on the subject of mother love were surprisingly similar to those of Watson. Freud's severe reprimand to Esti would seem pretty off-the-wall by today's standards, when a lack of affection is regarded as a form of deprivation in child-rearing.

In thinking back on Freud's anger at her tenderness toward her son, Esti remarked somewhat plaintively that nowadays doctors "would tell you the reverse," warning against the chilling effects of not giving a young child enough affection. There is even experimental evidence of how schizophrenic-like reactions can be induced in monkeys when their natural mothers are replaced by artificial feeding machines.

Freud never treated children himself, nor did Martha allow him to play much of a role in the rearing of his own offspring. Martin Freud wrote in his memoirs that it was simply a given that one could not go walking with "Papa" until one had been toilet-trained. Yet Freud had no qualms about giving Esti advice on child-rearing. For example, when her son was about two years old, someone had remarked that he looked so pretty he might have been a girl. Esti jokingly chimed in that she might try dressing him accordingly. Freud was horrified and made no bones about expressing his views on what he considered a serious matter. But Esti found she could also be criticized on a minor subject, like serving too many veal cutlets to her daughter, who had a sensitive stomach and had been ill. Esti was enmeshed in a large extended family where she felt her own views and reactions counted for little.

Esti had married Freud's eldest son, and in traditional Jewish families the father attached special narcissistic emotions to such a child: the first-born son was traditionally felt to be a replica of the father. I do not know how soon it happened, but Freud came to be sadly disappointed that none of his boys did well professionally. It is of course impossible to distinguish between cause and effect; what they were like must have had some influence on Freud's behavior. But it is worth noting that at least some of Freud's disciples thought he had neglected his own sons. Yet the barriers to their having successful careers were at least in part cultural: the end of the Hapsburg Empire meant that after World War I, Vienna had become a backwater town, and Austria itself an insignificant country politically. Hitlerism, which drove them all from continental Europe, was a second significant interruption in their lives.

Martin increasingly participated in what had come to be the family business; he assumed the role of the general manager of Freud's publishing house. Freud's daughter Mathilda helped out on the social side, assisting his foreign patients in conducting their lives in Vienna, and Freud could count on Tola Rank as a kind of adopted daughter-in-law. She had married Freud's personal favorite Otto Rank shortly after World War I, and even in confined living quarters Tola successfully gave dinners and social gatherings for Freud's foreign patients.

Esti said that for a time there had been a rivalry between Martin and Otto Rank, with Martin being a bit "jealous" of Rank's special standing in Freud's world. She thought that Rank was an unusually "ugly" man; she knew that Freud had grown disappointed in him, and that Martin had been "disgusted" with what Rank had done to Freud's financial affairs. Despite her divorce, Esti still had trouble overcoming her great sensitivity to the fact that Freud had referred to his favorite disciples as "my son." She was defensive about Freud having used such an expression, and tried to explain that it was just a German idiom that, in traditional Viennese culture, an older man would use to address a much younger pupil.

But the historical evidence was more substantial than Esti wanted to believe. For example, when Freud and Jung were on good terms, Freud had referred to Jung as his "son and heir." As Jones expressed it, "Jung was to be the Joshua destined to explore the promised land of psychiatry which Freud, like Moses, was only permitted to view from afar."[5] Freud's favoritism toward Jung, as Freud hoped to shift the center of psychoanalysis from Vienna to Switzerland, was enough to help mobilize the anger and resentment of Freud's Viennese followers, and in particular Alfred Adler. Wilhelm Stekel's so-called defection took place shortly thereafter.[6] While Freud's difficulties with Jung, Adler, and Stekel took place before Esti had joined the family, when I saw her she still was mirroring some of Martin's own sensitivities about Rank, whom Freud annointed as his psychoanalytic successor.

By 1926, when Freud was seventy, Rank was definitely out of Freud's circle, leaving the way clear for Martin. The loss of Rank was a bitter personal blow to Freud and helped ease Anna's way to mounting power. She characteristically magnified Freud's own dislikes, and in his letters Freud alluded to her special bitterness toward Rank. I also found evidence of Anna's acute displeasure with Ferenczi. The infighting amongst the circle of Freud's followers was of special interest to me, and as a political scientist I tried to determine where the power lay. Despite how dispersed the movement sometimes appeared to be, Freud retained control right up to his death.

However curious such a gathering of people around Freud might have seemed, Esti suggested that many great figures, whether actors, singers, movie stars, or thinkers, attract circles of flatterers and sycophants. The novelist Thomas Mann had modeled his account of Goethe on what Mann had seen of Freud and his followers. (Esti knew that Freud had never analyzed Mann, but she thought he had treated the writer Stefan Zweig.) In the midst of all the personal jealousies around Freud there was the realistic issue that his psychoanalytic press always had problems that Martin could help attend to. Yet Martin's part as a manager for his father was also an implicit confession that he was not good enough to stand on his own two feet.

Freud's success as an organizer continued to amaze Esti—as she reflected on the leaders of the psychoanalytic movement in the mid-1960s—for Freud's following remained closed and tight even thirty years after his death. She remained well-informed about people in the psychoanalytic world through her fortuitous contacts in New York City; for instance, she shared some doctors with them. But essentially the knowledge she gave me came from old Vienna.

The relationship between Freud's family and his work was unusual; that Esti knew as much as she did about psychoanalysis was in itself striking. For Freud, to ensure the privacy of his patients, had set up his office with separate doors for them to use. Family members were not supposed to leave the apartment when patients might be arriving or departing; the family was expected to exercise discretion. As people gathered with Freud for Wednesday evening meetings, they came and went without the family's knowing who they were or precisely what they had come to discuss.

Yet Esti knew about Ruth Brunswick's problems with the local police and how Martin had helped her. Esti also observed Freud's special inability to forgive when it came to Stekel's trying to get back in Freud's good graces; Stekel had left Freud's circle before World War I, and even though Freud acknowledged that Stekel had been in some sense loyal to psychoanalysis, Freud continued to resent what he regarded as Stekel's earlier betrayal. Esti commented on Freud's "hatred" of Stekel; she did not know what Stekel had done, but Freud spoke of him as "a despicable character." She also knew that Freud's antagonism toward Adler always remained. In connection with perhaps the most famous controversy in the history of psychoanalysis, Esti thought that by the 1930s there had been an attempt at a reconciliation between Jung and Freud; at any rate she remembered having gone with Martin to a lecture of Jung's in Vienna around 1936 or 1937. At the time of the Nazi takeover of Austria in 1938, however, there is evidence that Freud refused to accept money offered through Jung in Switzerland, on the grounds that Freud did not want to be beholden to his "enemies."

Esti suggested that in the Old World, there had been a definite split in how psychoanalysis was viewed, and although Freud was well regarded, his pupils were not. Stekel, for example, was apt to stress sex too much. It was commonly thought that among Freud's students there were too many "beards trimmed like Freud's." Esti quoted a passage from Friedrich von Schiller, which Freud himself had cited, about how a soldier laughs at his sergeant for going to ridiculous lengths to appear like his general:

> I grant you, your counterfeit perfectly fits
> The way that he hawks and the way that he spits.[7]

Freud's disciples might imitate him, consciously as well as unconsciously, but however they attempted to copy him, they could not match his mind and essential spirit. Esti added that some of Freud's books were written with words cut like jewels.

Imitation Freuds had to be a special contradiction, for since he stood for great spiritual freedom, to truly be like him might mean going off on one's own. Freud's disciples did succeed in becoming authentic extensions of at least his deep ambitions as a spiritual conqueror. Esti had early on sensed this need of his, and to express her understanding, she once ordered for Freud a special birthday cake baked by a famous Viennese chef; the icing on the cake pictured a map of the world populated by different readers of Freud's various books. By then Esti had a sure understanding of what would please him.

Esti regarded Martin as "a good son," which meant, in addition to his work for his father, that he lived less than ten minutes from "Papa's." Sometimes he would be in his parents' apartment twice a day—at the big midday meal, and again in the evening. Martin was, however, known to his cousins as a "sportsman"; he was as worldly as his sister Anna was unworldly. According to a relative, when Anna had free time on her hands, she would naively ask, "What am I supposed to do in town?" Even when she was a young woman recuperating from an illness in Italy, Freud would try to discourage her from feeling that she had to write home every day. Whatever she might have talked about psychoanalytically in connection with sexuality, her own asceticism was widely known.

In contrast to Anna's peculiar dowdiness, Martin was dashing and handsome. Esti said that her mother-in-law had always been careful to pick unusually unattractive servants, "hags," because of the temptation they might otherwise pose for her three growing boys. (The Freuds employed a staff of six: a nanny for the younger children, another for the older ones, a cook, a cleaner, someone to light the individual stoves in each room, and a maid to help patients off and on with their coats.)

An American cousin characterized Martin as simply "a case of arrested development." Esti referred to the same aspect of her husband by remarking that there was nothing wrong with him except that he liked women. Looking at Martin's behavior with detachment and as much as possible without moral judgment or psychoanalytic diagnoses, he was simply a Don Juan, which was in striking contrast to what seems to have been the puritanism of his father. Esti thought Martin certainly needed analysis as therapy, although she knew he had not been analyzed; she was under the mistaken impression that none of Freud's sons had been in analysis.

Esti said that she only discovered Martin's illicit love life when the Nazis annexed Austria; her daughter, however, could not believe how Esti could have remained blind for so long. In 1938 Martin had been temporarily forced to hide out at a separate apartment that he had been secretly keeping on the other side of town. Paradoxically, Esti claimed that it was at this same time that she had just risked her life to protect Martin from the Gestapo. Freud probably knew something about Martin's sexual escapades, in that one of the women Martin had been in love with was Dr. Edith Jackson, a rich (if unattractive) American psychiatrist undergoing a lengthy analysis with Freud.

A few months after I first saw Esti I also interviewed Edith Jackson, then vacationing with a relative on Cape Cod. Her background was impressive (her brother was a famous lawyer who had helped defend Sacco and Vanzetti), she had a fine education, and she

The Hague Conference in 1920. *Front row, left to right: first,* Karen Horney; *third,* Anna Freud; *fifth,* Eugenia Sokolnicka; *sixth,* Sandor Ferenczi; *ninth,* Helene Deutsch; *tenth,* Beata Rank; *twelfth,* Karl Abraham. *Second row, left to right: third,* Ernest Jones; *fifth,* Ernst Simmel; *seventh,* Sigmund Freud; *eighth,* Otto Rank; *tenth,* Melanie Klein; *eleventh,* Ludwig Binswanger (Courtesy of Han Israëls).

Carl G. Jung (Courtesy of Henry A. Murray)

Otto Rank (Courtesy of
Virginia Robinson)

Beata ("Tola") Rank
(Courtesy of Helene Deutsch)

Helene Deutsch
(Courtesy of Egone)

Felix Deutsch
(Courtesy of Helene Deutsch)

Erik H. Erikson (Courtesy of Stephen Schlein)

Edoardo Weiss in Lucerne, 1934
(Courtesy of Tim N. Gidal)

Grete Bibring in Lucerne, 1934
(Courtesy of Tim N. Gidal)

Freud in September 1939 (Courtesy of Esti Freud)

Dorothy Burlingham and Anna Freud at #20 Maresfield Gardens in 1979
(Courtesy of Michael Burlingham)

contributed to modern psychiatry. (Some of her life insurance was later bequeathed to Anna Freud.) In the course of asking her about the history of psychoanalysis and her personal contact with Freud, I tried to bring up the subject of her relationship with Martin.

I can only report that in the midst of a fairly extensive interview, Jackson grew distinctly chilly only on this one subject. She did go on to tell me, however, in the course of her other reminiscences, that she had resented Freud's having forbidden her to have sexual relations during the many years of her analytic treatment. I know that Freud did sometimes try to discourage other patients from masturbating, for instance on the grounds that it would interfere with the kinds of dreams they needed for analysis. But I know no other case among Freud's analytic patients that tallies with what Edith Jackson reported. For one young male patient, Freud even prescribed a contraceptive for the sake of making sexual relations better, and for a married patient, Freud sanctioned an extramarital affair. So his restriction on Edith Jackson, which was supposed to have been part of the analytic process, was not even remotely similar to anything his other patients told me. I think Freud's injunction to her might have been related to Martin's being the object of her affections. An experienced analyst nowadays might wonder how Freud had allowed things to develop so far between her and Martin.

While Esti was in Paris, on her way out of Vienna after finally being released from Austria, she said she decided on a separation from Martin. Although their relationship was already bad in Vienna, in France she had accidentally been given a letter by her brother-in-law for Martin, who was already in London. She opened it unthinkingly, without even looking at the envelope which had been addressed to Martin at her sister's; it turned out to be a passionate love letter intended for Martin.

Chance played one more part in adding to the indignities of his adulteries. When the books from their household were finally divided up, Esti found an album Martin had prepared of all his various conquests. Inside the covers of the mostly blank pages of a book— *Four Case Histories*, with Freud's name on the binding—Martin had pasted the pictures of his assorted lady friends, posing on street corners or at the beach. They were mostly beautiful women. There was also a stack of loose photos. Mozart's Don Giovanni had had a servant record the list of his collection of women, but in our century Martin had kept his own photographic album.

Freud's collection was his archeological treasures; he regarded himself as an adventurer in the world of the mind, and extended his conquests among a growing school of disciples. He was a spiritual seducer, in that he succeeded in changing the lives of so many that he came in contact with. His eldest son, however, chose to compete with him in a separate territory; Martin's being in love with Edith Jackson while she was in analysis with his father must have been a complicated act of filial insurrection.

Freud was sophisticated about sexuality and yet personally careful. I think that Freud knew about Martin's philandering even before the incident with Edith Jackson. Later in London, when Martin went to see a performance of *Romeo and Juliet*, Freud commented to a visitor that his son needed no further exposure to the role of Romeo, since he already was his own Romeo. Although the visitor could not have realized the full implications of Freud's remark, certainly Freud's wife, who was present, would have picked up Freud's meaning. Esti herself had never spoken either to "Papa" or "Mama" about the issue. It was unusual for Freud to exhibit what must have seemed like dirty family linen, and probably a sign that he felt that by then, everyone knew about Martin's goings-on.

It was a curious Freudian irony that Martin's precious photo collection wound up in Esti's hands. In her anger, she pulled this volume down from a bookshelf to show me exactly the kind of scoundrel Martin had been. Yet she refused to give him a divorce. Esti finally died in 1980 at the age of eighty-four, leaving six grandchildren and one great grandchild. Martin had long predeceased her. During one of our sessions Esti reported having been told that he was so ill as to be unable to recognize people. Martin had remained especially attractive to women almost to the end of his life.

Esti's daughter inherited the unusual heirloom of Martin's volume of photographs and she even published a few pages about it.[8] As with Freud's own relationship with Minna, there is reason to question whether anything physical took place between Martin and Edith Jackson. A skeptical observer who knew them both thought it might have done Edith, who was so straight-laced, some good to have had such an affair. Yet Esti had enough evidence about Martin's other entanglements. Her daughter had seen a letter from her father angrily demanding his album back, but Esti continued to carry a grudge and kept the book for the rest of her life.

Freud had overlooked Martin's sexual escapades as long as they remained a secret to Esti, or at least until she formally acted upon her knowledge. But when she left him in 1938, Martin was "punished" in London by having his family responsibilities taken away from him. As far as Esti knew, he ended up having nothing financially. Freud has been quoted as having said in 1925 to the aristocratic Marie Bonaparte: "in my private life I am a petit bourgeois. . . . I would not like one of my sons to get a divorce or one of my daughters to have a liaison."[9] After 1938, Martin's younger brother Ernst took charge of the publishing matters. There was no longer a press, but Ernst's career as an architect had been interrupted by the political upheavals in Europe and he had extra time, so Anna and he collaborated on editorial matters.

In hindsight, perhaps Esti should have realized that her own difficulties with Minna probably reflected Freud's own privately held views. It was recently disclosed that unknown to Esti, Freud was, as early as 1930, writing to an English nephew: "Martin you may have heard or guessed is in bad relations with an unreasonable, abnormal wife. . . ." Esti naively thought that Freud would not diagnose the family, but she failed to realize what an outsider she must have seemed like to Freud. Martha seems to have been more tolerant; in 1934, when Martin had a kidney stone Martha wrote to her son Ernst and his wife that Esti had behaved very well, "only he [Martin] cannot stand her." Then in May 1938, Freud wrote a letter to Ernst that was even more critical of Esti, and that implicitly white-washed Martin's extramarital conduct:

> Martin will probably leave before us with his family, leave wife and daughter in Paris, go to London with the boy. He hopes, and we all join him in this, that this will in practice be the end of his unhappy marriage. She is not only maliciously meshugge but also mad in the medical sense. But what will he do in England? He cannot live without a wife (women) and there he won't find again the type of freedom he allowed himself here.[10]

In Vienna, Martin had been accepted as a regular in Freud's card-games, but in London he was left to his own devices. A number of people who were well-disposed to Freud, prominent London analysts for example, tried to help Martin find work, but at his age and level of experience they were unable to do anything for him; eventually he ran a tobacco shop near the British Museum. After the separation it was Anna who sent Esti, at first, some regular monthly payments, but when Esti went to America, she got nothing further. Although Esti had little in the way of money, she claimed she had retained a certain irresponsibility about spending it which was more fitting for her youth.

At the time I saw Esti, I thought that since Freud himself had talked about the early decline of his sexual desire, perhaps both he and his wife had been mutually content with the effective end of their sexual relationship. By the age of forty, Freud had written to his close friend Wilhelm Fliess in Berlin: "sexual excitation is of no more use to a person like me."[11] Such a passage might be taken to reflect merely a depressed mood, but since it fits in with other comments of his, it may be deeply revealing about the nature of his private life. Martin would then seem to have been fulfilling an aspect of life which his father had securely sublimated.

Alternatively, Freud might have had special sexual difficulties. When I raised with Esti the issue of Freud's possible potency problems, she was genuinely thunderstruck and animated in a way that nothing else I had said evoked. In old Vienna, she indicated, the furniture in the room would have spontaneously combusted at my asking such a question; an inquiry like mine would have been that unmentionable. Yet she was open-minded enough not to rule out any possibility.

Freud became world-famous for having made so much about the role of sexuality in human conflicts. Yet a close reading of the tone of his texts reveals how distasteful much of human instinctuality remained to Freud, in spite of his effort to be accepting and tolerant. Freud, who so admired Leonardo da Vinci that he wrote a small book about him, said that Leonardo's asexuality meant that he had risen "above the common animal need of mankind."[12] Since Martha had borne six children within eight years, she was obviously easily impregnated by Freud; it may be hard to believe that throughout so many pregnancies she could have been a relaxed and enthusiastic sexual partner. It appears that Freud disliked, or could not tolerate, the available contraceptive means, and he recurrently wrote about the neurotic side effects connected with premature withdrawal, the practice of *coitus interruptus*.

Much that Freud published in the 1890s about the psychology of the lack of sexual gratification sounds to me autobiographical. The one emotion Freud surely knew about was anxiety, and he interpreted it as a result of incomplete sexual discharge. Although his theories about the sources of anxiety were to change in the 1920s, as a clinical matter he always attributed it to dammed-up sexuality.

During the 1890s Freud developed the concept of "actual neurosis," which he was determined to contrast with the idea of psychoneurosis. The notion of actual neurosis was designed to explain symptoms that have a physiological origin arising from unsatisfactory sexual practices such as masturbation, *coitus interruptus*, or abstinence. He distinguished such "actual" conflicts from the problems he later chose to specialize in—psychoneurosis—which could be traced to conflicts stemming from early childhood.

Freud held that psychoanalytic therapy could be of no special help in cases of actual neurosis. It seems as if Freud had become resigned to his fate, so he sought to work in an area of psychological dilemmas where he thought he could be uniquely effective. Esti remarked that within the Freud household, there were an unusual number of complaints of headaches; they would, according to Freud's thinking, be a sign of "actual" conflicts. Furthermore, "Mama" once remarked to Esti that she had mistaken as menopause the early stages of her pregnancy with Anna. Since Martha was only thirty-four years old when Anna was born, it was hardly likely to be time for her menopause. To both Freud and his wife it was an unwanted pregnancy. Freud did tend to think that normal sexuality should be confined to the purposes of childbearing. Other forms of sexuality could be classified, according to psychoanalytic theory, as "perverse."

From Martha's point of view, each pregnancy had been a strain on her energy. According to Esti, "Mama" had been "worn out" early.

Running the household for Freud required, in addition to Minna, many servants. Managing such a staff was chore enough for Martha. She had shared the Bernays virtues of being punctual and reliable; according to Esti she was thrifty, and especially would not spend money on herself. She may have been brought up strictly, but she went along with her husband and from the family's point of view she had not disapproved of his work. Martha was a self-contained woman who did not show emotion in public; her personality was said to have come out more after Freud's death. It is not known how she explained to herself the way she was pushed into the background by Freud's pupils.

But the place she came to occupy in Freud's life may pertain to her difficulties with her daughter Anna, and how in Martha's memory she could relate the menopause to Anna's birth. Apparently there were more than the usual mother-daughter tensions between Anna and Martha. "She *was* such a sweet child" was Martha's way of describing a transformation she felt had taken place in her youngest child; her "hardness" had "come out." In the end Martha was jealous of Anna. And on Anna's side, some resentment might have been natural in that her mother was not able to take over more of the responsibilities connected with her father's life.

At the time of Freud's death it was Anna, not Martha, who played a central role. Freud only died after terrible suffering. It was Anna who sustained him with her nursing care; she could not bring herself to allow him to die, until Freud himself was ready to ask for the right of euthanasia. Afterwards the physician, Max Schur, was resentful that the suffering had not ended weeks earlier. But when Freud made his decision, and Schur promised him the necessary sedation, Freud thanked him and then added: "Tell Anna about our talk."[13]

11

A "Precisionist": Oliver Freud

Oliver Freud was the only son of Freud's whom I succeeded in meeting. By the time I had begun my interviewing, his two brothers were already suffering from a variety of physical ailments. By 1966 Oliver was retired and living on a pension in Williamstown, Massachusetts, which is in the western part of the state in the Berkshire Hills; so it was a pleasurable outing for me to drive there from Cambridge on a beautiful spring day.

I had been warned by several people that although Freud's son had been named for Oliver Cromwell, I would find neither a powerful person nor a colorful individual but simply a bore. From experience, however, I had learned that there was never any sure way of predicting who would or would not be a good interview subject. Perhaps because of her extreme old age, I found Freud's sister-in-law Sophie, who had been married to his younger brother Alexander, tedious to interview; yet, I learned information from her that I could not have found out in any other way. (For example, I discovered that while Freud was on good terms with Adler, he had sent Sophie to him for an analysis.) In Oliver's case I had decided that as Freud's son, he would certainly have something to teach me, and I was not to be disappointed in that expectation.

The naming of Oliver, like that of his other children, seemed to be at Freud's discretion. Although "Frau Professor," as Martha Freud was so often known, may have kept Freud out of the nursery, where I doubt he much wanted to be anyway, he did have the ultimate say about the names of their children. As we have seen, that power extended to Martin and Esti's family. The naming of Oliver reflected Freud's admiration for English parliamentarianism and his respect for its liberties. It was also a way to maintain ties to the families of his two half-brothers, who had moved to England when his parents had first come to Vienna from Moravia. Nor can it have eluded Freud that Cromwell had allowed the Jews to come back to England; Freud's own family had been the beneficiary of a dispensation permitting them to return to Vienna.

When Freud took the night train from Paris to London in 1938, on his way from Vienna to exile in England, he told his son Martin that he dreamt he was landing at the same town in England where William the Conqueror had arrived in 1066. If one appreciates how physically feeble and tottering Freud was by 1938, the persistence of that inner sense of himself as a warrior of the spirit becomes all the more significant. In his letters to Fliess, Freud once wrote that he was "not really a man of science, not an observer, not an experimenter, and not a thinker. I am nothing but by temperament a *Conquistador*—an Adventurer, if you want to translate the word—with the curiosity, the boldness, and the tenacity that belongs to that type of being."[1] Repeatedly Freud found it agreeable to identify with great political leaders like Napoleon and Bismarck. Freud once recalled in a dream that his father on his deathbed looked like Garibaldi, which doubtless was an aspect of Freud's own self-conception. Cromwell, then, was only one of many such figures that Freud chose to admire.

Curiously enough, Freud's mother seemed to have shared similar aspirations for him. As an old woman she reported having dreamt she was at Sigmund's funeral; surrounding his casket stood the heads of state of the major European countries. It seems to me extraordinary for a Jewish mother, even as an old woman, to allow an account of such a catastrophe to cross her lips because it displayed the fame her son had achieved; the expectations she had for him were in harmony with his own.[2]

Since Freud's first visit to Britain at the age of twenty, he had been an Anglophile. Of course his half-brothers lived in Manchester, and

Freud corresponded with his other relatives there. But Freud's enthusiasm for all things British went beyond what can be rationally
explained. In the 1920s, for example, when Freud had to deal
mainly with analytic patients from abroad who spoke English as their
native tongue, he definitely preferred to spend time with his British
patients than with those from America. One of Freud's most prominent American patients at the time, Abram Kardiner, remained
lastingly resentful that when Freud found himself pressed for available analytic hours, he reduced the number of his sessions for his
American patients to five a week, while continuing to see his British
patients for the normal six times a week.

In the kind of interviewing I was doing, I had to fly by the seat of
my pants. Just as it was impossible to know beforehand who would
turn out to be most interesting, so I had to learn to evaluate for
myself the people I met. At times it was easy to be misled, but on
more than one occasion, my first impressions seemed almost mag-
ically fulfilled. I had, for example, been impressed with Mathilda
Hollitscher as a distinguished person in her own right. In 1991, years
later, I finally got to meet Ruth Brunswick's daughter "Tilly," who
had been named for Mathilda Hollitscher. My first reaction on
meeting Tilly was how strikingly she resembled photographs of her
mother. When I later went over my notes from my interview with
Mathilda Hollitscher, I found that she had commented at the beginning how Tilly had looked "exactly" like her mother.

Confirmations of my own judgments about people could also be
found by rereading Freud's own letters. Years after I first met Oliver,
in studying a revised edition of Freud's important correspondence
with Fliess, I was struck that Freud's description of Oliver as a boy of
eight was so much like the mature man I had interviewed in his mid-
seventies. (Despite Freud's fall-out with Fliess, Fliess's portrait always
hung in his father's office, according to Oliver.) The Freuds had been
on a summer holiday in 1899, a time when Freud was putting the
finishing touches on *The Interpretation of Dreams*. Freud wrote to
Fliess then of Oliver: "Oli classifies mountains here, just as he does
the city railroad and tram lines in Vienna." Freud thought his
children were getting on well, and without jealousy. A month later,
Freud had similarly observed of his middle son: "Oli is again practic-

ing the exact recording of routes, distances, names of places and mountains."[3] As much as I know about psychological theory, and how it maintains that one's basic character traits can be formed at a very young age, I am still astonished at the apparent stability in Oliver's personal qualities, since the man I met in Williamstown was so precise and exact in all the memories he offered me.

Freud was fifty-three years old when, in 1909, he traveled with Jung and Ferenczi to Worcester, Massachusetts, which is a bit east of Williamstown, to receive his honorary degree from the new Clark University. G. Stanley Hall, Clark's enterprising president, had invited Freud to give some lectures, but Hall was featuring many other dignitaries besides Freud. From Hall's point of view, the occasion was designed to promote his little-known university. Freud, however, took the opportunity to spread his teachings in new surroundings.[4]

The subject of Freud's relationship to America is intriguing. Just as Karl Marx detested Russia, precisely where his ideas proved most influential, it was also ironic how Freud had such infinite disdain for everything American. It is surprising, then, that according to Mathilda, a copy of the Declaration of Independence hung in the Berggasse, and she said that the date July 4th "always" meant something to her. Nonetheless the stories of Freud's witticisms at American expense are legion.

When I asked Oliver what in particular his father had so vehemently objected to about America, since he had such a constant variety of complaints, Oliver thought that Freud had not been able to "adjust" to the specifically American ways. Oliver's cousin Edward Bernays had the impression that when Freud stayed at a camp in western Massachusetts—which was partly owned by William James and by one of Freud's key American supporters, James Jackson Putnam, a professor of medicine at Harvard—Freud had been horrified at the idea of sitting on the ground while steaks were being charcoal-grilled; it seemed like a form of "savagery." Nor did Freud appreciate being addressed by his first name and asked to defend his theories. New World manners were bound to be startling to a European gentleman of Freud's years. And he could not have been impressed that he, coming from Austria, and Ferenczi (from Hun-

gary) along with Jung (a Swiss) were welcomed by having the camp
decked out with the flags of Imperial Germany. To the untutored but
well-meaning Americans, these were three visiting German doctors,
whereas Freud, Ferenczi, and Jung each had decided loyalties at
odds with the German state.

When I asked Oliver's sister Anna essentially the same question
about Freud's responses to America, her reply was a knowing smile—
implying "everything and nothing." She, like her father, much
preferred the British; dependency on American money must have
been an added irritant. Oliver had once visited Clark University in
1950, where Anna was being awarded her first honorary degree. He
said on that occasion he had met a university employee—whom
Oliver described as "a factotum"—who had memories of Freud's
1909 visit; the man had tried in vain to prevent Freud from smoking
where it was not allowed. Freud also had various stomach problems
in the States, perhaps from the change in water, and he was appalled
at the difficulty of finding public restrooms on street corners; instead
of understanding that it was the American manner to have such
facilities indoors, he attributed the custom to general American
prudishness. I assume he would have associated any ban on smoking
at Clark to a pervasive American lack of sophistication.

Freud is reported to have consumed about twenty large cigars a
day; even after his cancer of the jaw, he could not give up this habit.
No one who knew Freud could imagine him without either the
smoke or the smell of tobacco. That photograph of Freud holding a
cigar that Mathilda hung over her livingroom mantle was an expression of broad family feeling, since her brother-in-law was the photographer; but everyone who knew Freud took his cigar-smoking for
granted, and understood it as a major, if usually unspoken, characteristic of his.

One patient of Freud's from the 1920s felt wounded that Freud had
never offered the man, in analysis with Freud for years, a cigar. On
the other hand, if Freud did offer a favored disciple a cigar, and the
gesture was not accepted, Freud was reported to have been offended.
Ernest Jones knew how seriously Freud took his smoking. Jones, who
lived in Toronto before World War I, was bitter about what he
considered the provincialism of Canadians. Instead, he should have

been grateful for having received a Toronto academic post, after his career in London was ruined following his having been jailed for allegedly abusing a small girl who was a patient. But Jones characterized his Canadian hosts to Freud as "a despicable race, exceedingly bourgeois, quite uncultured, very rude, very stupid and very narrow and pious. They are naive, childish and hold the simplest views of the problems of life. They care for nothing except money-making and sport, they chew gum instead of smoking or drinking. . . ." Jones went on to complain about his life in Toronto: "their public meetings are monuments of sentimental platitudes. They are horror-struck with me because I don't know the date of the King's birthday, for they take their loyalty like everything else in dead seriousness and have no sense of humor."[5]

Freud was rightly proud of his own capacity for wit, but neither he nor any of his followers were apt to overindulge in alcohol. Smoking was another matter. Freud's addiction to nicotine, even though he struggled against it in the 1890s, was in striking contrast to his general insistence on self-reliance. For example, when Jones once appeared in Vienna with an umbrella, Freud, despite his admiration for the British and his understanding of their customary defense against the possibility of rain, told Jones that he should "break" himself of the habit of carrying it. Presumably Freud chose to interpret the umbrella symbolically.

In the 1880s and 1890s, Freud had pioneered in exploring cocaine's medical applications. Before anyone yet realized that it could be addictive, he had used more than was good for him. Freud even sent some to Martha to give her cheeks more color. It may be that part of his resentment toward the United States stemmed from his mistakenly having relied on premature medical advice from there about the properties of cocaine.[6]

Nevertheless, Freud continued to take the drug long after its worst dangers were known. One has to suspect that cocaine played a part in his interest in Fliess's curious theories about the nose. (Edgar Allan Poe's drinking was not enough to account for his immortal short stories, but no one would think of ignoring his alcoholism.) Typical of Freud's outlook was how, even in the last period of his cancer, he only would take aspirin to relieve the pain. Yet, in contrast to how he always smoked, he was curiously intolerant of alcohol. In a famous incident, he fainted in Jung's presence after an argument over wine. According to his own account, Freud had insisted that Jung defy his teetotaling mentor Eugen Bleuler, and join him in drinking some wine. Freud partly blamed the alcohol for his having lost consciousness. Years later, Freud told one of his artistic patients, who especially enjoyed scotch, that in England as a young man Freud had once sampled it enjoyably. The naivete of Freud's account implied that he had not tried the drink again.

Oliver Freud was born in 1891, fourteen months after his older brother Martin, yet Oliver had been the first to marry. He was married during World War I in December 1915, but then secured a divorce by September 1916. Oliver had been working as an engineer in an outlying part of the Austro-Hungarian Empire, twelve hours from Vienna, while serving in the military. According to Esti Freud, Oliver's young wife had not been able to withstand the strain of the social isolation combined with the primitive living conditions. He remarried by 1923, and his first wife evidently perished during the Nazi Holocaust. Perhaps Oliver's first marriage was so brief as to seem to Freud never to have legitimately occurred; for in 1925 Freud could commit the strange lapse of talking to Marie Bonaparte as if there had been as yet no divorces for any of his sons. However, Esti remembered, because while Martin was away during the war, she and Oliver had gone on some "walking trips" together and her family was shocked that she was willing to be seen in the company of a divorced man.

Oliver had been trained as a mathematical engineer. He spent five years at the Polytechnical School of Vienna, an institution entirely separate from the University of Vienna, and earned a degree in civil engineering. When I saw him, he had worked for some years before his retirement for the Budd corporation in Philadelphia.

Oliver had first come to Philadelphia in 1943. Before then, for almost ten years after leaving Berlin in 1933 because of the Nazis, Oliver had worked in Nice, France, where he owned a photography business; previously, photography had been a hobby of his. Jones thought that Oliver was expert at taking photographs of Freud when he was relaxed and unaware of being watched, but I have never seen any that struck me as remarkable; Freud's Halberstadt son-in-law had more natural artistic talent. Some months prior to Oliver's departure from France, where it had been impossible for him to reestablish himself in engineering, his photographic facilities and equipment had been taken over by an order of the Germans which applied to all Jews. Up until 1943 the Vichy regime in the south of France had protected people like Oliver and his family.

It is not clear to me why Oliver decided to come to the United States in 1943, rather than join most of his family in England. Of course America, being farther away, may have seemed safer, but I still wonder why Oliver had remained on the continent for so long after his parents, two brothers, and two sisters had left for England. From Freud's point of view, given the prejudices that he and Anna had about the States, any relatives of his there were automatically suspect. By 1943, however, Freud was already dead, and perhaps Oliver and his family somehow failed to get into England at that late date. Also, his wife did have some relatives in America.

Freud's posthumous influence was such that the famous American psychiatrist Harry Stack Sullivan, who had a special White House pass during World War II, called J. Edgar Hoover's FBI office to facilitate Oliver's being cleared in an investigation that was automatic for all incoming foreigners. Ruth Brunswick, whose father was a prominent jurist, also did what she could to smooth Oliver's way, and welcomed them when he and his wife arrived by boat. Some lingering estrangement between father and son may help account for Oliver's having chosen to remain in France when the rest of the family left for London, and why ultimately he opted for opportunities in the New World.

I knew from people in London that some mystery surrounded the death of Oliver's daughter, Eva Mathilda, who was born in 1924. The circumstances surrounding her death were something that the Freud family in London had never wanted to discuss. Esti, who had briefly lived in Nice before going to Morocco, told me that Eva had needed to have an operation which was, in fact, performed, but that she had died of a brain tumor. A recent French source maintains that Eva died of blood-poisoning, perhaps connected to an abortion, and that she had been in therapy after having refused to leave French territory.[7]

Oliver, his wife Henny, and Eva had obtained their U.S. visas in 1942, and then tried to cross the Spanish border to get out of France. But at the next to the last train stop they were told that at the approaching station, the Germans were taking Jewish passengers off the train for deportation; so the Freuds turned back to Nice. At that time, Nice had been occupied by the Italians rather than the Germans, and the Jews seemed relatively secure. Nonetheless, Oliver and his wife made secret plans again to leave France, once they had acquired the necessary fraudulent papers. One of Freud's French psychoanalytic followers, René Laforgue, who after the war stood accused of collaborating with the Nazis, also helped facilitate Oliver's effort to flee abroad.

Eva, however, was terribly frightened by the previous train experience. She developed what Oliver later called "a fear complex," and she felt safer staying in Nice, where she had a young boyfriend in the Resistance, than in trying to escape. She was eighteen years old, eager to complete her studies, and reasoned that it would be more dangerous for three to try to emigrate than for two. Oliver tried to ensure his daughter's safety through the help of the bishop of Nice, who assured Oliver of Eva's safe-keeping. The bishop had helped many refugees escape from France, and Oliver knew that Laforgue had entrusted Eva to a psychiatrist student of his. Although Oliver has been accurately described as a "precisionist,"[8] his leaving Eva behind was a terrible gamble that proved unsuccessful. Not taking her with them was a shock for her parents, and then Eva did not survive the war.

At the time I interviewed Oliver in April 1966, I did not know any of the tragic details connected with the loss of his only child. When I had first contacted Oliver by letter, and then telephoned him, about the possibility of his agreeing to see me, he said he was afraid that as a layman about analysis he was going to disappoint me. I knew from records I had seen amidst Jones's papers in London, that members of the family there suspected that Oliver had cooperated with an American free-lance author of a 1947 biography of Freud of which they disapproved.[9] Oliver's correspondence back then revealed that he was aware of their suspicions, but since it was a false accusation, he did not feel inhibited about seeing me.

I found him an exceptionally nice man, conscientious and truthful. For eight or nine years, ever since the death of Jones, Oliver said that he had been out of contact with leading analysts. Oliver knew that he had the reputation in the family of having the most accurate memory. He was unusually honest with me, although from time to time he was a bit bothered about how I might use the personal information he gave me. From my outsider's point of view, everything he said was worth preserving.

About half-way through the interview, his wife Henny brought in some sherry and crackers and proceeded to join the discussion. She had originally been a painter in Berlin. She held in her lap two autographed copies of books by psychoanalysts; one was Marie Bonaparte's study of Edgar Allan Poe. Such gifts were typical of how Freud's favorite pupils, members of his extended following, also played a part within his immediate family. Esti told me that in Vienna, Henny had been most severely criticized within the Freud household for having once dared to stay an extended period in "Papa's" rooms.

I thought Henny made the interviewing process more difficult. Since it was Oliver I had come to see, it seemed to me presumptuous of her to do as much talking as she did. Oliver was straightforward and open about his own family, at least when I knew enough to ask the right questions. But his wife tended not only to monopolize the conversation, but was also decidedly more politic and "discreet" about what she said. Her presence served to inhibit me from asking certain kinds of questions.

I did find out, however, that Freud once gave Henny an antique stone which she had made into a ring. Originally it had been Freud's highest compliment to give such a stone to his special pupils for purposes of having a ring made. While at first Freud had been selective about the people to whom he gave rings, in later years he tended to be less so. Nonetheless, those to whom he failed to give a ring never forgot the significance of the oversight. The rings were passed on from one generation to the next. Michael Balint wore Ferenczi's ring when I interviewed him, and Ruth Brunswick's daughter was wearing her mother's ring when I met her. (Jones had received his ring at the time Freud was first giving them out—to the handful of people Freud had assembled to form the "secret" committee after the loss of Jung, and whose members were to guard the sacred purity of psychoanalysis. Jones's ring had been stolen from the trunk of his car; his widow wanted me to suppress that fact, presumably on the grounds that Freud might have been disapproving of Jones for not having worn the ring. Leaving it in the car-trunk might have seemed to Freud a neurotically ambivalent symptomatic act, and one for which he might never have forgiven Jones.)

Freud's gift to Henny meant he was accepting her within his psychoanalytic family. Likewise, giving rings to his disciples meant that Freud was welcoming them into his personal family. When Henny and Oliver had been married on April 10, 1923, only Oliver's mother and his brother Martin had come to Berlin for the ceremony. As an excuse for his father's absence, Oliver mistakenly told me that Freud was already undergoing operations on his jaw by then, which was not true since it was to be another ten days until he underwent his first surgical procedure. Freud had known for a couple of months that something was wrong inside his mouth, but he did not seek medical advice until the third week in April.

As with others I interviewed, Oliver wondered how I had managed to find him. In his case, his cousin Edward Bernays, who lived in Cambridge, Massachusetts, had told me Oliver's whereabouts. Henny could not help resenting Edward for having been so slow in trying to get in touch with them. Henny also made remarks about how Edward, an immensely successful public relations expert, had made a profitable career out of being Freud's nephew. Edward did take care of translating and publishing matters in America, and knew how to help orchestrate celebrations in honor of Freud's hundredth birthday in 1956. But Edward, "a man of such means" from Henny's point of view, had done far too little for Oliver's aunts (Freud's sisters) in Vienna. According to Henny, Freud's brother Alexander had made some sarcastic remarks in Edward's presence in Vienna about what Freud's sisters (who were Edward's mother's sisters) might need from him.

Although I thought it was irksome that Henny took up so much interview time, Oliver and I did talk alone together. He said that he had read "most" of his father's books, but not all. For example, he had read the famous *Introductory Lectures on Psychoanalysis* which first came out during World War I, and was to be the most widely translated of any of Freud's work; but Oliver had never read the *New Introductory Lectures on Psychoanalysis*, a slighter book but still a standard text, which had been published initially in 1933. Some of his father's psychoanalytic papers Oliver considered too technical for him. Although he had once owned the first German collected edition of his father's works, it was lost when he fled France in 1943.

Oliver knew his father had been a great letter writer, but he considered it a chore to correspond by mail. Most of his letters from his father had been lost, and Oliver said he had only two or three of them left. Perhaps it was part of Oliver's unusual honesty that he admitted to being responsible for the disappearance of any of Freud's letters, all of which are precious historical documents. In the midst of so many emigrations from Europe, however, much of what people would otherwise have saved of Freud's failed to come down to us. Nonetheless it did seem peculiarly fitting in a topsy-turvy kind of way that, given how much actually survived, someone as exacting as Oliver could have lost so many letters from his father.

Martin's book about their father contained what Oliver considered some small errors of fact; Oliver had not, for example, ever studied with his brother Ernst in Germany, as Martin claimed. I was originally astonished that sophisticated people like James and Alix Strachey could think so well of Martin's book. Yet although it was lacking in literary grace, I learned that if one knows how to read between the lines, Martin had been exceptionally revealing. I found his text useful because once Martin had put various aspects of the family's life into print, it was fair game for scholars to inquire about relevant details without being accused of merely snooping.

According to Oliver it was not true, as Martin had maintained, that Freud had banned medicine as a profession for his children. It came to sound as if Freud had taken not too much, but too little, interest in his children's development. At least with his sons, perhaps out of disillusionment, he let them go their own ways, and rarely interfered with their career plans. Although I did not directly bring the matter up with Oliver, the consensus among Freud's followers seemed to be that he had spent an inadequate amount of time with his children. Yet despite Esti's disaffection from the family as a whole, she thought that that charge of neglect was unfair, when considered within the cultural context of what was expected of a father in Freud's time. Perhaps Freud's disciples, out of jealousy toward his natural family, preferred to think that he had been relatively neglectful of them as a way to make themselves more important in his life.

From boyhood on Oliver had been interested in mathematics and associated technical things. His mother used to say that when he grew up he would be an engineer, and this suggestion "worked." Oliver, the "precisionist," and Martin, with his artistic side, were about as different as brothers could be. Oliver thought that perhaps it was because Martin might have wanted to choose medicine that he exaggerated his father's potential opposition. And Anna could have her own motives for belittling the significance to Freud of the profession of medicine, given her subsequent career as a nonmedical analyst. In Oliver's view, Freud had only used to say, in a conversational way, that he did not think any of them would study to become physicians. Oliver thought it was the best way for Freud to achieve his objective, because if he had actually forbidden them to study medicine, it might have had the opposite effect.

Yet, Freud did play a notable role in Oliver's plans for his future. Shortly after World War I started, at a time when psychoanalytic patients became scarce and his father's earnings had dwindled, Oliver had finished his regular studies at the institute in June 1914, and had a well-paying job; he was scheduled to take his final exams in the winter of 1916. But in May 1915, Freud called Oliver into his "sanctuary"—as Freud's study was known in the family. Freud wanted to talk about Oliver's future plans. It was the only time that Freud tried to influence Oliver in a decision about his education, and Oliver said he was still thankful for it.

Oliver explained to his father that he thought he would spend all summer at his job, putting off his final exams. Freud countered that sooner or later he would be called up into the army, and then it would be hard to return to his studies. So Freud recommended that Oliver resign from his position and take the exams at the end of July. More or less unwillingly Oliver obeyed this suggestion, and then graduated in July. Oliver later thought that his father had been absolutely right, for the next year he was drafted into the army and was much better off for already having his degree. After Oliver read Jones's biography, he decided that his father had given this advice because he himself had postponed his own university exams for several years for the sake of continuing interesting work.

Most of my best exchanges with Oliver took place before Henny decided to join us. I know that her presence would have made it impossible for me to have asked Oliver whether his father had ever discussed sexuality with him. Luckily, I did raise the question before she finally settled in; and according to Oliver, neither his father nor his mother had explained anything about "the birds and the bees." Esti told me that she had heard from Martin that the boys had been sent to a family doctor to find out about sex. In his book, Martin reported how once there "had been a discussion in the family about cattle when it became clear to father that none of us children knew the difference between a bullock and a bull. 'You must be told these things,' father had exclaimed; but, like the majority of fathers, he had done nothing whatever about it."[10] Therefore Freud had not had to explain what castration meant.

In this context of sexual education and enlightenment, Oliver said that only once did he have a talk with his father about sex, and that was concerned with masturbation. The discussion took place in 1907 when Oliver was sixteen years old. His father had "warned" him against the practice; although I inquired as best I could what Freud's objections might have been, Oliver could not remember. But Oliver did recall his emotional reaction to the incident; he said that he was "quite upset for some time" as a result of the conversation with his father. Oliver volunteered that this particular talk with his father had created a definite barrier between them, and had prevented Oliver from having as close contact with his father as his brother Martin had.

It would seem that within his own family, Freud lacked the distance and detachment that he recommended to others psychoanalytically. Not unnaturally, he felt uncomfortable about facing such an issue with one of his own sons. Among his disciples Freud could be dry and cynical; the problem with masturbating, he once observed, is to know how to do it well.[11] But with patients, and in his conversation with Oliver, Freud sometimes viewed masturbation moralistically, as a neurotic symptom if not an old-fashioned vice. In an analysis, Freud could discourage masturbation because it might stir up symptoms of an "actual" neurosis, and therefore cause confusion about which material was properly psychological as opposed to being the result of sexual self-abuse.

Although the subject of sex turned up surprising information from Oliver, it took less daring on my part to ask about Freud's political views. As far as Oliver was concerned, his father had typically old Austrian attitudes: a general discontent with the nominally parliamentary government combined with patriotism toward the aging emperor. According to Martin, "we Freud children were all stout royalists, delighting to hear, or to see, all we could of the Imperial Court."[12]

By the 1930s, Freud was determined not to leave Austria, but he was at odds with the socialist convictions of most Viennese. Although the Freuds had been neutral during the first Austrian upheaval of 1927, when the bloody antisocialist civil war took place in the summer of 1934, "the Freud family were anything but neutral . . . all our sympathies were with the Chancellor Dollfuss and his successor, Schuschnigg."[13] It was acutely distressing to some of Freud's politically idealistic followers to have him defend the authoritarian actions of the Austrian regime. One patient temporarily stopped seeing Freud because of Freud's defensiveness about what was happening politically.

Whereas Martin was a competent authority on Freud's politics in the 1930s, since Martin was still living in Vienna then, Oliver was able to describe his father's political convictions during the earlier period when Oliver was growing up. As the saying went about old Austria, it was an absolutism mitigated by inefficiency and negligence. Oliver thought that the whole family voted for the "small minority" of Liberals in the elections, when any of them ran for office; the Liberals stood between the Christian conservatives and the Social Democrats on the left. Esti had thought that Freud's brother Alexander was more "worldly," and would come to the Berggasse to discuss politics and money with "Papa."

My questions about religion, compared with those about sex and politics, required no special daring on my part. Oliver said that he had never attended Jewish High Holiday services until the mid-1920s, after his marriage to Henny. Freud's life was completely removed from religious practices, yet he retained a powerful feeling as a Jew. Oliver remembered that Freud's own father had been sufficiently "liberated" that he liked to eat ham. Although Freud and his wife did not observe the Jewish holidays, Oliver's paternal grand-parents did keep Passover.

From Oliver's point of view, it was "rather late" before the family realized his father's importance. Oliver thought that the years when foreign visitors started coming, from 1906 to 1909, had signaled a decisive break with Freud's past. Freud had liked to dramatize the degree of his own professional isolation, both from his predecessors and his contemporaries. In particular, he made a great fuss out of his disaffection from the Viennese, and Oliver agreed that Freud's recog-nition had come more from abroad than locally: "of course the isolation lasted much longer in Vienna than anywhere else."

Oliver echoed what I had already heard from the others in his family that psychoanalytic terminology was never used at home. Although Oliver knew some of his father's physician friends in Vienna, most of them did not seem to share Freud's special con-cerns. Freud had only seldom spoken about any professional matters within the family. But by the end of World War I, when foreigners were pressing Freud for his time and patients were eager to move there to be treated by him, the family certainly knew that Freud had achieved world fame.

12

"My Pride and My Secret Hope"

Oliver knew a substantial amount about Freud's psychoanalytic movement, most of it first-hand, although part of his knowledge came from having read some of the relevant books. In talking with both Oliver and Esti, I was struck by how important and especially "charming" they had found Max Eitingon in particular to have been. Since Eitingon wrote so little in the way of papers, and was notably lacking in flamboyance in a circle full of colorful people, it took repeated personal testimony from those I interviewed to alert me to his full scope and genuine standing in Freud's world.

During World War I, Oliver had also been "very personally in contact" with Otto Rank. Rank was in Cracow, using his experience as Freud's editorial assistant and private secretary to help run a military newspaper. Even after his break with Freud became public, Rank never succeeded in creating much of a separate following, but Oliver understood Rank's special relationship with Freud. It was clear that his father considered Rank "somewhat of an adopted son." Unlike Martin, whom Esti said was jealous of Rank's place in his father's affairs, Oliver just took it for granted that Rank had been Freud's "efficient helper in everything." For example, Oliver mentioned that even during World War I, Rank had been able to provide cigars for Freud "from obscure sources": they could be smuggled from abroad packed inside manuscripts or galleys. Oliver also knew that the estrangement between Freud and Rank did not occur until around 1924.

Like everyone else in the family, Oliver remembered the "very strict schedule" his father had adopted for his daily routine. From eight in the morning until the one o'clock break, Freud saw patients for regular analytic treatment, six days a week. From one to two was dinner time. From two until three Freud used to go out, and then from three to four, he would reserve time for consultations. Freud resumed his analytic practice until seven o'clock, which was the regular time for supper. After the evening meal he returned to work, and according to Martin it was "not uncommon" for him to continue "until perhaps three o'clock the following morning. . . ."[1] Esti thought that Freud stopped work by midnight, but so far as I know, no one has yet challenged in print the version of things Martin publicized.

In the early days, when the children were still living at home in Vienna, Freud would usually take one of them along on his afternoon outings. On these trips Freud made some purchases or did errands, like collecting proofs or delivering them to his publishers. In his memoirs Martin made it very clear that it ought not to "be imagined that these excursions took the form of leisurely promenades designed to enjoy the beauty of the Ringstrasse and its flowering trees in springtime. My father marched at terrific speed."[2] Oliver remembered that in November 1899, he and his father had walked by the Deuticke bookstore, which was then Freud's publisher, and Freud pointed out in the window the first edition of *The Interpretation of Dreams:* "That was the book I was finishing last summer at Berchtesgaden." Oliver was then eight and a half years old.

Freud's vacations were as regular as every other aspect of his routine. He set aside Wednesday evenings for monthly meetings of psychoanalysts, and Saturday nights for lectures at the university, followed by card-playing with old physician friends. (At home, Freud might relax for part of the evening playing cards with Minna.) Every other Tuesday night was set aside for meetings of B'nai B'rith. Although after he fell ill with cancer he stopped his public speaking engagements, the rest of his timetable remained pretty much the same, and his summer holiday remained a fixed part of his life.

Oliver's precisionism reflected one aspect of his father's character, just as Martin's adventuring was an expression of a different side of Freud. I wish now that I had asked Oliver what he thought of his older brother's philandering. It is not so much that I lacked the courage to ask; it was just that I was proceeding with such caution in interviewing Oliver that I did not even think of looking into that sensitive area.

I did manage to raise one key question—even if I failed to follow it up correctly—for I asked Oliver whether his father had ever offered to analyze him. Oliver's answer was a quiet, matter-of-fact "no." He explained that it was not done with any close relatives, although in "later" years there was one exception—Anna. Oliver was talking to me about Anna's analysis before it was public knowledge, and I thought I was getting away with enough by opening up this one critical channel without being greedy and looking for too many others. Oliver never tried to conceal the fact that Anna had been analyzed by their father.

Oliver did not seem to know when Anna's analysis had started, but he could confirm that it went on into the 1920s. Oliver finally left Vienna in the summer of 1920, and then in the spring of 1921 he passed through town, staying with his parents. He said that he noticed that every evening Anna disappeared into the "sanctuary" with "Papa." Oliver wondered what was going on, and then she told him that she was being analyzed.

I also asked Oliver whether he thought that the analysis had been good for Anna, and he said "yes," although he did comment with a gentle reservation that she had never married. We both understood that her having remained unmarried was presumably a sign that, according to Freud's own theories, the analysis had not fulfilled all its possible objectives. Esti thought of the analysis in terms of Freud's training Anna and promoting her future; for being analyzed by Freud granted one a special status, even before it had become a formal rule that all analysts must themselves be analyzed. Esti was also sympathetic to Anna's difficulty in finding a mate who came up to Freud's own standards. When I suggested that Mathilda had managed to marry, Esti reminded me how much older Mathilda had been, implying that Freud's stature in later years would have been more intimidating for Anna. But none of the Europeans I was talking to assumed that marriage by itself was a necessary constituent of an ideal of so-called normality. Everyone who knew Freud well understood that the daughter of such a great man would find it especially difficult to find a suitable husband, and that any arrangement two such unusual people chose to work out had to be accepted as an aspect of their uniqueness.

Oliver was sure that his father had not analyzed his brother Ernst, for he thought he would have known had it been so. (I had been checking out a rumor about Ernst, which apparently was unfounded.) He reported that he never wondered why his father was making an exception with "Annerl," as she was known in the family, since Oliver said he as not well acquainted with psychoanalysis and its methods. But Oliver did point out that during World War I, "Annerl" was the only child left living in "the house."

Unfortunately, it did not dawn on me to ask Oliver if he had ever been analyzed by someone other than his father. But it turns out from pieces of Freud's correspondence which have been allowed to be quoted that Oliver in fact was treated psychoanalytically during the early 1920s by Dr. Franz Alexander. Alexander was a brilliant young Hungarian who became the first to graduate from the Berlin Psychoanalytic Institute; he was already a prominent analyst in Berlin where Oliver lived, and in later years he had a remarkable career in the States. Alexander developed an intensive correspondence with Freud, which has still not appeared, so we do not know what they almost certainly wrote each other about Oliver. Alexander may have learned from Oliver about Freud's analysis of Anna. Alexander is known to have had an abiding interest in problems of technique and therapy, an area in which he later became a notable innovator. (Anna Freud, like Kurt Eissler, remained unremittingly hostile to the changes that Alexander had introduced.)[3]

On October 31, 1920, Freud wrote Eitingon that he was "often" worried by Oliver, and that Oliver needed "therapy."[4] Oliver was showing all the signs of "the excessive cleanliness, ritualistic orderliness, and indecisiveness symptomatic of an obsessional neurosis."[5] What had once amused Freud about Oliver as a child had become in adulthood a source of real concern. On December 13, 1920, Freud told Eitingon that before the onset of what Freud thought of as obsessional symptoms, Oliver had been "my pride and my secret hope."[6] Was Freud exaggerating here, with that Viennese charm of his which can be so misleading? Or was there more to his relationship with Oliver that only the future publication of his letters can hope to clarify? We do know that Freud wrote Eitingon that he was suffering "very much with my feelings of helplessness."[7] Inasmuch as Eitingon was more an administrator than either a therapist or a theorist, it is fortunate that Oliver wound up being treated by Alexander. It would be too much like orthodox psychoanalytic party-line reasoning to propose that "Eitingon did not take Oliver because of his closeness to the family. . . ."[8] Thanks to Hans Lampl, a friend of Freud's sons in Vienna, Oliver was referred to Alexander.[9]

It is hard to imagine how it can be said that Oliver was "successfully treated,"[10] since he remained so much the same. Freud himself seemed unimpressed by the alleged success of the therapy. In 1934 he told another correspondent, novelist Arnold Zweig, about Oliver's "extraordinary" qualities and the extensiveness and accuracy of his knowledge. "His character was faultless, then the neurosis came over him and stripped off all the blooms." It would be typical of Freud to regard individual symptoms as separate from character, but it is not clear what change for the worse he thought he had detected. He described Oliver in 1934 as being "unfortunately strongly inhibited neurotically," and said that he had had "bad luck" in life. It has been said that "Freud found Oliver's problematic life, he told Zweig, a heavy burden to bear."[11] Oliver was then living with Henny and their daughter in Nice. Freud did not live to learn of his granddaughter Eva's death during World War II, but others in the family said that however repressed Oliver had been before, he became even more withdrawn and inhibited after his daughter died.

Even if I missed out discussing his analysis, just by meeting Oliver I could later evaluate Freud's own comments. Post-Freudian psychoanalysts were not happy with Freud's distinction between symptoms and character; whatever he might have done in practice, Freud had often written as if he were not interested in alleviating symptoms but only in altering fundamental character structure. Both Carl Jung and Wilhelm Reich, each in different ways, would challenge Freud's effort to distinguish symptoms from character. And all the early analysts, despite their protestations to being unconcerned with the curing of symptoms on the grounds that substitute formations could too easily crop up, were in practice eager to report good practical therapeutic results.

I did ask Oliver why he thought there had been so many estrangements in Freud's professional life, and he answered that "many people cannot stand living under the influence of superior spirits." Oliver said that he had learned from his father that people have difficulty being grateful to someone else, and that a disaffection takes place, even if only unconsciously. He gave as an example an incident with one of his Bernays cousins, whom Oliver had befriended in Berlin, yet who subsequently turned against him.

Esti Freud had told me that she considered Oliver "the most neurotic" of Freud's children; Ernst was, in her view, the least troubled, and made a notably successful marriage. Esti claimed that she herself had considered in Vienna becoming an analyst, even though she said her husband had treated her as if she were "an idiot." She reported having gone so far as to see Helene Deutsch, in her capacity as head of the Training Institute, but that Helene had not been encouraging. Of course, had Freud wanted one of his relatives, other than Anna, to be accepted as an analyst, he would have been sure to let Helene know. When I asked Helene about Esti, she could no longer remember much one way or the other. Part of the fascination of my interviewing work was that I could try to piece together what might be a plausible narrative of events. As the years passed, with more of Freud's letters appearing, what I had learned became even more significant.

Of the three Freud children I met, I found it easiest to talk to Oliver. Maybe it was because we were both men, but I am certain that the fact that we were away from the rest of the family in London, and from the whole politics of the dynamics of the movement there, meant that I felt relatively unconstrained about what I asked. Anna had recently been in the States, where she had been in a minor automobile accident; Oliver and his wife knew the exact details.

Anna had not had time to see them, but had telephoned the day before she returned to London. She was apologetic about finding it impossible to combine professional and family visits, but said she would be certain to see Oliver when she was back in the States at the end of the year—when she was scheduled to receive an honorary degree from the University of Chicago. Martin was to die in 1967, and then Oliver himself in early 1969; Anna went to Massachusetts to represent the family and to put Henny in a nursing home. So even though, when I was interviewing Oliver in 1966, he was geographically separated from Anna, the magic circle of the family still was a powerful influence.

Without implying any possible sexual hanky-panky between Freud and Oliver's Aunt Minna, I did ask Oliver about her role in Freud's life. Unhesitatingly Oliver immediately replied that Minna was "surely more intellectual" than his mother. Minna, for example, read foreign languages like English and French, a talent that was "not among my mother's strengths." Oliver made it quietly clear that, from his point of view, the family had had "a nice equilibrium," partly accounted for by the balance of three boys and three girls. (As a child, Oliver had been known as "Oli," and in my presence Henny addressed him that way too.) As the middle son, Oliver was in a position to be able to appreciate the merits of balance. Freud's brother Alexander was ten years younger, so they were the oldest and the youngest in the family; the five sisters had come in between. Oliver recited a childhood expression of his father's, which Oliver learned from his grandmother: "Our family is like a book," Freud had gallantly said. "We are the covers and the girls are the leaves between."

Oliver agreed with a description of his grandmother Freud as having been "very self-willed"; but somehow I feel sure that he would not have emphasized the point, or even brought her up, if I had not been especially interested in what Freud's mother had been like. One of Oliver's American cousins whom I had interviewed said she had found it hard to take what she called their grandmother's "authoritarian character." When I questioned this description, Henny interjected—perhaps correctly—that children in earlier generations had been brought up differently from what later people were apt to expect. But Henny was generally so eager to put the best face on things that I could not regard her contributions as especially trustworthy. Yet, she did offer one interesting quotation from Freud, which I have never seen reproduced elsewhere. At his 70th-birthday celebration in 1926, foreign friends and disciples were present at his apartment. Freud then said, "If you want to change something [in psychoanalysis], do it, but never to please the public!"

Oliver did not contradict anything Henny said, although she would jump in and answer questions that I had directed at him. In my experience with biographical work, I have found that those who have married into families are apt to be defensive, and therefore more protective about the intrusions of outsiders like historians. Oliver could be more secure if only because of his own confidence in his biological ties as a Freud.

Oliver was clear that his grandmother Freud deserved to rank as a "disciplinarian." In my second book, *Brother Animal* (1969), I later wrote:

> Freud . . . perhaps partly in the tradition of the nineteenth century . . . rarely discussed his tie to his mother, except in terms so unrealistically loving as to make one suspicious. He never seems to have acknowledged how dependent on his mother he always was. She was in fact regal and self-sufficient, an opposite type from the woman he married, and the prototype of the kind of woman who in much later years would have power over him. Curiously enough for the discoverer of the Oedipus complex, Freud's mother was the dictatorial person, whereas his father seems to have been kindly and improvident.[12]

There are many reasons, not all of them connected with my interviewing, that led me to these ideas. Freud's own theories of human psychology were always in the back of my mind, as I tried to imagine how his subjective experiences might have led him to particular conclusions. For example, he once proposed that "a mother is only brought unlimited satisfaction by her relation to a son; that is altogether the most perfect, the most free from ambivalence of all human relationships."[13] Based on Esti's experience, she doubted that Freud had been right. But if he idealized the mother-son tie, then it might have been as a cover—as Ferenczi had thought—for his own poorly understood relationship to his mother.

Anna Freud took great offense at my *Brother Animal*, although it was not until 1989 that I fully realized the extent of her distress. She made a detailed list of her objections for Kurt Eissler, in an effort to encourage his polemical attacks on my book. Although this is not the place to recount the behind-the-scenes story of her opposition to *Brother Animal*, she did take exception to my account of Freud's mother in a way which is relevant here. Although she ignored my allusion to an affair between Martin and Edith Jackson, Anna bristled at the suggestion that in obscure ways unknown to himself, Freud might have been dependent on his mother. She did not see her Grandmother Freud as "regal and self-sufficient," nor the prototype of women who later acquired importance in Freud's life. Anna wrote nothing to challenge my account of her own mother or paternal grandfather, but she did describe her grandmother, Amalia, in her own distinctive style:

> She was . . . rather infantile, if not to say childish, excessively devoted and proud of her sons, as Jewish mothers are, and unintellectual to a degree that even the word does not fit. She probably had a good stock of common sense of a very primitive kind, but she was neither dictatorial nor self-sufficient and until her very old age, rather charmingly vain of her appearance. My father suffered her as a good Jewish son, but dependent on her??[14]

Anna did not readily acknowledge weaknesses in her father, and any dependency on his part conflicted with her own idealizations of him. Nor would she take well to any suggestion that there might be more to the mother-son tie than he had himself suggested; hidden ambivalences were not aspects of his character she was likely to talk about. I know of no other passage of hers which so directly recounts her own memories of Amalia Freud. It is not a flattering portrait, and I suspect that Anna's choice of words reflected her distaste at the thought of the old woman. Describing her as "rather infantile," with "a very primitive" stock of common sense, was not exactly complimentary, relying as it did on diagnostic-sounding terms. Yet to describe her as "rather infantile" was not so different from a more down-to-earth notion of her being queenly in self-conception. Since Anna herself felt so alien to all things Jewish (she declined to accept an honorary degree from Brandeis University), every time she characterized the relationship between her father and his mother in those cultural terms, I think she was trying to dissociate her own conception of Freud from that whole Jewish world.

Yet Oliver, in characterizing Amalia as a "disciplinarian," was saying something about her which was not only at odds with what Anna Freud later wrote, but far more in keeping with what could be gathered from other members of the Freud family. Oliver had not meant to imply that his grandmother's character had been a source of any great family conflict. On the contrary, the fact that her power went unchallenged was exactly why I think that my choice of the word "regal" may not have been so far off-base. The Viennese analyst Robert Jokl told me that in his opinion, Amalia Freud had had "a court" around her. Doubtless Anna would have objected to the term "regal" in any connection with her father.

One of Oliver's American cousins told me that Dolfi—Freud's youngest sister and the one who remained unmarried—sacrificed her life "on the altar of motherhood." Freud's mother was supposedly a terrible tyrant, and both Freud and his brother Alexander were criticized by the extended family for allowing Dolfi to be so abused. A niece of hers said that "nowadays one would think of hiring a companion." At the age of sixty-eight, Dolfi said, "Unfortunately I am not married," and her mother, who lived to be ninety-five, retorted, "Is that any way for a young girl to talk!" Even in her extreme old age, Freud's mother held sway, and on Sundays, Freud, the family, and sometimes visiting analysts came to see her. Dolfi was not allowed to have a life of her own; the only place she could go alone was the dentist, a niece told me, because she "had to have her teeth along." Neither Freud's wife, nor his brother Alexander's, wanted to take care of Amalia Freud. And it was said that Dolfi "went to pieces" after her mother finally died. In the view of at least one analyst I interviewed, Willi Hoffer, a nightmarish aspect to American public relations intrusions would be for someone to ask Freud about what he thought of his sisters.

In my interviews with Freud's family members, I never expected to gain an entirely new picture of Freud. But I did hope that a knowledge of the people would enable me to pinpoint aspects of the available literature that rang true to life, and those that had been undervalued. The written evidence about Freud is still so lacking that it has been possible for a writer in 1988 somehow to claim, without any backing whatever, that Dolfi was Freud's favorite sister, "the one he appreciated the most."[15]

What Martin Freud wrote about Amalia Freud is quite instructive. He emphasized her origins in East Galicia, and expressed a common prejudice that Jews from there were "absolutely different from Jews who had lived in the West for some generations. They, these Galician Jews, had little grace and no manners; and their women were certainly not what we should call 'ladies.' "[16] I was probably remiss to have used the word "regal" to describe Amalia, if that term implies graciousness, for Amalia had the power, while Freud's wife possessed the manners. I still think that it would be true to Freud's own teachings if we examine his family background for the models of people he later got involved with. There is good reason to believe that self-involved women, whom Freud called narcissistic, exerted a special influence on him. An analyst who knew Freud intimately once privately observed that Freud had a special countertransference conflict with beautiful narcissistic women.[17] When I once read that passage to Helene Deutsch, she broke in to observe, "I always thought so," implying she knew she was among those to whom Freud was especially susceptible.

Martin indicated how such a prima donna, whom Freud had not been foolish enough to marry, can be difficult. He attributed Amalia's characteristics solely to her being a Galician Jewess:

> These people are not easy to live with, and grandmother, a true representative of her race, was no exception. She had great vitality and much impatience; she had a hunger for life and an indomitable spirit. Nobody envied Aunt Dolfi, whose destiny it was to dedicate her life to the care of an old mother who was a tornado. Aunt Dolfi once took Amalia to buy a new hat—and she was not perhaps wise to recommend what seemed to her 'something suitable.' Studying carefully her image crowned by the hat she had agreed to try on, Amalia, who was on the wrong side of ninety, finally shouted: "I won't take this one; it makes me look old."[18]

Martin wrote that Dolfi "was not clever or in any way remarkable, and it might be true to say that constant attendance on Amalia had suppressed her personality into a condition of dependence from which she never recovered."[19] Freud's own kind of dependency on his mother, which I still believe to be a hypothesis worth entertaining, was obviously of a different sort from that of his sister Dolfi. In a sense, he re-created in his relationship with Anna the same sort of apparently conflict-free perfection that he thought was exclusively true for mothers and sons.

In 1911 Freud made some remarks that sound like an autobiographical version of his relation to his mother: "I have found that people who know that they are preferred or favored by their mother give evidence in their lives of a peculiar self-reliance and an unshakeable optimism which often seem like heroic attributes and bring actual success to their possessors." Not surprisingly, Freud thought he derived only positive attributes from Amalia. In writing about Goethe in 1917 Freud elaborated:

> if a man has been his mother's undisputed darling he retains throughout life the triumphant feeling, the confidence in success, which not seldom brings actual success along with it. And Goethe might well have given some such heading to his autobiography as: 'My strength has its roots in my relation to my mother.'[20]

Anna could see nothing but strengths in her father; nor could one expect Martin to be psychologically distant from Freud. Although Martin's book is an uncritical and often superficial approach, it does offer some special insights. He reported, for example, that Dolfi "died of starvation in the Jewish ghetto in Theresienstadt," while the three other Viennese sisters "were murdered, probably at Auschwitz."[21] (It was not unusual for the people I interviewed to read some background material before seeing me. Mathilda, however, never got beyond the first two volumes of Jones's biography. One woman, a psychiatrist and former patient of both Freud's and Jung's, laughingly admitted to having read a whole book about her psychoanalytic institute before speaking with me. This sort of self-consciousness has to be distinguished from those who regarded Jones's books as a successful act of statecraft, and who did not want to see his picture of things challenged.)

It would have been only human for Freud to have absorbed traits from both his parents. When I asked Freud's sister-in-law Sophie,

Alexander's widow, whether Sigmund had been like Amalia, I got an emphatically positive response. Yet, while Amalia was obviously hard to get along with, I never met anyone within Freud's family who directed such a complaint against Freud himself. But then he gave up, I think, on his own sons fairly early on, directing his attention to his psychoanalytic pupils—his spiritual sons. He was tolerant of his own sons in letting them go their own way, but he was more patriarchal with his students than with his real children. Many of his disciples would later complain about his authoritarianism.

Esti had been defensive about Freud's quest for a successor. Freud may have written about Oliver as his pride and secret hope, but when I raised the issue of succession with Oliver, I drew a blank stare of uncomprehension. After Freud's difficulties with Adler and Jung, Freud entrusted the future of psychoanalysis to a small group of leading analysts. Freud then wrote to one of them: "That assurance that the children will be provided for, which for a Jewish father is a matter of life and death, I expected to get from Jung; I am glad now that you and our friends will give me this."[22]

Although Freud invented the concept of neurosis, for which he designed psychoanalysis as a method of treatment, few within his family or among his followers detected in him any signs of nervousness. When I asked Oliver about it, he said that he never observed any neurotic features in his father, and that he was aware of Freud's neurosis only from reading Jones. Anna had written Jones that the family had never seen Freud's preoccupation with death which is so striking in his letters; she cannily suggested that some of his complaints about his health were designed to protect him from demands coming from others. I think that Oliver's and Anna's perceptions were typical, and were matched by many others in Freud's circle, who saw in him someone extraordinarily self-controlled who rarely revealed his inner conflicts. An American niece only could think of how he could be extremely punctilious, and thought his punctuality and regularity an aspect of his being neurotic. It is due to Freud's great capacities as a writer that we know as much as we do about the emotional sources of his ideas, and how intensely tormented he could be.

From today's point of view, Freud's family life may look like a museum piece. But it is important to realize that in the context of

Freud's time and place, Oliver was correct in specifying the quality of "equilibrium." The large family functioned as a harmonious system, although there had been tensions that bothered people at the time. Freud was inevitably a man of his era; he had pulled himself up by his own bootstraps, but they were the bootstraps of someone born in 1856. He was so different from the rest of his family, siblings included; he alone had so penetrating a mind and such unique curiosity. In a purely intellectual sense, both his parents could be considered simple-minded. Once we see Freud in the context of his family life, we can begin to understand the human and social premises under which he worked. And we can gain some perspective on how he came to exert such an influence on his followers, who in turn were to have such an impact on twentieth-century thought.

Afterword

Psychoanalysis has been such an influential movement that the ideas it has promoted are bound to have stirred up a powerful reaction. Freud's impact on our century is at least as great as that of Charles Darwin earlier. For just as Darwinism came to pervade all aspects of social and political thinking, not to mention religious beliefs, so psychoanalysis has succeeded in decisively reshaping our broadest psychological notions. Freud's teachings have affected the nursery as well as the bedroom, and the intimacy of his message has provoked a fierce response.

Freud himself has attracted both extraordinary veneration and critical scrutiny, more so with each passing decade of my own long-standing work in this field. The world had changed at least as much in 1964, which was twenty-five years after Freud's death, as it has in the quarter of a century since I conducted my interviews. Meeting Helene Deutsch in 1964 was decisive in bringing me into the circle of Freud's original followers. The personal knowledge I acquired then has proved increasingly relevant as the years have passed.

Freud had inspired Helene Deutsch in a unique way. His example had breathed life into her career and thinking. I am reminded how, during an interview with Leonard Woolf, who had been Freud's publisher in England, Woolf's face had been transformed when he momentarily turned to look toward a manuscript of his wife Virginia that he was then editing. Genius does have the capacity for making us more of ourselves. Freud released something special in Helene Deutsch, and some portion of that inspiration came through in the course of my contact with her.

Each of Freud's disciples, many of whom are unique in their own right, have increasingly drawn a special kind of attention, sometimes due to their difficulties in getting along with Freud. Jung, probably the most famous "dissident" in the history of psychoanalysis, ended up having a major influence on literature and the arts, and a formidable school of his own has perpetuated his point of view. But Jung's collaboration with the Nazis in the 1930s has been enough to close more than a few minds to him. Adler, a socialist, was younger than Freud or Jung when he died, and his independent Austrian following was decimated by World War II. Freud's own loyal movement was more international; although it is rarely acknowledged today, Adler laid the groundwork for much of later psychology, especially because of his interest in normal, as opposed to psychopathological, human development.

Another analyst who ran afoul of Freud was Rank. Despite Rank's unique interest in creativity and his personal relationship with both Anaïs Nin and Henry Miller, Rank is even less influential today than Adler. To continue this catalogue of Freud's most notable students, Reich made many important contributions to modern psychotherapy and helped promote the sexual revolution; but he also made therapeutic claims that the federal Food and Drug Administration objected to, and when Reich failed to defend himself adequately, he was imprisoned. Melanie Klein has had a lasting effect on British intellectual life, even though Freud viewed her as a heretic and his daughter Anna fought against her work for years. And Jacques Lacan, after being kept with his Parisian group from the International Psychoanalytic Association, is regarded today as a central thinker among all those influenced by French theorists. One could go on, detailing the way analysts have repeatedly been involved in controversies while playing a central role in this century's life of the mind.

With Karl Marx, "perhaps the most remarkable thing . . . is his extraordinary success in the personal relationships that mattered most."[1] And the same could be said of Freud. Although both men lived amidst a series of public squabbles, in Freud's case—as I think the preceding material makes clear—his private family life was noteworthy for its harmoniousness. In assessing Freud's life and character, one must keep in mind that Freud was not only born in another century and lived on a different continent than our own, but that the whole world of old Vienna has long since disappeared.

Nothing I have written about Freud should be taken as some kind of magic formula to understanding his genius. Even though we know so much about Freud's life—probably more than about any other historical figure that one might imagine—still there has to be an element of mystery about how creativity works. Freud sometimes saw himself as an ally of Copernicus and Darwin; for with his concept of the unconscious, and the limits it sets on our conscious awareness, he too helped dissolve man's self-important image of his place in the universe. As we have seen, Freud has recently been compared to Plato, Montaigne, and even Shakespeare. How bewildering it must have been for Freud himself to try and place himself within Western thought. He sought out heroes like Leonardo da Vinci and Moses; in writing about them, Freud was also trying to come to terms with his own talents. Yet even Freud thought that something inexplicable had to elude our understanding of the greatest cultural achievements. As he once wrote in an essay on Dostoevsky, "Before the problem of the creative artist analysis must, alas, lay down its arms."[2]

I believe it is impossible to understand Freud apart from his relationship to his own family. This should be a truism, in that psychoanalytic psychology has taught us how much everyone necessarily owes to his or her forebears. Aside from Freud's obvious indebtedness to his family, they also mattered to him in a way that is all too easy nowadays to miss. To explore this aspect of Freud's character is neither to discredit him nor to portray him as a saint in order to promote further psychoanalytic cultism.

Since Grete Bibring's retirement at Beth Israel back in 1964, there has been an avalanche of books about Freud and early psychoanalysis. At the time I began my research, I was naive about the degree of sectarianism associated with the field. Given the psychiatric power that psychoanalysts then had in the States, it was too easy to ignore the extent of the ideological partisanship that was pervasive. Within psychiatry, however, I think that those years must represent one of the high tides of the influence of Freudian teachings. And the reaction since has been so great, largely in the direction of biological psychiatry, that it has been possible to forget that Freud made at least one lasting contribution to modern psychotherapy: he concentrated on the human interaction between therapist and patient in a way that no other school of thought had done.

In 1964 his students, like Grete Bibring, were still waving the banner of orthodox psychoanalytic teachings. Anna Freud was to live for almost another two decades, and as long as she reigned at #20 Maresfield Gardens, Freud's movement remained more or less cohesive. He had, through his youngest child, left psychoanalysis in the hands of his family. But, like Freud, Anna governed partly by creating a large extended family made up of psychoanalysts.

Without Helene Deutsch's help I would never have been able to see Anna Freud or to sit in on case conferences at the Hampstead Clinic. As I undertook my research, there was nothing that I came across that I did not try to discuss with Helene. She was in effect a supervisor of my ongoing interviewing. I was not proceeding as a muckraking journalist, and therefore did not seek the kind of sensationalism that someone like Janet Malcolm has specialized in. I was working as an intellectual historian with a compelling interest in the history of ideas.

I was up against a preposterous series of attempts at secrecy, so that while the Freud Archives locked up the interviews of Esti and Oliver Freud, for example, I was able to meet them and learn for myself. I think it has to be in the context of all the idealizing about Freud that Anna Freud took such sharp offense at my publications. I was consciously publishing while she was still alive and I was therefore able to correct any possible errors. But when *Brother Animal* first came out, Anna Freud not only took a series of steps to combat me, but she also sent to a prominent London analyst a copy of Helene Deutsch's letter recommending me in the first place, in order to explain why she had ever agreed to see me. In 1974, when Eva Rosenfeld, who had continued to help my work despite the controversy that Anna had helped to promote, wrote about me to Anna, Anna's reply was as harsh as any she ever composed: "All I can say is that Roazen is a menace whatever he writes."[3] Any independent writer should, I believe, be proud of such a tribute.

However upset Anna remained about me, she never tried to contact Helene directly. Instead, intermediaries on her behalf in New York City communicated between Helene in Cambridge and Anna in London. Eventually the storm died down, and by 1978 I had officially embarked on my biography of Helene. But I had gained a much better appreciation for those famous "dissidents" who earlier had been accused of treason to the cause. In spite of what had happened over me, when in 1980 Anna went to Cambridge to receive an honorary degree from Harvard, she accepted the suggestion of a Boston analyst that she pay a visit to Helene.

The next year a scandal broke out at the Freud Archives, instigated by Jeffrey Masson's allegation that Freud had only abandoned his early theory about the significance of childhood sexual seduction in order to curry favor with Viennese medical circles. At this point, even though I was in the midst of working on my biography of Helene Deutsch, my name was dragged into the Masson affair. (The world is a small place, for I had known him in Toronto.) Supposedly, the Masson episode was "a similar situation" to what had happened to me years earlier. As an eminent London analyst wrote confidentially to Kurt Eissler, "Jeff Masson is no different in character to Paul Roazen. . . ."[4]

Readers can judge for themselves the accuracy of these various allegations. I have inquired about Freud's role as a family man and have presented the principals as best as I could. I thought they were all fascinating people, and as the years pass and further correspondence of Freud's is allowed to come out, I think that my having known them will add immeasurably to an appreciation of the written texts.

Oral history is no substitute for all other types of inquiry. What can be learned from the kind of field work I conducted has its definite

limits; not only does any investigator have blind spots and inade-
quacies, but it is impossible to check fully what one person says as
opposed to another. Despite these pitfalls, I would contend that
being able to meet these people and ask them direct questions was an
invaluable opportunity, one that I hope will serve to supplement the
kind of documentation that eventually gets published. Written history also has its own special ways of being misleading; even if letters
succeed in not being destroyed, either by events or design, such
material should be questioned and examined with all the skepticism
that trained historians are experienced in. How one distinguishes, for
example, between some old Viennese puffery as opposed to a genuinely held feeling is not something that can be established by any
objectively available standards.

In the mid-1960s I made an implicit wager that meeting Freud's
family would be worthwhile. In the time since then, mythologizing
about Freud has continued, and a whole new set of controversies has
arisen. In time, I hope that the places where I might have erred will
become evident, and that they will not seem the result of any undue
partisanship on my part.

I would like to conclude on a separate note, as I attempt to
examine the past for the sake of the future, for I think that the study of
history should lead us to question the present. Unlike those who
think that family life is getting progressively better, I want seriously to
question whether our own time can be said to have evolved in any
way superior to the Freud family circumstances. It is too easy to be
dismissively patronizing about Freud's kind of patriarchalism.

Even though the past is gone irrevocably, I look to the past to
challenge some of today's preconceptions. First of all, we should be
highly reluctant to pass judgment on previous generations, for are we
really better off now? Helene Deutsch was self-critical enough to
wonder whether psychoanalysis had really succeeded in making
people happier. Freud's influence helped promote a kind of individu-
alism and encouraged a break with customary family life, and yet I
wonder whether what we now have is an improvement. We struggle
with too much normlessness, and our children have different dis-
abilities from Freud's own.

In major cities of the world today one finds an enormous population of extremely lonely people who sometimes can only connect with others by means of psychotherapeutic involvements. Freud lived in a world where family came first, but that is now gone. What we have instead is the egoistic ideal of self-development. Although psychoanalytic therapy supposedly sets out to try and combat human narcissism, being in treatment can foster just the kind of self-absorption that such therapy is trying to overcome. Is the history of psychoanalysis merely a version of the tale of the Sorcerer's Apprentice? Not only do current therapists fail to share the unique qualities of Freud's original followers, but Freud may have actually undermined more than he ever expected. When the Viennese satirist Karl Kraus maintained long ago that psychoanalysis was the illness for which it purports to be the cure, he was on to something tantalizingly complicated.

There is little question that ours is a more individualistic and egocentric era than Freud's. I find it hard not to be more than a bit nostalgic at the loss of those large extended families of old. We have gone from a time when divorce was an almost unheard-of scandal to one in which there are almost no social supports left for those who are in principle opposed to divorce, and who want to preserve such family life as is still possible. Compromise is an integral part of civilized life, and it is as if we have forgotten how splendid it can be for children to grow up with a variety of family models around them. The Freud sons and daughters, for example, were free to grow in different directions, and none of the people I met struck me as stifled by circumstances. I do not want to go to the opposite extreme of too much nostalgia, instead of excessive self-congratulation. For just as it is mistaken, I think, to see the present in terms of having progressively evolved from the past, so it would be an error to talk only about what has been lost over time. But history does indicate that we have paid a price for the way we are today. Egocentricism is another name for selfishness; Freud himself may have sometimes shown a striking lack of consideration for others, but one does not have to be an apologist to recognize that he was Freud. And if family bonds were once perhaps too tight, we must still work to find suitable substitutes for those supports that nurture humanity.

None of the people I met struck me as having led frustrated lives.

There was to be sure a good deal of tragedy, and such suffering can be painful to behold. But I would question, for example, to what extent highly talented women are necessarily better off now than they were almost a century ago. I do not think we can view creative people as helpless victims of social circumstances, for such talk robs people of the possibility of autonomy. I believe that basically Freud was right in thinking that under most social conditions, people are obliged to make choices. That means that we have the ability to make our lot better than might otherwise be the case.

Women in Freud's era, such as Helene Deutsch or Grete Bibring, for example, managed to make their mark, and they did so while remaining married. The example of Anna Freud has to be an exception, but then Freud taught that we ought to approach other human beings as if they are all potentially exceptions. Although it is common to think that social conditions have improved for women over this past century, and it may be true for most of them, strangely enough there were more prominent women at the top of the psychoanalytic profession in Freud's day than is the case today.

Although it is often overlooked now, within the Vienna Psychoanalytic Society Freud had been in favor of admitting women members, and he took this stand over the opposition of his much younger disciples.[5] Thus, within the context of his time and place, Freud helped many women with emancipating opportunities. It is possible to believe, as Freud did, that human biology leaves men and women with unequal burdens; people have bodies, and sexual reproduction, which is not all that can be said about anyone, does color how we think. As long as the biological inequalities between the sexes are acknowledged, and not associated in any way with alleged inferiorities or imputed superiorities, then Freud had something of lasting importance to teach. Despite all we may think we already know about Freud, his challenge to us still retains its fundamental vitality.

I was interviewing Esti Freud at a time when the incipient feminist movement was criticizing some traditionalist psychoanalytic thinking. Today, things have moved in an entirely new direction; after a quarter-century of Freud-bashing, feminist theorists are finding that there is more to psychoanalytic psychology than first met the eye.

Freud's terminology has been easily misunderstood. For example, when he wrote about masochism, he took for granted that all civilized people are self-punitive, and that it was the task of therapy to relieve unnecessary stress; his theory that men are more sadistic than women was not intended as any kind of compliment to his own sex. Freud's concept of penis envy may sound laughable now, an obvious expression of sexist bias; but he intended to have offered a theory of female castration anxiety, and the equivalent complex in men was supposed to explain the sources of the neurotic belittling of women. Lately we have had volumes attempting to bridge feminist thinking with psychoanalytic theorizing; the problem, as I see it, is that so much of this work remains ahistorical. There is almost a century's worth of thinking about these issues, and it would be myopic to think we have recently reinvented the wheel.

Psychoanalytic psychology represents a tradition of thought that should enrich us. By examining past theorists, from Freud to the present day, we can enlarge our imaginative capacities. The early Freudians had an attractive kind of idealism, and if their sectarianism can be put aside, and all the old shibboleths about heretics or deviations are ignored, past theorists can be examined on their own merits and limitations.

In order to make any sense of what Freud was saying, it is necessary to see him in the setting in which he lived. The moral dilemmas that people faced in Old World culture are bound to be different from our own, but that does not mean we cannot benefit from examining their experiences. Freud helped to change modern ethics, and assuming that the question of how we ought to live is universal, then the complex example of Freud's life can teach as much as any coherent body of doctrines.

So along with all the new criticisms that have been leveled at psychoanalytic thinking—much of it entirely justified—books on the subject will continue to appear. I have tried here to show a side of Freud that is apt to be neglected. Freud once alluded to his "father complex,"[6] which he said he knew so well. His critics have been apt to maintain, along with Ferenczi, that Freud as an old man did "not love anyone, only himself and his work. . . ."[7]

Still I think that there are humanly attractive aspects to Freud which are easy to miss. On April 12, 1929, for example, he noted in a letter to Ludwig Binswanger, a Swiss psychiatrist, that Freud's daughter Sophie, had she lived, would have been thirty-six years old that day. In the same note to Binswanger, Freud said he had not been able to decipher the handwriting in Binswanger's previous letter to him.

> I considered returning the letter to you with a jocular expression of my indignation, and the suggestion that you send it back rewritten. Then my sister-in-law offered her assistance, and gave me the deeply moving news contained in the latter part of your letter, whereupon I understood why you had not dictated it into the machine.

Minna had been able to help Freud by determining from Binswanger's scrawled text that he had lost a son. Freud had his own special sort of condolences to offer:

> Although we know that after such a loss the acute state of mourning will subside, we also know we shall remain inconsolable and will never find a substitute. No matter what may fill the gap, even if it be filled completely, it nevertheless remains something else. And actually that is how it should be. It is the only way of perpetuating that love which we do not want to relinquish. [8]

Anyone who could write that way about human feelings deserves to live on, entirely aside from our need to emancipate ourselves from the storybook legends about the saints and heretics of the secular religion which have become, alas, so dominant in much of the discussion about psychoanalysis. Freud's compassion for Binswanger was a direct consequence of Freud's own loss of Sophie. And if his thirst for knowledge was unquenchable, there are worse ways for people to live. It ought to be possible, I think, to use the example of Freud and his family to help bridge the tragic chasms which too often persist between today's various schools of different branches of psychology and psychotherapy.

Notes

Introduction. Looking Back on How I Began

1. Harold Lasswell, *Psychopathology and Politics* (1930; reprint ed., Chicago: University of Chicago Press, 1986). Cf. Paul Roazen, *Encountering Freud: The Politics and Histories of Psychoanalysis* (New Brunswick, N.J.: Transaction Books, 1990), pp. 241–44.

2. Paul Roazen, *Freud and His Followers* (1975; reprint ed., New York: Da Capo Books, 1992), p. 135.

3. Elliot S. Valenstein, *Great and Desperate Cures: The Rise and Decline of Psychosurgery and Other Radical Treatments for Medical Illness* (New York: Basic Books, 1986).

4. *The Diary of Sigmund Freud: 1929–1939, A Record of the Final Decade*, trans., annot., and introd. by Michael Molnar (New York: Charles Scribner's Sons, 1992), p. 195.

1. Helene Deutsch Gets My Foot in the Door

1. Helene Deutsch, "Some Forms of Emotional Disturbances and Their Relationship to Schizophrenia," in *Neuroses and Character Types: Clinical Psychoanalytic Studies* (New York: International Universities Press, 1965), pp. 262–81; Helene Deutsch, "On a Type of Pseudo-Affectivity (the 'As If' Type)," and "Clinical and Theoretical Aspects of 'As If' Characters," in *The Therapeutic Process, the Self, and Female Psychology: Collected Psychoanalytic Papers*, ed. Paul Roazen (New Brunswick, N.J.: Transaction Books, 1992), pp. 193–207, 215–20.

2. Paul Roazen, *Helene Deutsch: A Psychoanalyst's Life*, 2d ed. (New Brunswick, N.J.: Transaction Books, 1991), pp. 303–4.

3. Paul Roazen, "The Rise and Fall of Bruno Bettelheim," *Psychohistory Review* (Spring 1992): 221–50.

4. Paul Roazen, "Tola Rank," *Journal of the American Academy of Psychoanalysis* 18 (1990): 247–59.

2. The Family Freud in Perspective

1. Cf. Emanuel Rice, *Freud and Moses: The Long Journey Home* (Albany: State University of New York Press, 1990).

2. Anna Freud Bernays, "My Brother Sigmund Freud," in *Freud As We Knew Him*, ed. Hendrik M. Ruitenbeek (Detroit: Wayne State University Press, 1973), p. 142.

3. *The Clinical Diary of Sandor Ferenczi*, ed. Judith Dupont, trans. Michael Balint and Nicola Zarday Jackson (Cambridge: Harvard University Press, 1988), pp. 187–88. Cf. Paul Roazen, "Book Review of *The Clinical Diary of Sandor Ferenczi*," *American Journal of Psychoanalysis* 50 (1990): 367–71.

4. *The Clinical Diary of Sandor Ferenczi*, p. 188. See also Roazen, *Freud and His Followers*, p. 258.

5. *The Clinical Diary of Sandor Ferenczi*, p. 188; Roazen, *Freud and His Followers*, pp. 503–6.

6. Harold Bloom, "Freud, the Greatest Modern Writer," *New York Times Book Review*, March 23, 1986, pp. 1, 26–27.

7. "Freud's Last Will, with an Introduction by Paul Roazen," *Journal of the American Academy of Psychoanalysis* 18 (1990): 383–91.

3. Maresfield Gardens

1. Bruno Bettelheim, *Freud's Vienna and Other Essays* (New York: Knopf, 1989), p. 20.

2. Roazen, *Encountering Freud*, pp. 183–86.

3. Elisabeth Young-Bruehl, *Anna Freud: A Biography* (New York: Summit Books, 1988), p. 287.

4. Janet Malcolm, *In the Freud Archives* (New York: Knopf, 1984), p. 33.

4. On First Encountering "Miss Freud"

1. Paul Roazen, "Book Review of Joseph Sandler, Hansi Kennedy, and Robert L. Tyson, *The Technique of Child Analysis: Discussions with Anna Freud*," *Journal of the History of the Behavioral Sciences* (July 1991): 281–83.

2. Peter Gay, *A Godless Jew: Freud, Atheism, and the Making of Psychoanalysis* (New Haven: Yale University Press, 1987), p. 139; quoted in William J. McGrath, "Freud and the Force of History," in *Freud and the History of Psychoanalysis*, ed. Toby Gelfand and John Kerr (Hillsdale, N.J.: The Analytic Press, 1992), p. 79. Cf. also Paul Roazen, "The Historiography of Psychoanalysis," in *Austrian Studies*, vol. 3, ed. Edward Timms and Ritchie Robertson (Edinburgh: University of Edinburgh Press, 1992).

3. Young-Bruehl, *Anna Freud*, p. 440.

4. Paul Roazen, *Erik H. Erikson: The Power and Limits of a Vision* (New York:

The Free Press, 1975); Paul Roazen, "Erik H. Erikson As a Teacher," *Michigan Quarterly Review* (Winter 1992): 19–33.

5. The Hampstead Clinic

1. Martin Freud, *Glory Reflected* (London: Angus & Robertson, 1957), p. 60.

2. Anna Freud, *The Ego and the Mechanisms of Defence* (London: The Hogarth Press, 1937), chap. 10.

3. Ibid.

4. Ibid.

5. Stephen Schwartz, "Intellectuals and Assassins—Annals of Stalin's Killerati," *New York Times Books Review*, January 24, 1988, pp. 3, 30–31; "Letters to the Editor," *New York Times Book Review*, March 6, 1988, pp. 2, 33; Theodor Draper, "The Mystery of Max Eitingon," *New York Review of Books*, April 14, 1988, pp. 32–43; "The Mystery of Max Eitingon: An Exchange," *New York Review of Books*, June 16, 1988, pp. 50–54; Robert Conquest, "Max Eitingon: Another View," *New York Times Book Review*, July 3, 1988, pp. 22–23; "Letters to the Editor," *New York Times Book Review*, September 11, 1988, pp. 37–38; Theodor Draper, A *Present of Things Past: Selected Essays* (New York: Hill & Wang, 1991).

6. Michael John Burlingham, *The Last Tiffany: A Biography of Dorothy Tiffany Burlingham* (New York: Atheneum, 1989), p. 266. Cf. Paul Roazen, "Book Review of Burlingham's *The Last Tiffany*," *Psychoanalytic Books* (1991): 32–40.

7. Burlingham, *The Last Tiffany*, p. 230.

8. Anna Freud and Dorothy Burlingham, *Infants without Families* (New York: International Universities Press, 1944), p. 103.

9. Cf. George MacLean and Ulrich Reppen, *Hermine Hug-Hellmuth: Her Life and Work* (New York: Routledge, 1991).

10. Quoted in Burlingham, *The Last Tiffany*, p. 156.

11. Quoted in Ibid., p. 180; Roazen, *Freud and His Followers*, p. 448.

12. Roazen, *Helene Deutsch*, p. 287.

13. Quoted in Burlingham, *The Last Tiffany*, p. 287.

6. The Movement: Jones and Kleinianism

1. Paul Roazen, "Nietzsche and Freud," *Psychohistory Review* (Spring 1991): 327–49.

2. Sigmund Freud, *The Origins of Psychoanalysis: Letters to Wilhelm Fliess, Drafts and Notes: 1887–1902*, ed. Marie Bonaparte, Anna Freud, and Ernst Kris, trans. Eric Mosbacher and James Strachey (London: Imago, 1954); *The Complete Letters of Sigmund Freud to Wilhelm Fliess, 1887–1904*, trans. and ed. Jeffrey M. Masson (Cambridge: Harvard University Press, 1985); *Letters of Sigmund Freud, 1873–1939*, ed. Ernst L. Freud, trans. Tania Stern and James Stern (London: The Hogarth Press, 1961); Sigmund Freud, *Psychoanalysis and Faith: Dialogues with the Reverend Oskar Pfister*, ed. Heinrich Meng and Ernst L. Freud, trans. Eric Mosbacher (New York: Basic Books, 1963); A *Psychoanalytic Dialogue: The Letters of Sigmund Freud and Karl Abraham 1907–1926*, ed. Hilda C. Abraham and Ernst L. Freud, trans. Bernard Marsh (pseud.) and Hilda C. Abraham (New York:

Basic Books, 1965); *The Letters of Sigmund Freud and Arnold Zweig*, ed. Ernst L. Freud, trans. Professor and Mrs. W. D. Robson-Scott (London: The Hogarth Press, 1970); *James Jackson Putnam and Psychoanalysis*, ed. Nathan G. Hale, Jr., trans. Judith Bernays Heller (Cambridge: Harvard University Press, 1971); Sigmund Freud and Lou Andreas-Salomé, *Letters*, ed. Ernst Pfeiffer, trans. William and Elaine Robson-Scott (London: The Hogarth Press, 1972); *The Freud/Jung Letters*, ed. William McGuire, trans. Ralph Manheim and R.F.C. Hull (Princeton, Princeton University Press, 1974); Edoardo Weiss, *Sigmund Freud As a Consultant*, 2d ed. with new intro. by Paul Roazen (New Brunswick, N.J.: Transaction Books, 1991).

3. Paul Roazen, "Tampering with the Mails: Book Review of *The Letters of Sigmund Freud to Eduard Silberstein 1871–1881*," ed. Walter Boehlich, trans. Arnold Pomerans, *American Scholar*, Autumn 1991, pp. 613–20.

4. Paul Roazen, *Freud: Political and Social Thought* (New York: Knopf, 1968; 2d ed. with new pref., New York: Da Capo Books, 1986), pp. 77, 315.

5. Paul Roazen, *Brother Animal: The Story of Freud and Tausk*, 2d ed. with new intro. (New Brunswick, N.J.: Transaction Books, 1990), p. 140.

6. Interview with Dr. Smiley Blanton, January 25, 1966; interview with Professor Lionel Penrose, August 31, 1965. Penrose was attributing the latter saying to Dr. John Rickman.

7. Young-Bruehl, *Anna Freud*, p. 68.

8. Quoted in ibid., p. 171.

9. Roazen, *Freud and His Followers*, pp. 355–71.

10. Ibid., pp. 392–418.

11. Young-Bruehl, *Anna Freud*, p. 17.

12. Roazen, "Rise and Fall of Bruno Bettelheim." p. 241.

13. Sigmund Freud, *The Standard Edition of the Complete Psychological Works of Sigmund Freud*, ed. James Strachey (London: The Hogarth Press, 1953–74), vol. 20, "Psychoanalysis," p. 266. Hereafter this edition of Freud's works will be referred to simply as *Standard Edition*.

14. Roazen, *Encountering Freud*, pp. 24–26.

15. Anna Freud, "Personal Memories of Ernest Jones," *International Journal of Psychoanalysis* (1979): 287.

16. Young-Bruehl, *Anna Freud*, pp. 181, 172, 171–72, 259.

17. Paul Roazen, "Book Review of M. Masud Khan's *The Long Wait*," *Psychoanalytic Books* (1991): 19–25.

18. Roazen, "Tola Rank," p. 251.

7.   *My Discovering about Anna's Analysis*

1. Weiss, *Sigmund Freud As a Consultant*; Young-Bruehl, *Anna Freud*, pp. 434–35.

2. Young-Bruehl, *Anna Freud*, chap. 3.

3. Roazen, *Encountering Freud*, p. 105.

4. *Letters of Sigmund Freud, 1873–1939*, p. 314.

5. Roazen, *Freud: Political and Social Thought*, epilogue.

6. Roazen, *Encountering Freud*, p. 264.

7. Anna Freud, *Psychoanalysis for Teachers and Parents*, trans. Barbara Low (Boston: Beacon Press, 1960), p. 78.

8. Sigmund Freud and William C. Bullitt, *Thomas Woodrow Wilson: A Psychological Study* (Boston: Houghton Mifflin, 1967), p. xiv.

9. Quoted in Peter Gay, *Freud: A Life for Our Time* (New York: Norton, 1988), p. 433. Cf. Paul Roazen, "Book Review of Gay's *Freud*," *Psychoanalytic Books* (1990): 10–17.

10. Hannah Decker, *Freud, Dora, and Vienna 1900* (New York: The Free Press, 1991), p. 254.

11. Paul Roazen, "Book Review of Brownell and Billings's *So Close to Greatness: A Life of William C. Bullitt*," *American Scholar*, Winter 1989, pp. 135–40.

8. *"Altogether Feminine": Mathilda Freud Hollitscher*

1. Quoted in Young-Bruehl, *Anna Freud*, p. 306.

2. Roazen, *Freud and His Followers*, pp. 420–36.

3. *Letters of Sigmund Freud, 1873–1939*, p. 281.

4. *New York Times*, February 24, 1978; See also Anna Freud, "Mathilda Hollitscher Freud," *Sigmund Freud House Bulletin* 2, no. 1 (1978): 2.

5. *Letters of Sigmund Freud, 1873–1939*, p. 281.

6. Young-Bruehl, *Anna Freud*, p. 42.

7. *The Complete Letters of Sigmund Freud to Wilhelm Fliess 1887–1904*, p. 364. Cf. also, Freud, *Origins of Psychoanalysis*, p. 289.

8. Young-Bruehl, *Anna Freud*, p. 309.

9. Esther Menaker, *Appointment in Vienna* (New York: St. Martin's Press, 1989), p. 134.

10. Martin Freud, *Glory Reflected*, p. 125.

11. Ibid., p. 129.

12. Theodor Reik, "Years of Maturity—Review of Vol. II of Jones," *Psychoanalysis* 4 (1955): 72.

13. Cf. Erich Fromm, *Sigmund Freud's Mission: An Analysis of His Personality and Influence* (New York: Harper & Brothers, 1959), chaps. 2 and 3.

14. Martin Freud, *Glory Reflected*, pp. 108–9.

9. *"The Black Sheep": Dr. Esti Freud*

1. *Reich Speaks of Freud: Wilhelm Reich Discusses His Work and His Relationship with Sigmund Freud*, ed. Mary Higgins and Chester M. Raphael (New York: Noonday Press, 1967), pp. 3–131.

2. Roazen, *Encountering Freud*, ch. 6. See also Paul Roazen, "Reading, Writing, and Memory: Dr. K. R. Eissler's Thinking," *Contemporary Psychoanalysis* 14 (1978): 345–53, and Paul Roazen, "Book Review of Eissler's *Freud As an Expert Witness: The Discussion of War Neuroses between Freud and Wagner-Jauregg*," *Contemporary Psychology* (1988): 213–14.

3. Decker, *Freud, Dora, and Vienna 1900*, p. 109.

4. *Letters of Sigmund Freud, 1873–1939*, p. 344.

5. Interview with Therese Benedek, August 2, 1951, Freud Collection, Library of Congress.

6. Helene Deutsch, *Psychoanalysis of the Sexual Functions of Women*, ed. Paul Roazen (London: Karnac, 1991).

7. Sharon Romm, *The Unwelcome Intruder: Freud's Struggle with Cancer* (New York: Praeger, 1983).

8. Sophie Freud Loewenstein, "Mother and Daughter: An Epitaph," *Family Process* 20 (1981): 5.

9. *The Diary of Sigmund Freud: 1929–1939*, p. 304.

10. Jones, *The Life and Work of Sigmund Freud*, vol. 3, p. 182.

11. Peter J. Swales, "Freud, Minna Bernays, and the Conquest of Rome: New Light on the Origins of Psychoanalysis" (privately printed).

12. Peter Gay, "Freud and Minna? The Biographer As Voyeur," *New York Times Book Review*, January 29, 1989, pp. 1, 43–45; Cf. Paul Roazen, "Of Sigmund and Minna," *New York Times Book Review*, April 9, 1989, p. 36.

13. Cf. Letter of Marie Bonaparte to Ernest Jones, December 10, 1953 (Jones archives).

10.   Like a Cuckoo Clock

1. Melitta Schmideberg, "A Contribution to the History of the Psychoanalytic Movement in Britain," *British Journal of Psychiatry* 118 (1971): 64.

2. Burlingham, *The Last Tiffany*, pp. 144–45.

3. Peggy C. Davis, " 'There is a Book Out. . . .': An Analysis of Judicial Absorption of Legislative Facts," *Harvard Law Review*, 100 (1987): 1545.

4. Quoted in Burlingham, *The Last Tiffany*, p. 145.

5. Ernest Jones, *The Life and Work of Sigmund Freud*, vol. 2, *Years of Maturity*, 1901–1919 (New York: Basic Books, 1955), p. 33.

6. Roazen, *Freud and His Followers*, pp. 174–211, 211–22.

7. *Standard Edition*, vol. 18, quoted in "Group Psychology and the Analysis of the Ego," p. 134.

8. Sophie Freud, "The Heirloom," in *My Three Mothers and Other Passions* (New York: New York University Press, 1988), pp. 291–97.

9. Quoted in Celia Bertin, *Marie Bonaparte: A Life* (New York: Harcourt Brace Jovanovich, 1982), p. 155.

10. *The Diary of Sigmund Freud: 1929–1939*, pp. 55, 166, 304.

11. Freud, *Origins of Psychoanalysis*, p. 227; cf. also *The Complete Letters of Sigmund Freud to Wilhelm Fliess*, p. 276.

12. *Standard Edition*, vol. 11, "Leonardo da Vinci," p. 101.

13. Jones, *The Life and Work of Sigmund Freud*, vol. 3, p. 246.

11.   A "Precisionist": Oliver Freud

1. Quoted in Ernest Jones, *The Life and Work of Sigmund Freud*, vol. 1, *The Young Freud*, 2d ed. (London: The Hogarth Press, 1954), p. 382; cf. also *The Complete Letters of Sigmund Freud to Wilhelm Fliess*, p. 398.

2. Roazen, *Freud and His Followers*, pp. 41–42.

3. *The Complete Letters of Sigmund Freud to Wilhelm Fliess*, pp. 358, 364.

4. Roazen, *Encountering Freud*, pp. 54–63. Saul Rosenzweig, *Freud, Jung and Hall the King-Maker: The Expedition to America (1909)* (St. Louis: Rama House Press, 1992).

5. Quoted in R. Andrew Paskauskas, "Ernest Jones: A Critical Study of His Scientific Development" (Ph.D diss., Institute for the History and Philosophy of Science and Technology, University of Toronto, 1985), p. 213.

6. Silas L. Warner, "Freud's Antipathy to America," *Journal of the American Academy of Psychoanalysis* 19 (1991): 141–55.

7. Elisabeth Roudinesco, *Jacques Lacan & Co.: A History of Psychoanalysis in France, 1925–1985*, trans. Jeffrey Mehlman (Chicago: University of Chicago Press, 1990), pp. 159–60. Young-Bruehl maintains that Eva died of influenza: Young-Bruehl, *Anna Freud*, p. 279.

8. Young-Bruehl, *Anna Freud*, p. 41.

9. Helen Walker Puner, *Freud: His Life and Mind*, foreword by Erich Fromm, 1978, 2d ed., with new intro. by Paul Roazen (New Brunswick, N.J.: Transaction Books, 1992).

10. Martin Freud, *Glory Reflected*, p. 80.

11. Letter from Edward Hitschmann to Ernest Jones, March 26, 1954 (Jones archives).

12. Martin Freud, *Glory Reflected*, p. 29.

13. Ibid., p. 196.

12.   "My Pride and My Secret Hope"

1. Martin Freud, *Glory Reflected*, pp. 26–27.

2. Ibid., p. 27.

3. Cf. Roazen, "Review of Sandler, Kennedy, & Tyson."

4. Quoted in Gay, *Freud*, p. 387.

5. Young-Bruehl, *Anna Freud*, p. 41.

6. Quoted in ibid., p. 115.

7. Quoted in ibid.

8. Ibid. Cf. Paul Roazen, "A Partisan Biography: Book Review of Young-Bruehl's *Anna Freud*," *Virginia Quarterly Review* (1989): 749–55.

9. Young-Bruehl, *Anna Freud*, p. 471.

10. Ibid., p. 41.

11. Gay, *Freud*, pp. 429–30.

12. Roazen, *Brother Animal*, pp. 119–20.

13. *Standard Edition*, vol. 22, "New Introductory Lectures on Psychoanalysis," p. 133.

14. Letter from Anna Freud to Kurt Eissler, December 7, 1969 (Library of Congress).

15. Young-Bruehl, *Anna Freud*, p. 32.

16. Martin Freud, *Glory Reflected*, p. 11.

17. Letter from Max Schur to Ernest Jones, September 30, 1955 (Jones archives).

18. Martin Freud, *Glory Reflected*, p. 11.

19. Ibid., p. 16.

20. *Standard Edition*, vol. 5, "Interpretation of Dreams," p. 398; *Standard Edition*, vol. 17, "A Childhood Recollection from *Dichtung und Wahrheit*," p. 156.

21. Martin Freud, *Glory Reflected*, p. 16.

22. *Letters of Sigmund Freud, 1873–1939*, p. 308.

Afterword

1. J. Hampden Jackson, *Marx, Proudhon and European Socialism* (London: The English Universities Press, 1957), p. 48.

2. *Standard Edition*, vol. 21, "Dostoevsky and Parricide," p. 177.

3. Young-Bruehl, *Anna Freud*, p. 434; cf. letter from Anna Freud to Eva Rosenfeld, February 19, 1974 (Library of Congress).

4. Letter from M. Masud Khan to Kurt R. Eissler, November 10, 1981 (Library of Congress).

5. *Minutes of the Vienna Psychoanalytic Society*, vol. 2: 1908–1910, ed. Herman Nunberg and Ernst Federn, trans. M. Nunberg (New York: International Universities Press, 1967), p. 477.

6. Quoted in Gay, *Freud*, p. 361.

7. *The Clinical Diary of Sandor Ferenczi*, p. 160.

8. *Letters of Sigmund Freud, 1873–1939*, p. 386.

Index